THE MASTERS OF WISDOM

John G. Bennett

TURNSTONE PRESS LIMITED
Wellingborough, Northamptonshire

First published 1977
First Paperback Edition 1980
Second Impression 1982

ISBN 0 85500 069 4

Printed and bound in Great Britain

Contents

– the gospel of Matthew – the Sermon on the Mount as a *legominism* – sending out of the disciples – the Transfiguration – the secret of love – humiliation of James and John – humiliation of Peter – the Last Supper – Judas taking away the sins of the world – the new commandment – the way of the first Christians

Illustrations

Foreword

When a writer dies leaving work unfinished, his executors have to face several decisions. They must decide first of all whether or not the work is to be published at all. If it is to be published, the form must be agreed. Is the book acceptable as it is, does it need additions, pruning, editing, explaining and so on, and who is available to do this work? With this book the problem was complicated still more by the fact that the manuscript was in the stage only of a "first draft", and therefore quite unfit to be presented to a publisher. At the same time there is material here both useful and interesting to the reader, and by good fortune the publisher was sufficiently enthusiastic and understanding to accept the manuscript as it stands.

John Bennett died on the day he had decided to write the last chapter of *The Masters of Wisdom*. He left a handful of notes on Chapter Ten but what he intended to say about the present day Masters of Wisdom never materialized.

J. G. Bennett excelled as a speaker. He was able to convey a subtle or complex idea to an audience with a simplicity that compelled understanding. He wrote with difficulty, but he thought it important that he should express some of his ideas in written form. He was always inventive and creative. He lost interest in his writings as soon as they left his hands to go to the publisher and before one book was finished he would be preparing his mind for another. He had plans to write books on the Law of Three and the Law of Seven; on the Law of Reciprocal Maintenance and on What Makes the Future.

He told fantastic fairy stories to his children in which the protagonists, a hedgehog, a prince or a magic starfish passed from one world to another, from one dimension to another, making a picture of the possibilities open to man. I regret that these stories were not recorded. They were truly original.

I believe the idea of "The Masters of Wisdom" came to him soon after Gurdjieff's death in 1949 when he heard someone referring to Gurdjieff as a phenomenon standing alone, who had come, presented us with a system of work and disappeared without trace. That was the first time I remember hearing my husband speak about a hierarchy of Masters. He originally intended to use much of the material contained in this book in *Gurdjieff – Making A New World*, but the subject became so important to him that he decided to use it in a book of its own. He was immersed in the material for *The Masters of Wisdom* for about a year and a half before his death. It was his habit to read very little. He considered casual reading a practice harmful for the psyche of man, but in the last months before his death his bedside books were the *Rashahāt* and the *Nafahāt al-Uns* and for the purposes of research he revived his reading of Ottoman Turkish. He wrote only in his spare time. Normally his day was fully occupied with his students at Sherborne House, correspondence, lectures, etc. and his writing had to be done in odd moments, a rare free evening or during a summer holiday. He was never able to give it as much attention as he wished. He regarded it as a hobby rather than as a duty and all his other activities came first. He considered it important that *The Masters of Wisdom* should be published and it is for that reason that we have put it together.

I intended, with the co-operation of the most helpful and sympathetic of publishers, to bring out the book exactly as it stood, without the alteration of a word. J. G. Bennett's writing was always so condensed and his choice of words expressed his thought so precisely that no one felt competent to touch the manuscript. Fortunately Simon Weightman, Anthony Blake and George Bennett undertook to check the references, standardize the spelling, verify dates, etc. throughout the book. Trilby Noon undertook the final typing for presentation to the publisher, who waited patiently for the work to be finished.

I am more than grateful for the long hours of thought given by this dedicated team. There is no doubt that without the help of

Simon Weightman, who also wrote the Epilogue and Anthony Blake who wrote the Preface, the work could not have been published in its present coherent form; and John Bennett's last and profoundly interesting book would almost certainly have been lost.

I would like to emphasize that the published book is as my husband wrote it; apart from the Preface, Epilogue and a few minor alterations for the sake of continuity, nothing has been added and nothing taken away.

Elizabeth Bennett

Preface

In history, there are the things that happened. History, especially modern history, is concerned with arriving at more and more detailed and reliable knowledge of what has happened. Our representations of the past are weighed against the evidence. We establish a more and more exact chronology and our information about what has happened becomes increasingly precise in quantitative and statistical terms. There is still a heavy reliance on the testimony and descriptions made by people of historical times so that we tend to have vastly more information about the policies of rulers than about the everyday lives of ordinary people. In the same event, the historian may know about a single conversation, a political structure, economic conditions and the movement of populations. All of this is to do with what happened.

If this were all, history would not interest us — unless we happened to belong to the profession whose aim was the acquisition of such knowledge. Such a history describes an empty world: we are not in it; human experience is not in it and it does not touch us. When we entertain the reality of experiencings we are on to something different, something not amenable to the methods of pinning down what has actually happened.

Bennett gives this illustration from an event that he himself witnessed: ". . . the forced exchanges of Greeks and Turks in 1925 which were described by historians as causing great misery and loss of life. The really important feature of these events, as I saw it, was the great courage with which people overcame their

difficulties and the benefit to their countries in the new blood
that was brought across the sea."

Suffering and courage are the stuff of fiction but they are also
the kind of thing that makes history interesting. There are deeper
and more superficial experiencings; and our own experiencing is
mingled with that of the people whose history we study.
Without experiencings, history is a shadow-play. With them, it
is elusive and imprecise. We cannot know about the state of
mind that a people had as we can about their movements; but, in
a sense, it is the state of mind that really matters.

Surely, it matters what men and women go through, for this is
the medium in which the event arises! We must enter the domain
of values as well as deal in facts and give weight to what men
experience. It is problematic whether we give special weight to
the ecstasy of Baha ad-dm by a tomb in Bukhara. At first glance,
this and the course of events seem separate and can be considered
separately. But that is not as it is. The ecstasy of Baha ad-dm was
connected with events that eventually influenced millions of
people all over the world.

Essentially, however, experiencing gives us something about
the value or worth of an event as a moment in the totality of
human history. It is how men and women feel and sense their
situation. This in its turn does influence what happens, but there
is something here which stands in its own right. It is experiencing
that gives the depth of events, not the magnitude of external
happenings.

This is not all. History is also a matter of deeds and we have to
face the problem of intelligence. Some of the most important
questions we can ask are about the power of men to influence the
course of events. To what degree are events predetermined? Do
we, like certain historians, conclude that it is all a nexus of
contingency, with neither rhyme nor reason? Is man so immersed
in the material world that he is under the sway of its laws? Is he
entirely a conditioned being able to act and react only in ways
established in him by the past? Is there any genuine freedom in
human life and, if so, what is its scope? Is there some mode of
action that is quite free of conditioning and, if so, how does this
penetrate into the affairs of men?

In our time, traditional views about man as being a responsible
free being have been severely shaken. This has an important
bearing, since intelligence is a matter of purposeful acts. A

jaundiced view of history is that it shows that man is getting nowhere. Certainly, there is little evidence that he is capable of directing the course of history except in the negative sense of destroying possibilities through short-sightedness, egoism and lack of intelligence. If we feel that in spite of appearances man is getting somewhere, then it must be a very hazardous business. We must also conclude that a rare kind of intelligence is at work which cannot be reduced to ordinary capacities.

All the evidence is that the vast majority are completely blind to the repercussions of their acts. Peoples and governments today continue to do things seemingly in full knowledge of their harmful effects. But it is only a theoretical knowledge, not a perception. The men who transformed our view of the cosmos, the astronomers of the seventeenth century, have been rightly called "sleepwalkers". They had a dream which helped to create the modern world, a world many of them would have abhorred or failed to understand. If we study the lives, actions and writings of men involved in the French Revolution all that is visible is a chaos of emotion and ambition combined with an unrealistic idealism. They were dreamers also.

We know that reformers produce as much misery as they relieve. It is difficult to find an action that is genuinely and intentionally connected with the outcome of events – that is, an intelligent action.

Taken by itself, the element of deeds in human history is a record of intentions that misfire. Such a conclusion may be unacceptable. But at the very least we must agree that intervention on whatever scale in the course of events is a hazardous undertaking and that there are degrees of accomplishment.

Yet great things have come about. The most obvious is the evolution of life and man. Almost on a level with this we can place the emergence of creative powers. The creation of languages and the creation of ideas of the cosmos and human destiny thousands of years ago reverberate in the human mind. The proof is in the pudding: we cannot conclude that there is no action that is really intelligent; that is, purposeful and able to embrace the complexities of the human situation. It is this that Bennett calls "Demiurgic intelligence".

We can look to the coalescence or unity of happenings, experiencings and deeds as *significance*. This is the core of history.

Significant history happened, was experienced and was intended. Clearly, there is a relativity of significance and at the lowest level the three elements are liable to be disjointed: this is the dream-world of ordinary life where something is happening, what we imagine is going on is quite different, and our intentions get us nowhere.

The writing of history itself can be a deed. This is how it is in stories and legends, some of which have played a major role in the historical arena. A similar role is played by the vision of a great leader, such as Chinghis Khan who was able to create in his followers a new image of the Mongol people. In our time, it has been explicitly recognised that the writing of history is a factor in controlling the future.

The modification of the experiencing of men and women in relation to what has happened and is happening is little understood but no-one can deny its importance. At its lowest it is political demagogy; at its highest it is the voice of the prophet.

One thing that is difficult for people to understand is how the spiritual life influences the material life. The spiritual is not powerful through strength or force but through perception. Those who have "seen God" see the world differently from ordinary men. They cannot communicate their vision in words; but they do better, they communicate by what they do and how they live. The deeds of men and women who have become free of self-interest, and even entirely of themselves, brings into human life an element that no great leader or genius can. The leaders cannot understand what the spiritual men are or what they see, but they are affected. They can see a singleness of purpose that exceeds even their own and through this affinity find a response in themselves to spiritual guidance.

The response to guidance from a higher order of perception is recognised by everyone as important, no matter who or what they suppose has such a perception. But a great mistake has been made in supposing that spiritual men are so other-worldly that the affairs of men are forgotten. This cannot be so. We are all bound into the common action of the great human event. The higher perception must penetrate into what actually happens. Baha ad-din turns away from the affairs of the world after seeing the labours of Khalil Ata destroyed, but in the long run he serves mankind as he was destined to do.

A history that looks to significance is as hazardous as the stuff of history itself. The historian will be faced with making judgments on the relative intelligence of men, that is, on their capacity for intentional action in terms of human progress. This will not produce a simple chronology of what has happened, nor will it be chronology enlivened with a sense of human experiencing. It must involve a search to discover and reveal intelligence at work – using the same material of stories, records and traces that are the raw data of every historian.

In this book, the judgment of intelligence includes distinguishing a special class of men, the Masters of Wisdom, who are treated as the bearers of a degree of intelligence that is vastly superior to anything attainable by planning, reasoning and organization. This intelligence is itself portrayed as Wisdom, a high order of action that is not confined to man, but brought into existence all the endless wonder of life on this planet and even constructed the human mind. The conditions for partaking of this wisdom are the overcoming of illusions about the world and the self and the liberation from self through "conscious labours and intentional suffering".

To give form to a history of higher intelligence is not easy. It is supposed that all actions of this high order belong to one whole and that therefore one should find this reflected in links between groups of men at different critical times in history. This is, in part, the notion of a chain of transmission; which includes the methods or know-how of how to attain Wisdom. Bennett has endeavoured to follow this notion by tracing a linkage between the Sarmān brotherhood of three thousand years ago and the Khwājagān of the eleventh to sixteenth centuries after Christ. The Sarmān themselves are supposed to have arisen from a earlier phase when the high intelligence was concentrated in a few exceptional individuals who guided early man in the development of his powers; and who, in their turn, arose out of the intelligence that guided evolution before man arose.

If there is no such linkage to be found anywhere we are faced with the conclusion that the incursion of higher intelligence is gratuitous. In this connection, there is the unresolved problem of the emergence of extraordinary figures in Christendom such as St. Benedict and Meister Eckhart who clearly belonged to the company of the Masters yet had no apparent antecedents. Certainly, the chain of transmission is only part of the story; but it has the convenience of enabling us to portray the influence of higher intelligence in accordance with established chronologies.

Bennett's account takes us through the time of Christ with its range of difficulties including the well-acknowledged fact of the extreme editing and distortion of material in the known gospels. Bennett has to introduce the Magi as a link between the time of the Sarman and the rise of spirituality in Islam. The whole drama of the schools of Syria and Alexandria responsible for shaping the Creed and liturgy is left obscure. The influence of Buddhist, Shamanist and Christian know-how on the emergence of the methods of the Masters is only hinted at. The Magi and their role may be only a fiction. They are introduced because of the conviction that Zoroaster had an influence that far surpasses what we now assume. However it may be, the Magi here serve the same role as a fictional entity in physics like the 'quark' which may or may not prove to exist – whatever existence means in physics these days – but which does take research forward.

The important thing is that Bennett keeps the three elements – happenings, experiencings and deeds – in balance. His is a history of significances through which we can confront the central practical issue of whether or not there is a high order of intelligence at work in human history and, therefore, whether we can work in hope.

Introduction

We all agree that this world is in trouble. Many feel that events are totally out of control and that our leaders can do no more· than paper the cracks while the edifice of human society on this earth is falling apart. We are accustomed to seek expert advice when we are up against a problem we cannot solve; but here it is the experts themselves who are defeated. We look in vain for an effectual lead from politicians, economists, scientists, psychologists, historians or philosophers. Theory and practice are equally at sea. We neither see what can be done on the global scale, nor do we put into operation the commonsense measures, the need for which is obvious to everyone. For all our bluff we know we have lost our way. In this book, I shall attempt to answer the question whether or not we can look for experts of a different kind. I have called them 'Masters of Wisdom' from the Persian word *Khwājagān* that was introduced a thousand years ago to designate an extraordinary body of men who influenced the history of central Asia for five hundred years by the possession of an expertise of a kind we see little of today.

If the Masters of Wisdom of central Asia were an isolated phenomenon they would be interesting for oriental scholars, but not for all the rest of us who look anxiously into the future to see where help can come from. I believe that there have been Masters of Wisdom on earth since the time of Adam, and that before Adam there were intelligences that guided the evolution of life on this earth. I hope to show in this book that this belief is consistent with all that we know about the historical process and that it is the one sure foundation for a hopeful view of the future of mankind.

There have been great crises in the past, such as the fall of the Roman Empire, the destruction of the ancient cultures of Asia by the Mongols in the thirteenth century, and the French Revolution; they were severe blows to the fabric of human society but they were local and great areas of the world were virtually untouched. I shall give reasons for concluding that in these local crises the Masters of Wisdom played an important part in guiding mankind into safer waters. We need to look at the history of the earth and the appearance of man in order to see the full significance of the belief that a higher wisdom has intervened in history at all critical moments. If we can accept this, then we can found our hopes for the future upon an intervention that will compensate for our human weakness, folly and sheer ignorance.

If this belief is ill-founded, then either mankind must continue to flounder until the sheer pressure of events forces us to change our way of living, or there must be an Act of God that is beyond our understanding. We cannot readily accept the thought that the course of events is already out of control, because we can see that commonsense actions that are technically possible could remove many of our troubles. The universal acceptance of a static economy related to needs rather than greed has been so earnestly advocated by good and influential people that we might have expected governments and people to make at least a small move towards it. We continue to do just the opposite, and this is the crux of the matter. Our ignorance is exceeded only by our impotence. Fifty years ago Gurdjieff came to the West with his message of transformation, saying that man is a machine with no will, no 'I', no conciousness and that 'he cannot do'. The truth of this is becoming so obvious that even professional optimists are beginning to see it. But the full message of transformation is not taken: man as he is cannot do and he has no will, no consciousness; but he has the potential for becoming a 'real man'. Only a real man, in the full sense, can be a Master of Wisdom. Those who are in power are unable to do even what is obviously needed, because neither they nor those whom they rule are more than 'machines' that can behave only as they are conditioned to do. It is useless to preach to machines, or to encourage or frighten them: they continue to function according to their own mechanical pattern. This is how it is with mankind and will continue to be until our evolution has gone a long way further.

Some people have learned tricks that can be played with human machines and so gain power over them, but as long as they themselves remain machines, their power is worse than useless. We can see this in the manipulation of public opinion by those who know the tricks. As Gurdjieff put it: "People can be made to believe any old tale and frothing at the mouth will set themselves to convince òthers that it is so and cannot be otherwise." Neither the tricksters nor the tricked can see or do anything that they are not conditioned to do by their heredity, their upbringing, their environment and by their fundamental egoism.

The Masters of Wisdom differ from 'experts in manipulation' by their ability to see the reality of the situation, by their freedom from egoism and by their ability to co-operate with one another. They do not work only on the external, visible level, but in domains to which ordinary people do not have access. They are in contact with the higher wisdom that surveys life on this earth as a whole and can see whence it has come and whither it is destined to go.

What is written in the last paragraph is no more than an expanded definition of the term Masters of Wisdom. It gives no reason for believing that there are now or ever have been such transformed people; or, if there are, that they concern themselves with the human crisis. Many people will agree that there have been in the past not only individuals but groups and societies who have been transformed, but they look upon them in an 'other-worldly' context. They were saints and prophets, visionaries and reformers whose work was not for this world but for the next. They shunned power and fame and made no attempt to 'change the world.' We have to look much more closely to find evidence of the Masters at work.

At this moment in human history the question of a higher wisdom has become supremely important. If it must be answered in the negative, our chances of survival as a species for more than a hundred years are very doubtful. We can see the difficulties ahead for the next twenty or thirty years, but assume that if we can surmount them, the twenty-first century of the Christian Era will see the triumph of man over nature and a world society that will regulate human life in such a way as to eliminate poverty, war, famine, disease and even, perhaps, death itself. Such predictions are indeed being confidently made by experts in 'futurology'. A realistic prediction that takes account of the basic facts of human nature leads to just the opposite conclusion. Every technological advance creates three problems for every one it solves. Every increase in man's power over nature results in more destruction. Human society is not moving towards the brotherhood of man, but towards worse manifestations of human selfishness and greed. We shall no doubt survive the twentieth century; but unless there are great changes few will survive the twenty-first.

We reach the conclusion that many have come to: there is no way out unless human nature can be changed. If it is true as Gurdjieff says, that the 'man-machine' can be transformed into a real man only if he receives help from those who are already transformed, then the search for the Masters of Wisdom begins to look serious. However hard they may be to find, and however doubtful their very existence may be to those who have not searched, it behoves us to look into the evidence.

Aldous Huxley in *The Perennial Philosophy* traced the ancient belief that a higher wisdom is accessible to man. It is a belief conveyed in the creation myths of all people, in the myth of a Golden Age and in Promethean and Apollonian mythology. It is expressed in fairy tales, so many of which turn upon the Wise Old Man who helps the hero or heroine to achieve impossible tasks. We must recognise that the belief in a higher wisdom only proves that men have wanted to believe it. Many would like to believe it today and they invent new myths of flying saucers and all the marvels of science fiction. There are more serious attempts which present a teacher or teaching as the great hope of mankind and many claim to know how the social, political and economic life of mankind is to be redeemed and regenerated. So much of this is unconvincing and even repellant to the unconverted that it is more an obstacle than a help to reaching a positive conclusion as to the reality of a higher wisdom.

We have also to look at the traditional repositories of divine inspiration: the great world religions and their institutions. We may recognise the sincerity of their members and even accept the reality of their beliefs; but we cannot see in their manifestations evidence of a greater wisdom than that of non-spiritual peoples. "Physician heal thyself!" can be said to every religious community that preaches brotherly love and fails to set the example we need.

It is a hazardous undertaking to seek to penetrate beyond the visible unwisdom of the would-be wise and search for evidence that there is an operation that is not only genuine but effective. What in times of prosperity, peace and progress would be an undertaking for the lunatic fringe, becomes in a crisis such as mankind faces today a task that we dare not neglect.

Our only hope is to search for traces in the past. We should look particularly at times of crisis, where the situation looked desperate, and see if we can detect the work of people who can be regarded as Masters of Wisdom.

I shall start before the time of Adam, by which I mean the appearance on earth of the modern race of man proudly called *Homo sapiens sapiens.* According to my reckoning, this occurred between 35,000 and 40,000 years ago. Until then the higher wisdom operated outside of man. Since that time it has entered into people who were capable of receiving it. By tracing the origin and evolution of life and the appearance of the first men, and reconstructing the history of mankind during the last Ice Age, we can see how strongly the magnificent event suggests a creative genius, infinitely patient, infinitely ingenious, whose vision was realised in the coming of Adam. Then, we might fancy that this same genius decided to engage upon the hazardous enterprise of withdrawing his guiding hand, leaving his brain-child to find itself and become like himself.

The history of the past twelve thousand years can be seen and interpreted as the awakening of the human mind to its responsibilities. This awakening is constantly set back by two elements in human nature. One is man's animal origin and the other is his arrogance and egoism. His chequered history is a succession of failures and fresh starts, but on the whole there has been a gradual progress. At each crisis, man has been helped to make a new start and this should give us hope that it will be so again. The present crisis is of almost unprecedented magnitude, because we are at the midpoint of a great cycle that started twelve thousand years ago. For the first time since the end of the last Ice Age, the present human race is in real danger of extinction. There is a maximum imbalance between man's outward powers and his inward weakness. This imbalance is beyond the capacity of man to rectify for himself. We must look for help from the higher wisdom and be prepared to accept it.

Chapter One

The Demiurge

In this book I ask the reader to look at life on this earth and at human life in particular, from the standpoint of a very high intelligence engaged in an almost impossible enterprise. The task is to bring into existence beings capable of providing the earth with a soul, by achieving such a degree of mutual love and such wisdom as to be able to act as one and yet retain their individual freedom. Mankind today represents an early stage in the accomplishment of this task.

The very high intelligence I am postulating is neither human nor divine. It is neither perfect nor infallible, but its vision and its powers far transcend those of the wisest of mankind. I shall call it the Demiurge, from the word used in Athens to designate 'worker for the people', the artisan or craftsman who provided the *demos,* citizens of Athens, with the instruments of well-being and culture. The word was taken over much later by Aristotle to stand for the Great Artificer, the power that creates and maintains life on the earth. In Aristotle's day, the earth was the most important component of the world. The sun, moon and stars were luminaries that existed to provide the earth with day and night. Even the gods lived on or near enough to the earth to visit it when it suited them to do so. It was natural to think of the Great Artificer as the prime mover, the transcendental source from which all existence flows.

Very great changes have come in our world picture in two thousand three hundred years. Copernicus and Galileo made us see the earth as a minor planet in the solar system. Modern astronomy tells us to look on the sun as but one star in a hundred billion that form our galaxy and our galaxy as but one in countless millions of galaxies stretching further than our imagination can reach. We are bound to think quite differently of an intelligence that governs our earth than of one – if there be such – that rules the universe. By keeping the word Demiurge for the postulated spirit of the earth, we can put aside, as beyond our grasp, the idea of a deity that created and rules the *entire* universe. In doing this, we should breathe a sigh of relief and thankfulness. The earth is our home and its destiny should be our main concern.

We must remember that the conception of an absolute God was foreign to all ancient peoples. Jahweh was the greatest God, but limited both in His powers and His concerns. So was Ahura Mazda. The Buddha accepted the existence of gods, but regarded them as limited and by no means omnipotent. The early Christians kept to the Jewish notion of a limited God. It was only the influence of Greek thought that equated God with the Absolute. If we can accept the notion of a limited God we are bound to admit the notion of a limitless Source "beyond God."

We need no longer distress ourselves brooding over Hume's dilemma: "God is either loving but not omnipotent, or omnipotent but not loving: He cannot be both." The truth is that the omnipotence of God is a silly idea thought up by men with narrow, logical minds. It must be obvious to anyone whose feelings have not atrophied that love and omnipotence can never be united. When I became convinced that there is a great and benevolent but limited intelligence working behind the scene of this world, and also saw that man cannot exist only for his own benefit but must have been created to serve some higher purpose, I experienced an enormous relief. Life could be full of meaning and I could play a useful, even a necessary, part in it – just because everything is not controlled by the overwhelming power of an almighty God.

The picture shown to us by the history of the earth is that of a slow but accelerating transformation from lifelessness to life, from primitive sensation to a developed consciousness. The transformation has gone forward uncertainly and even precariously, but the result is already a marvel. We see the amazing adaptation of life to the nature of the planet; of one form of life to another. We see the utmost ingenuity of construction, we see beauty and we can see the play of a vast cosmic spirit. If all this came into existence blindly by the working of mechanical laws and accidental combinations, it is a double marvel. If we look at it as an achievement of a great intelligence, we must be ready to bow before it and acknowledge that it is incomparably greater than ours.

When we look at the solar system we see a closely knit family of sun, planets, satellites, asteroids, comets and fields of force. We know that life on earth depends upon the heat, light and other radiation it receives from the sun. Scientists agree that the sun's radiation must have played a decisive part in the first appearance of life on this planet. I want to go further, and ask you to think in terms of the sun as a higher intelligence, as the creative power that acts throughout the solar system. We can look upon it as the Creator and Father of all life, including our own. Compared with the Sun, the Demiurge occupies a subordinate position. It does not itself create life, but has undertaken the task of nursing it and guiding it towards the moment when it can become responsible for itself. There is nothing that should astonish us in the thought of an intelligence behind nature. Biologists, who would reject any suggestion of a divine creator, find themselves talking and writing on Nature as if she were an intelligent being. You can scarcely open a book or read a paper about the evolution of life without finding passages in which the author personifies Nature. If questioned, he would assure us that this is only a figure of speech and is not to be taken literally. Sometimes, however, our speech betrays us; we say truer things than we intend. As we come to know more and more about life, we shall certainly come to the conclusion that there is an intelligence behind it all. It would be wrong to look at this intelligence as life itself and we should therefore separate Nature from the Demiurge.

The Sun was the creator of the eternal pattern of life. Through life soul could appear and the Earth itself be transformed into a divine being and become the bride of the Sun. The Earth as pure intelligence without mind and without a living body could accept the Sun's intention but could not bring it into the existing world. This task was therefore allotted to the Demiurge whom we may discern in the creation myths of many cultures. I am asking the reader to look at it as history. Myth and history are twins: they represent the ideal and the actual faces of the same reality. The difference is nevertheless important, for history connects us with past and future, whereas myth belongs to the eternal present.

In this chapter I am summarising a presentation of ideas that can be found in detail in my book, *The Dramatic Universe*, and I am therefore not writing so much to convince the reader as to set down a language in which I can speak freely about the way that I look at the world.

We have four concepts. The first is that of an absolute Unfathomable Source from which the whole existing universe proceeds. We must postulate such a source because we have separated the solar system, as our own proper subject of study, from the universe in which it is so minute and, apparently, insignificant. By making this separation, we have to look at the solar system as a unit complete in itself with its own presiding intelligence, the Sun, whom we may think of as God, Creator and Father of life on the earth, and ruler of the solar system. If you reflect deeply, you will see that it is possible for us to form the conception of a supreme being, upon whom every living creature depends, while remaining within the limits of the solar system.

When we come to this earth, we have nature – sometimes referred to as Great Nature. Vernadsky called the film of life that covers the earth "biosphere" and he and many other scientists have been ready to regard the biosphere as a unit that is a being.

The fourth conception is that of the Demiurgic intelligence that stands between the creative power of the Sun and the slowly evolving nature on the planet.* I must, before going further, try to bring the picture of the Demiurge into better focus.

We come here against an unexpected problem: I have written of the Demiurge in the singular but we shall find it necessary to think also of Demiurgic intelligences in the plural and even to say that the Demiurgic intelligence can enter into the human individual. Because orthodox logical thinking is atomic and we tend to look upon a number as having an absolute quality, we

* *Editor's note.* Bennett, in fact, uses in addition a fifth concept, which is that of the Cosmic Reconciling, or God as Love. Love comes from beyond the limits of the creativity of the sun. Love is inherent in life and it is from within life that Love can operate. In a very true sense, then, Nature is sacred. Just as our first experience of love is from our mother, so mankind's first experience of Love came through the love that Nature, his mother, has.

find it unreasonable to suppose that anything can be one and many at the same time. We can admit, for example, that the human body is one whole but also that it is manifold, consisting of limbs, organs, systems and parts large and small. This relationship of whole and part is easy to accept. The difficulty comes when we want to speak of one and many, without the many being subordinated to the one, or the one regarded as the sum of its parts. A better analogy could be found with colour: there is one colour that we call 'blue' and each surface that has a blue colour is as blue as any other. Where 'blue' is present, it is altogether present; size and number have nothing to do with blueness. We have to make a mental leap and think of the Demiurgic intelligence in the same way. Wherever this intelligence is present, it is wholly present. It is neither one nor many; neither large nor small. We also have to say that the Demiurge is both unlimited and limited. It is able to communicate with the creative power that is above it and also enter into every living thing.

We have to add one more element to our picture of the Demiurge, and that is to think of it as a will without a body and, therefore, without an instrument of its own.* It is only when the Demiurge enters into Nature that it has the means of action. It has always been, to me, a remarkable experience to turn back to the first chapter of Genesis and to see how well the notion of an intelligence presiding over the development of an already created world is expressed by the word *Elohim*.** The Elohim preside over the successive stages of differentiation that first prepare the earth for the coming of life, then bring life and finally man to be the ruler of life. The first chapter of Genesis is myth, but myth and history are different languages for speaking about the same reality.

I am going to write about the arising and evolution of life on the earth. It does not matter whether this is taken as history or myth because what matters is that we should have a feeling for the working of a higher intelligence. This will prepare the way for the main understanding of this book, which is to trace the stages by which the Demiurgic intelligence has entered human life and manifested through the Masters of Wisdom.

* *Editor's note.* That is a physical body working through the material energies.
** *Elohim* is a Hebrew word having a plural form; it can mean either the Spirit of God, or the Spiritual Powers.

The earth took its present shape more than two billion years ago. When the time came for life to appear, the Demiurge entered into the only available instrument, namely the active molecules dancing in the primitive atmosphere. The capacity for response to intelligent will was very small indeed, but it was enough to increase the chances of complex molecules arising, composed of hydrogen, carbon and nitrogen, that had the properties of self-aggregation, or polymerization.

We usually look upon the instrument that increases the probability of improbable reactions as a passive agent which we call a catalyst, or, when it comes to life, an enzyme. There is no doubt that catalysis played a decisive part in the synthesis, under the influence of the sun's radiation, of amino-acids, which are the building bricks of life. There is, however, a gap to be bridged even here because the primitive rock surfaces which acted as catalysts could not provide the required pattern to bring about the formation of self-reproducing molecules. Given enormous periods of time and great number of molecules taking part, scientists have assumed that even the most complicated and most improbable reaction could occur by blind chance. Calculations have shown that this will not work and there is, therefore, considerable justification for concluding that an Intelligence must have intervened even before life appeared.*

Even if a biochemist succeeds in synthesising living matter, he will do so not by blind chance but by the exercise of a very high order of intelligence. He will certainly be awarded the Nobel Prize and be rightly regarded as a great genius. He, and his fellow biochemists, may claim to have shown that life arose spontaneously. All that really will have occurred is that man will have succeeded in copying, with great skill and immense perseverance, what the Demiurge accomplished on the primitive earth a billion years ago.

I owe a great deal to my friend Dr Maurice Vernet** for his convincing demonstration that life cannot be understood in terms of any non-living mechanism. Life is sensitive; its activity is always directed towards a goal. Inert matter is insensitive and its activity is governed by laws of causality and probability. The behaviour of material systems can be known and predicted with as much accuracy as we please. The behaviour of living things is

* Editor's note. c.f. *The Dramatic Universe*, Vol. IV, pp 107–13
** c.f. M. Vernet, *La Sensibilité Organique* . . .

never wholly predictable. The gap between the non-living and the living could not be bridged from the side of the non-living. It required intelligence. There is already an intelligence in the most primitive life which is absent from the most complex non-living formations.

I have already indicated the role of the Sun. The Demiurge gave something to bring life but it could not have done so without the higher creative power. In life there is also something beyond intelligence and creativity. In my book, *The Dramatic Universe*, I associated the coming of Life with an act of Divine Compassion.*

This earth was destined to give birth to life from the time it came into its existence. The vast mass of water that stabilizes its temperature; the atmosphere that provides the essential elements of hydrogen, carbon, oxygen and nitrogen while at the same time transmitting the life-giving radiation from the sun and absorbing the lethal ultra-violet; the solid earth itself containing in its crust all the known chemical elements: these provide life with its perfect birth place and home. If the sun is the Father of life, then earth is certainly its Mother.

Life began as a thin film of blue-green algae spreading over the surface of the ocean. The atmosphere contained little oxygen and the ocean little salt, but an intense activity of photosynthesis continuing for five hundred million years fixed great quantities of carbon and released an equal amount of oxygen into the atmosphere. We must here pause to look at the marvel of photosynthesis, the mechanism by which green vegetation can use the light of the sun to convert carbon dioxide and water into carbohydrates and, oxygen. The secret of this marvel is the molecule of chlorophyll which must have appeared on the earth more than a billion years ago, for it is present in all but the most primitive algae. All life depends on chlorophyll: a combination of carbon, hydrogen, oxygen and nitrogen with an atom of magnesium nestling in its heart. Chlorophyll has for half a billion years performed the prodigious task of supplying all life with carbon to build bodies and oxygen to breathe. By the middle of the first billenium before our time, the land surface, the oceans and the atmosphere were ready for another great step.

Up till now, reproduction had been mere proliferation of

---

* c.f. *The Dramatic Universe*, Vol. IV, p. 117

protoplasm. There were no cells and so no sex. There were no beings to be born or to die: just a thin film of algae feeding on air, water, light and the chemicals of the earth's crust. The transition to simple life – the protozoa – was a step of staggering simplicity that simply could not have occurred spontaneously. It consisted in enclosing a drop of protoplasm within a membrane and giving it a nucleus that held the pattern of its own construction. For the first time on earth, an individual being appeared. So far as can be judged from the scanty remains in the most ancient rocks, this step took half a billion years, that is five hundred times as long as man has existed on the earth.

The creative genius that produced a cell can be dimly conjectured if we reflect that the simplest cell contains more than a hundred million atoms of hydrogen, carbon, nitrogen and oxygen and special elements like iron, magnesium and sulphur, all built into the most intricate structure of interacting molecules.

Cells can float in water so they can meet one another and fuse to give a new individual. With this, sexual reproduction became possible. Life passed from self-renewal to reproduction. Two cells could produce new cells and having thus perpetuated their existence could die and their bodies dissolve. Sex and death came together: sex with its limitless potential for transformation and mortality with its limitation of existence in space and time. Sex and mortality – the hope and the hazard of life – are to us so commonplace that we cannot readily picture the intelligence which foresaw that they would be the means of creating free and intelligent individuals.

For a long time cells either floated freely or aggregated in colonies like sponges. The next great step was the appearance of the metazoa, animals with differentiated functions and plants that could provide life with carbon and oxygen. The rocks of the dry land, weathered by wind and rain for hundreds of millions of years and carried down to the sea by the rivers, formed the soil on which vegetation could find a hold and prepare for the evolution of the higher animals.

The early animals had no organised sensitivity. Their reactions were as automatic as those of the inert chemicals on which they fed. Even sex was devoid of attraction – an accidental meeting and mating of similar organisms. Death held no fear, for there were no perceptions beyond the awareness of light and darkness, heat and cold.

A great catastrophe occurred to the earth about five hundred million years ago. It was probably connected with the arrival of the moon, which has ever since been closely associated with sex. The surface of the earth was torn open and new rocks, those of the Cambrian series, appeared. Nearly all life was destroyed, but that which remained developed in variety and potential for sensitive experience. It is important to realise that evolution has not been a continuous progress towards 'higher' forms of life. There have been many promising starts that came to a dead end and some biologists regard this as evidence against any theory of guided evolution. To produce skeletal tissues required experimentation and elimination. If we look at the development of life in this way, we can see that the apparent failures sometimes made most valuable contributions to the solution of life's problems. Not all forms of life can justify themselves on utilitarian grounds. We must here look at Nature in Her other aspects. She is beautiful and playful. To disregard these features is crass ingratitude.

The Demiurge reveals to us not only the purposeful drive towards higher levels of being, but also the joy of life and the love of play. This is beautifully expressed in the Book of Proverbs,* where Wisdom describes her part in the creation of life on the earth:

"The Lord possessed me in the beginning of his way,
Before his works of old.
I was set up from everlasting, from the beginning,
Or ever the earth was.
When there were no depths, I was brought forth;
When there were no fountains abounding with water.
Before the mountains were settled,
Before the hills was I brought forth:
While as yet he had not made the earth, nor the fields,
Nor the highest part of the dust of the world.
When he prepared the heavens, I was there:
When he set a compass upon the face of the depth:
When he established the clouds above:
When he strengthened the fountains of the deep:

---

* *c.f. Proverbs* 8:22–31. *Editor's note.* Bennett considered Wisdom and Demiurgic intelligence to be the same.

When he gave to the sea his decree,
That the waters should not pass his commandment:
When he appointed the foundations of the earth:
Then I was by him, as one brought up with him:
And I was daily his delight,
Rejoicing always before him;
Rejoicing in the habitable part of his earth;
And my delights were with the sons of men."

Some of the most primitive forms of life, sea-weed and sponges, sea-anemones and even the microscopic diatoms, are among the most beautiful. Biologists seek to explain natural beauty in terms of sexual selection or protective mimicry, but these apply only to advanced forms of life and by no means always to these.

Four characteristics of Nature cannot be understood without reference to intelligence. These are:

1. *Progress*. Life has moved in a definite direction towards the emergence of conscious creative beings. There are all the marks of intelligent experimentation to discover the most suitable forms.

2. *Interdependence*. Ecological science reveals the extent to which all life is interlocked in bonds of mutual dependence. The structure is so complex and improbable that it could not have come about without wisdom.

3. *Beauty*. This is usually explained in human terms: we see beauty in Nature because that is how we see. The explanation does not make sense. Beauty is superhuman. It is an attribute of the Demiurge. He creates beauty because He loves beauty. Fantasy is divine: Life was not created on this earth for strictly utilitarian ends. The Demiurge is artist and poet and our art and our poetry are a gift to us that enables us to share in His enjoyment.

4. *Play*. Play is timeless, it has no past and no future. It does not ask 'why'? Can we associate play with so great a will as that of the Demiurge who unites Sun and Earth to create Life? We can and must do so. Without play, history would have no meaning until its ultimate consummation. Play is creation in the present moment; it is fulfilment that has no tomorrow. When we look at all that is comic, even grotesque, and all that is absurd and

Demiurgic intelligences made use of the rich capacity of the mammals to transform sensitive energy in order to prepare the 'mind-stuff' needed for man.*

The creation of man as he is today involved four distinct stages. First came the primates, monkeys and apes, who developed throughout the Miocene and especially the recent Cainozoic ages. There were no signs of human characteristics until about four million years ago, when the first hominids appeared in Africa. These were still only experimental men, but they could do things that animals cannot. They could adapt themselves to different modes of life, for example, from arboreal fruit eaters to life on the ground. It was not until much later that true men came, with massive brains, who were capable of remembering the past and foreseeing the future. These are marks of the conscious energy that is on a higher level than life itself.

Man became conscious because the Demiurge had concentrated the energy this required. He did not become conscious by accident, for consciousness cannot arise accidentally. If domestic animals are sometimes conscious, it is because they borrow from their human friends. This we can see for ourselves in our dogs and cats and horses. Man acquired consciousness, not as a temporary loan but as an element in his essential nature. More simply, we can say that half a million years ago the Demiurge succeeded in providing man with a *mind*. This was the second stage. The mind of man is not a property of his body, although it normally requires a *brain* in order to connnect it with the world of bodies.**

The Demiurgic incarnations gained their ascendancy over the people, not only by their superior knowledge but also by the display of powers. They were the first magicians, the precursors of the Masters of Wisdom. There is evidence of the survival of

* *Editor's note.* Sensitive energy is the highest energy of life. In man, it is the 'stuff of mind', but only in the presence of conscious energy. The notion of energies different in quality was central to Bennett's work.

** *Editor's note.* In the present book, Bennett refers several times to the Sufi scheme of three worlds. These are, in simple terms: the world of physical bodies, the world of mind and the world of will. The Sufi technical terms are, respectively: *ālam-i ajsām, ālam-i arvāh, ālam-i imkān*. The second world is also called in English the 'world of spirits', referring to the psychic or mental energies that are not totally confined by physical existence. It is this world that most people ordinarily confuse with the truly spiritual world 'beyond the mind'.

Neanderthal magic in the northern valleys of the river Lena, a region as desolate as the Ice Age could have given man to live in. The Swedish explorer Ivar Lissner has given us detailed accounts of a surviving bear cult similar to that practised in the famous Drachenloch cave in the Swiss Alps more than fifty thousand years ago. The bear is venerated because it is believed to be the wisest of animals, and by sacrificing it according to an elaborate ritual its wisdom was transmitted to the tribe. For tens of thousands of years, the needs of man for assurance in front of the terrors of nature were satisfied by his confidence in the Demiurgic magicians. This second stage was a long period of waiting. For no apparent reason the step to true manhood was delayed right through the hundred thousand years that separated the glaciations of Riss and Würm. The first period of the Würm glaciation came and went, and there was a relatively mild period of ten thousand years during which the next great step was made, thirty-five to forty-five thousand years before our present time.

The third stage was the advent of creativity. We can call this the *creation of Adam*. For more than half-a-million years, men had all the characteristics of humanity except creativity. This is a higher energy than consciousness and is characteristic of the Demiurge. By 'Adam', I mean the first man who had all the characteristics of man as we know him. He could speak as we do, he could enjoy creative fantasies and translate them into action, he could become aware of past and future and understand that events could occur beyond the reach of his senses.

Such characteristics are not direct operations of the creative energy, but they are not possible unless it is present to stimulate consciousness. Where did this come from? Creativity is the energy that responds directly to the will, but men of the Mousterian* and early cultures were not individualised. They could not initiate. The power to initiate new activity was still with the Demiurge alone. How was it transferred to Man?

There is little doubt that a mutation occurred which resulted in a far-reaching change in human anatomy. This is a recent discovery of which I was not aware when I wrote the last volume of *The Dramatic Universe* ten years ago. It has considerably changed my picture of the coming of the first Masters of

* *Editor's note.* The Mousterian culture was Neanderthal spanning the period four-hundred to one-hundred thousand years ago.

Wisdom; it has not weakened but rather reinforced my
conviction that between thirty-five and forty thousand years ago
the event occurred which in the Book of Genesis is called the
Creation of Adam. The discovery is simply that Neanderthal
man could not articulate speech sounds as we can and that the
new man could. Until recently, it was supposed that apes could
not learn human speech because their brains could not handle
complexities of language. It has recently been shown that a
chimpanzee can learn a large number of gesture-words and use
them to communicate more than he learns by imitation. Apes
cannot form human speech sounds because of their anatomical,
not mental, limitations. Neanderthal man had the same
limitation. The great mutation around thirty-five thousand years
ago removed this limitation and the new race could articulate
speech sounds.

The hypothesis I want to put forward is that this was the
long-awaited moment when man could be endowed with
creativity to enable him to make full use of his powers. The
nature of creativity is such that it cannot be transferred from one
person to another. It is an integral part of the essence, the
instrument of the will and the source of freedom. Creativity must
enter us at the moment of conception and this gives us the key to
understanding how it entered the human race. The Demiurge
can take the form of a man or a woman and can beget children.
We have an echo of the event in the Book of Genesis. Adam was
created by the Elohim: the Demiurge acting directly. The
complete transformation whereby man acquired the new bodily,
psychological and spiritual powers of the Adamic race is
described in a very ancient tradition: "And it came to pass, when
men began to multiply on the face of the earth and daughters
were born unto them, that the sons of God saw the daughters of
men that they were fair; and they took them wives of all which
they chose. And the Lord said, 'My spirit shall not always strive
with man, for that he also is flesh: yet his days shall be a hundred
and twenty years.' There were giants in the earth in those days;
and also after that, when the sons of God came in unto the
daughters of men and they bare children to them, the same
became mighty men which were of old, men of renown".
(*Genesis* 6:1–4).

All this happened towards the end of the mild climate known
as the Gottweig Interstadial when the glaciers in Europe, central

Asia and north America receded, but did not withdraw.* There
was freedom of movement. It may be that the legend of the
Garden of Eden refers to this time, when man became creative.
The old Neanderthal race disappeared in a very short space of
time, probably not by conquest but by sexual selection. The
Neanderthal race could in no way hold its own against the dread
return of the Ice Age without the support of its magicians, and
they had their hands occupied with the new race, *Homo sapiens
sapiens.* Twelve thousand years were needed to come to terms
with the new creativity. This was the fourth stage. They were
years of amazing achievement. Art and science moved rapidly
ahead to produce the great cave paintings. Men learned the art of
weaving and clothed themselves in garments.

In the regions south of the glaciers there was a band of equable
climate. To the south again there was dense and almost continual
rain. The new men, the Aurignacian and Gravettian as they have
been named by prehistorians, learned to speak, but their language
was very different from ours. They retained much of the gesture
language of their forebears. Of all their great achievements only
traces remain, mostly buried deep in limestone caves in Turkestan
and the Caucasus, in France and Spain.

The seas were lower in those days and there were probably
centres of initiation in what is now the Atlantic continental shelf.
They left behind them a message that remained undeciphered for
twenty thousand years, until Gurdjieff went with me to the caves
at Lascaux on the last journey he made before he died on the 29th
October, 1949. He showed me that the herds of deer depicted as
crossing a river represented an initiation rite. The number of
antlers on the deer indicated the level of development of the men
whose emblem they were. In these and other caves we can see the
work, not of magicians of the Mousterian culture, but of Masters
of Wisdom who lived, according to the calculations of the great
authority on parietal art, the Abbé Breuil, thirty to thirty-five
thousand years ago.

Gurdjieff told me that he had learned about these ancient
schools of wisdom from researches he himself had made in caves
in the Caucasian mountains and in the great limestone caverns of
the Syr Darya in Turkestan. I have since learned that there is a
Sufi tradition in central Asia that claims to go back forty
thousand years.

* *Editor's note.* About thirty-seven thousand years ago. See above p. 38.

I cannot claim that anything that I have written is convincing evidence; nevertheless, I am pretty sure that the Adamic age did begin at the end of the Gottweig Interstadial, that the onset of the new and final glaciation of Würm did put the new race to the supreme test and that it survived. For twelve thousand years all went well. This period, curiously enough, is exactly the length of time mentioned in the Avestan chronicle for the duration of the first race of men.

The first 'great cycle' * of twenty-five thousand years ended twelve thousand years ago, 10,000 BC, when the glaciers began their slow retreat from the northern temperate zone. That was the start of the modern age. The great change came when the Demiurge ceased to take possession of the magicians. It is true that shamans, the descendants of the great magicians, have remained to this day to testify to the permanence of tradition; but even in the great days of shamanism three thousand years ago, they did not possess the Demiurgic power that could survey human history in a vision of twenty thousand years and prepare for events in the distant future.

The new self-hood of man had fully established itself with the three-fold nature of body, mind and will, capable of being transformed into a perfected individual. The changes in the visible world were only a part of the story. There is a second world, called by the Sufis the *ālam-i arvāh* or world of spirits. This world has in it different levels, three of which concern us here. There is the region of sensitivity which man shares with the animals. Until the time of Adam, men had no place in the second level of consciousness. This is where the souls of men go after the death of the physical body and there they exist timelessly. I have called this the 'Mind-Stuff-Pool' because the energies composing it provide man with the material from which his mind, as distinct from his brain, is drawn. The third is the creative level, the domain of the Demiurge and of the fully-formed souls of men. This transforms mind-stuff into soul-stuff. Creativity is the essential ingredient of soul formation. Man could not embark on the next stage of his evolution until the third level was prepared. This took twenty-five thousand years by our reckoning.

Before we leave the first Adamic age, I want to emphasize its totally different character from any state of affairs we know. First

* *Editor's note.* The notion of cycles is explained at the end of this chapter.

of all, the climate was dominated by glaciers in the temperate zones and by almost continuous rains in the tropics. The human race was still few in number and existed precariously in a world dominated by mammals: mammoths, moose, deer of many species, wild horses. Bears, tigers, wolves were all a threat to men armed with primitive weapons. The tribes were always on the move; the seasons determined the movements of the herds that they hunted and the location of fruit and roots on which they fed. Without their magicians, they were helpless, and the magicians were like a race apart. They lived differently from the cave-dwellers, engaging in arts and sciences that the common people could not begin to understand. Their domination was complete and many of them misused their powers. Towards the end of the great cycle, from twelve to fifteen thousand years ago, these cultures degenerated, as we can readily confirm if we visit the prehistoric section of any museum and see how poor were the implements and how few the works of art from this period.

It was as if mankind had entered a period of waiting for the sun to rise again. The magicians, who could read the signs of the times, knew that the glaciers were soon to melt and a new age was to start. Those who could communicate with the Demiurge prepared for the great event.

Here I must say something about the duration of what I call the "epochs". There is a well-known view that associates the cycles of history with the precession of the equinox and divides the great year − or great cycle − of twenty-five thousand sidereal years into twelve signs of the zodiac. I have not been able to verify this and have noted that the most ancient records divide the sky into ten and not twelve regions. This gives the duration of two thousand five hundred years for each minor cycle or epoch, which fits the historical evidence very much better. In this book, I am not concerned with astrology or the calendar and cannot, therefore, go into any detailed discussion of ages and epochs. It seems clear to me that there have been great changes in human life at intervals of twelve thousand years − that is, roughly half a great cycle − going back to the origin of Adam thirty-seven thousand years ago. I also feel sure that there have been shorter cycles or epochs, each characterised by an attitude towards human life that was spread all over the world. The beginning of these cycles coincides with the end of the Ice Ages and it is convenient to call it the "second Adamic Period". This was the time when the forces acting on human life divided into those that were concerned to preserve a stationary condition and those that were directed towards the further evolution of man. The magicians were drawn into one or another of these two opposing tendencies. In this way there came about the division that has since been called the separation of the black and white paths.

It must be understood that the great cycles start slowly and gather momentum to reach their maximum activity about half-way through. We are now at such a mid-point and we can see for ourselves how fast events are moving. In the first great cycle (35,000 – 10,000 BC) creativity entered by slow degrees as the mind-stuff of man was gradually impregnated with the new energy. In the second great cycle, there was at first a slow concentration of soul-stuff. The difference between mind-stuff and soul-stuff needs a few words of explanation. Mind-stuff is the blend of energies from sensitivity to consciousness out of which the mind of man is made. Soul-stuff consists of these together with creativity. The three-fold combination of sensitivity, consciousness and creativity is the raw material of the soul. In order to *become a soul*, it must be united with the will. This is what I mean by *transformation*.

The retreat of the glaciers made life easy and there appeared to be no reason for continuing to struggle to find a better way of life. On the other hand, it was the very moment when mankind could make use of favourable climatic conditions to develop new powers. In the next chapter, we shall try to reconstruct the events that occurred under the direction of the first Masters of Wisdom. From this period onwards there is much more material for reconstruction, until we come to modern times, when we know so much that our difficulty is to recognize what really matters.

Chapter Two

The Early Masters

In this chapter, we shall trace the history of ten thousand years to the first millenium before Christ. Because of the great changes which came over the earth it is more than a history of mankind. It is a significant period for the evolution of life itself.

Epoch of Withdrawal and Concentration

Hitherto tribes had been dependent on their shamans to know where and when to go for food. Now their animal nature reasserted itself. Some of the magicians succumbed to the temptation to make life easy. The domestication of animals advanced rapidly and hunters became herdsmen. Those magicians who had received the Demiurgic initiation knew that a great task awaited them. They withdrew from the broad prairies rich with wild horses, deer and domestic cattle, taking with them groups of candidates for initiation. For this reason, I have called this the epoch of Withdrawal and Concentration. It lasted from 10,500 to 8,000 BC. The visible culture was Neolithic, a new creative impulse to produce better tools, such as the Azilian microlithic culture, better clothes and dwellings and better conditions of life.

The task of the true initiates was to provide mankind with adequate language to express abstract ideas, to lay the foundations of belief in a communication with the spiritual world* and to teach ordinary men and women to think for

* *Editor's note.* Bennett refers to the world beyond the spirit world.

themselves. The first Masters of Wisdom were the creators of traditional wisdom. They were initiates who were not simply guided by the higher intelligence, but were the Demiurge itself.

We can reconstruct the way they worked by studying the results which remain to our day in the form of three great language systems, four basic beliefs and four kinds of social system. There was also probably a fifth centre in the Andes. The four that I have studied in detail* are:

1 *The Great Mother* This had its roots in the fertility cults of remote antiquity. It was predominant in the near and middle East and in the eastern Mediterranean, especially in Asia Minor. The Great Mother was associated with a matriarchal society engaged in agriculture, and this culture gave rise to the first settlements. It originated no special language since none was needed.

2 *The Great Spirit* This became prevalent in central Asia and the far East and soon crossed over into northern America. Its primal origin was in the Demiurgic presences who took the form of magicians and established the technique of possession. The form of society was nomadic, where guidance came through the shamans who were inspired. The subtle polysynthetic and agglutinative languages created were capable of conveying the sense of an unseen spiritual presence and the timeless pattern of situations.

3 *The Creator God* This probably originated in north-east Africa and developed in later millenia traditions to do with the creative "magical" powers of the human psyche. From this source came the triliteral Hamito-semitic languages which are so well-suited to a description of the variety of creative manifestation. The social form was that of an aristocracy with a divine ruler.

4 *The Saviour God* This, as we shall see, probably originated within the Arctic circle in the region of northern Siberia. It was the Hyperborean culture. It produced the inflected Indo-European languages. The culture was based on a sense of the uncertainty of existence and the idea of the need for man to co-operate with creative intelligence to maintain his life and to progress. The languages produced were well-suited to deal with actions in space and time. The caste society was developed.

---

* *The Dramatic Universe* Vol. IV, chap. 47.

I will briefly trace the history of the four cultures during the first epoch.

Each of the four cultures represents a different Way of Transformation. Each of them was created by Masters of Wisdom – the first on earth.

The Great Mother

The traditions of the near and middle East bear witness to a time when the Great Mother was the fount of life and the originator of the domestic arts, especially of agriculture and husbandry. Cybele of the Phrygians, Innana of the Sumerians, Ishtar and Rhea were the names given to Nature as the mother of beasts and men. The region contains traces of the earliest permanent settlements and of the origins of agriculture that go back twelve thousand years, that is to the epoch of Withdrawal. Matriarchal societies predominated and still survive in more remote places. There was not a true withdrawal, because the Great Mother cult was easily established, nor was a new language created in this region.

The true functions of the Mother – to give birth and to cherish the new-born; to give stability to society and to remain sensitive to the Demiurge within – could be expressed in the simple ritual of fertility and the change of the seasons. No special language was needed and the language of the first Adamic cycle could still serve. When the great migrations brought people from other cultures into the area, the old language was forgotten but the cult of the Great Mother remained. The Masters of Wisdom of this region were concerned with teaching mankind the practical arts. Copper and iron, weaving and pottery, the wheel and the plough all originated in the region. It was an exoteric society that spread because the early farmers did not know how to care for the land and when it lost its fertility they moved on. In this way the Mother culture was able to reach Europe by way of the valleys of the Volga and the Danube, and drive the microlithic hunters to the west.

The Great Spirit

Over a vast area, half of Asia and most of the Americas, the Demiurgic power was looked for in the sky. It was the Great Spirit which possesses man and makes him creative. In its most sophisticated interpretation, the Great Spirit is *tao*, the all-pervading spirit from which come yang and yin, the male and female principles which give rise to the triad and so to all the diverse manifestations of Great Nature. In south east Asia the Great Spirit is *mana*.

The home of the Great Spirit culture was central Asia, long before the deserts destroyed its rich pastures and decimated the great plains on which the nomad tribes lived. This is the region where the old magic remained longest. The Masters of Wisdom were shamans, though not many shamans were Masters of Wisdom. I believe that the schools of wisdom were not nomadic, but groups who settled in the valleys of the Hindu Kush and Altai mountains and developed the remarkable linguistic system based on syllabic tonality that includes the Turkish languages, Chinese and Malay.

The Great Spirit culture led to the incomparable achievements of Chinese art and science, but an even more important contribution was the development of the techniques of transformation. Nowhere on the earth* were the secrets of the spirit world** so well understood. This started no doubt with the technique of *possession* employed by the shamans; but the most ancient traditions of the region confirm that a brotherhood of wise men has existed for thousands of years and that many of the secrets of yoga, Sufism and the tantra have emanated from that centre.

The Creator God

When northern Europe and Asia were covered with glaciers, Africa was subjected to heavy and continuous rain that turned most of the low-lying land into swamps unfit for human habitation. The uplands were inhabited by palaeolithic tribes governed by magicians whose methods were very different from those of the shamans.

To understand the tradition created by the Masters in Africa, we must remember the overpowering presence of the sun in those regions. It must have been truly astonishing for tribes accustomed for thousands of years to life in an atmosphere of rain and mist to see the sun drying the earth and bringing new forms

* Except, perhaps, in the Andes. I have done little research on this region and cannot say.
** *Editor's note. Alam-i arvāh*, the world of energies such as the sensitive, conscious and creative. See note on the three worlds, p. 37.

of life everywhere. The African magicians were the very embodiments of the power of the sun. They could kill and bring to life, they could make their presence felt through scores of miles of dense forest. They were not like the shamans, mere vehicles of the Great Spirit who reverted to ordinary human beings when they were no longer possessed, but supermen, even Demiurgic beings, who were altogether different from the ordinary people and even went to a special heaven when they died. These beliefs, which even now have not completely disappeared in east Africa, are relics of a very ancient tradition when there were real Masters of Wisdom in that region.

During the epoch of withdrawal, there were centres in Ethiopia and perhaps also Uganda and Kenya. Here sun-worship, creator-worship and king-worship were developed together with the marvellous linguistic system called Hamito-semitic. It is in some ways the most artificial language ever created by man, for it assigns totally different roles to movement and rest, that is to vowels and consonants. The latter express the basic meaning and the former the action associated with it. One cannot look at Hebrew or Arabic and be surprised that these are sacred languages in which God Himself has spoken.

One cannot fail to notice the remarkable unity of vision that combines the concept of One Creator God, the autocratic and theocratic state and a sacred language. The creators of the Semitic tradition must indeed have been Masters of Wisdom.

The Saviour God

We now come to the strange, almost unbelievable, story of the origin of the Aryan tradition. I could never have guessed it myself but for the researches of that remarkable man B. G. Tilak, one of the founders of Indian Nationalism, a profound scholar and a man of the deepest spirituality.* He published his researches in learned journals and they are splendidly presented in his book *The Arctic Home in the Vedas*. When I found this book, thirty years ago, I devoured it with amazement, unable to see why his thesis was not universally known and accepted. Since then, I have conducted my own researches and have found much evidence not available in his day.

---

* I can claim a remote connection with him as my father-in-law, Frederick Elliot of Baroda, had known him when he was tutor to the Gaekwar.

In short, Tilak shows that the oldest Vedic hymns must have been written by priests living in the Arctic Circle. I have no room in this book to summarise the evidence,* but will give a single example. *Ushas* in the Vedas are the goddesses of the dawn. They are very popular, appearing over three hundred times in twenty different hymns. Now the dawn in India is nothing special: day comes quickly as in all sub-tropical latitudes. But in the Arctic the dawn is spectacular. The sun moves in a circle round the Pole star and as the six months' night is ending the dawn appears again and again. On the Siberian shores of the Arctic Ocean it moves in a majestic dance coming close to the horizon, rosy and full of hope and dipping again to darkness. The number of false dawns increases until there are thirty in all. Now the Vedas describe the Ushas as thirty sisters who go round in five groups before the sun rises. It is hard to conceive how the picture of dawn going round the sky could have arisen in the minds of people not living in the far north. There are numerous other evidences of a Hyperborean origin of the Vedic hymns. The same is true of the Avestan hymns and the Norse sagas. Even in Homer some passages suggest that his hymns must have come from the Arctic regions.

Since Tilak's time, it has been proved that the Siberian Arctic had a much milder climate twelve thousand years ago than it has today. Traces of human settlements have been found on the shores of the Arctic Ocean. Hesiod tells us that when Zeus gained ascendancy over the Titans, they went north and lived: "their hearts free from anxiety in the Islands of the Blest on the shores of the Ocean where the great maelstrom whirls" **. This and other references to the Hyperborean region extol the mild climates to be found near the "petrified sea", i.e. the ice-pack.

Let us assume then that there could have been a school of Wisdom in the far north and that the Titans in Hesiod's account were the initiates who withdrew when the fight for power that came with the milder climates made it necessary to prepare a better future for mankind.

The external conditions were totally different from those of the other three centres. I believe that the withdrawal took place

* I give more details in *The Dramatic Universe*, Vol. IV Ch. 47 but the reader who wants to judge for himself must read Tilak's book.
** Hesiod *Works and Days* 172–3.

by sea, up the west coast of Europe. At that time, the level of the oceans rose owing to the melting of the glaciers and this may have been a factor in deciding the exodus. Once the Arctic Circle was reached the colonists were completely free from interference and remained so for more than two thousand years. During this time, the original Indo-European language was created and an amazing tradition was established. The overwhelming sense of human impotence in the face of the prodigies of nature, enacted before people day and night, brought with it the feeling that not even the gods are omnipotent. The long cold nights when the waters froze, the procession of the dawns rosy and beautiful, the break up of the ice-floes when the sun reappeared, the turning of the wheel of heaven: all these were made the theme of the salvation of the home of gods and men from the jealous serpent power lurking in the south. In one of its oldest forms in the Vedas it is found in the ritual that celebrates the conquest of the saviour god Indra over the serpent power Vritra who has taken the sun captive in the nether regions.

The myth gains added poignancy in the light of the colonists' escape from the evil powers that had taken possession of their homeland. Thus the notion of good and evil became linked with the Arctic day and night.

Now comes the all-important element that distinguishes the Aryan tradition from all others. *The God needs human help.* This is the origin of the ritual sacrifice by which man is associated with the Saviour God. For this purpose, a new language was created, a sacred language to be used only on sacred occasions. To be initiated into the language, a man must start by proving his worth. Hence the subsidiary myths and legends of heroes and their exploits.

The language created was one of the greatest achievements of the Masters of Wisdom. It made possible the expression of the most complex and the most refined experiences of which man is capable. We have only the degenerate remains of the original creation. In very old languages, like Sanskrit, Lithuanian and Romany we can find evidence of a structure that corresponds to the pattern of the Universe. It was also highly flexible and could adapt itself better than the other two root languages to all the changes that have occurred in the last ten thousand years.

Generation after generation passed. Slowly, the new language became familiar, for the entire life of the community turned upon the ritual practices. The Masters transmitted their secrets to the priests and remained in contact only with a select few destined to succeed them. The long winters encouraged exchanges after the day's work was done. The fascination of the drama of summer and winter was expressed in song and dance. The Masters of Wisdom, step by step, introduced their followers to the idea of a life that went beyond the satisfaction of animal needs and the search for Truth began. A very great event had occurred. Men had learned to think.

The Epoch of Diffusion

The earth enjoyed the best climate for a hundred thousand years during the period from 8,000 to 5,500 BC. The only area where conditions deteriorated was the far north which was cut off from the benefits of the Gulf Stream. The glaciers had melted, the Steppes were covered with rich moraine on which the luxurious grass supported immense herds of bison, wild horses and many species of deer. The population of the earth grew rapidly. In the first Adamic age the entire human race scarcely exceeded two million; it grew to ten times this number by the sixth millenium before Christ.

There now began the first migrations directed by the Masters. The Aryans moved southward up the valleys of the Ob, the Yenisey and the Lena and entered the plains of Turkestan where they met with the Great Spirit people. These latter prospered greatly as their nomadic habits enabled them to take full advantage of the increased food supplies. They went south to India, east into China and crossed by the long-established land bridge into America. The Creator God people occupied Egypt and some groups reached Mesopotamia. The groups that migrated brought with them their tradition, their language and their way of life.

The epoch was the most peaceful and happiest since the creation of Adam. No weapons have been found in any of the settlements that existed between 8,000 and 5,500 BC. The evil influences that threatened the earth at the end of the Adamic age had been neutralised and did not reappear until the close of the epoch. It may well be that this was the Golden age referred to in so many traditions.

In the region of the Great Mother culture, agriculture went ahead with the domestication of all the principal grain crops.

Fermentation was discovered and grapes were cultivated for wine making. Fine instruments made from obsidian, the beautiful volcanic glass, allowed fine crafts to develop. The first permanent settlements grew and prospered. We have an example at Catal Huyuk founded at the beginning of the epoch, about 8,000 BC. The evidence of peace, prosperity and the enjoyment of beauty are everywhere. In Europe the Great Mother was venerated from the Swiss lake villages to the Windmill Hill people in England. The culture spread slowly as the farmers went in search of land, taking their cattle with them. Traces can be found from the Indus Valley in India to Libya. The Mother Goddess was worshipped in the great centres of Harrappa and Mohenjo-daro before the coming of the Aryans.

The most remarkable achievement of the Great Spirit people was the colonization of America.* Mammoth, bison and antelope had crossed into the great plains. The Great Spirit found a home where it has remained for eight thousand years. The linguistic form gave shape to speech and in north America the tranquil existence of the Golden age seems to have persisted longer than in any other part of the world.

I cannot say, from simple ignorance of the facts, what happened in South America. There may have been a fifth centre or it may be that the Creator God culture was brought across the Atlantic ocean. The remarkable similarities of the monuments, symbols and beliefs of Mexico and the Andean cultures to those of Egypt have led many to believe that the extraordinary feat of navigating the Atlantic was first achieved six or seven thousand years ago. We have confused echoes of the event in the legend of Atlantis.**

It seems that the Mediterranean countries were open to the Creator God and the Semitic languages at a very early date. The old Maltese language and the Etruscan culture give this support.

The Creator God did not penetrate far into the East until much later. If one looks at the maps of the world, it is easy to see that

* Editor's note. There is evidence of crossings fifteen thousand years ago. What is talked about here is the special migration inspired by the creative action of the Great Spirit centre ten thousand years ago.

** Editor's note. There are two distinguishable elements in the Atlantis myth. One of these is the possible Atlantic crossing from Africa referred to here. The other, much later (second millenium BC) is found in the Timaeus of Plato and plays an important part in the story later on in this chapter.

the three cultures would meet naturally in the region between the Caspian and Aral Seas. Tradition tells us that this region was the seat of the most ancient school of Wisdom which united all teachings and all beliefs. Here the Great Mother was understood in her relationship to the Saviour God and here the Great Spirit was known as the link between man and the Creator from which he came.

By the sixth millenium BC the Aryan tradition was established in its new home in central Asia. The human race had greatly increased in numbers and had spread all over the earth. A sense of confidence in the permanence of human society came with the constantly improving conditions of life.

Alas for human belief in permanence. About six thousand years ago great changes of climate occurred all over the world. There were also great natural disasters. The great Siberian meteorite struck the earth with the violence of a thousand atom bombs. It must have been felt everywhere as a warning of coming disaster. The earth entered a period of wind storms and drought. Trillions of square miles of rich prairies turned to desert: the Sahara, the Arabian, the Kara Kum, the Gobi. The inhabitants were forced to migrate and the struggle for land began. The first wars of invasion changed the entire human situation.

The Epoch of Conflict

Between 5,500 BC and 3,000 BC, power and authority passed from the initiates who had preserved the tradition to the leaders* who could assure their people of land. Only where great tracts of land were irrigated from the mountains could the old nomadic life of the Great Spirit tribes and their shamans continue.

It was at this time that the Masters of Wisdom set themselves to establish hidden sanctuaries where their teachings could be preserved for the future. This was the beginning of the 'great work'. It was inevitable and foreseen long before, that as men learned to use their creative powers to dominate over others, there would arise divisions of castes and nations and that there would have to be a visible exoteric authority to maintain the integrity of society. The Masters could not occupy such positions, nor were men ready to look for advice.

* *Editor's note.* The language here is taken from that of *The Dramatic Universe* Vol. III chapter 41. The leader is the highest grade of *psychostatic* man, that is, man divorced from transformation.

By the end of the epoch the climatic conditions again changed. One result of the drought had been to dry the great valleys of the Nile, the Tigris and Euphrates and the Yellow River in China, making them habitable.

The ritual practices, the languages and the basic attitudes to life that had been established from the start of the great cycle remained but they came under the control of priests and leaders. Another effect of the migrations had been to establish commerce rather than barter as a means of exchange. Money had been invented, writing was in use in many places. City states began to grow in importance. We are entering the historic period the visible events of which are recorded in epic poetry confirmed by inscriptions and even, in some cases, written accounts on clay tablets or stone.

The Heroic Epoch

About five thousand years ago, mankind turned its attention to mortality and immortality in a new way. Man believed in immortal Gods and looked for immortal men. This was the start of the Heroic epoch. The first known hero was Gilgamesh whose legend is preserved in a number of cuneiform inscriptions.

The hero had a two-fold function. He had direct access to the gods and he could ensure prosperity to his people. Very often he was looked upon himself as half-god, half-man. This is how it was in Egypt where the divine pharaoh was immortal and could confer deathlessness on those near him. This interpretation of the hero was characteristic of the Creator God culture. The Great Mother culture admitted heroes, who as consorts of the goddesses themselves became immortal. The Great Spirit culture accepted heroes as incarnations of the Great Spirit later known as *Shang-ti.* The Saviour God Aryans very naturally saw their heroes in men who gave their lives to help the gods in their struggle with the powers of darkness.

In all this, the Masters of Wisdom played an unseen role. It was they who saw that the time had come when mankind must be divided according to their capacity for transformation. I shall use here the names I gave to these divisions in *The Dramatic Universe.*

Those men and women who do not or cannot from natural deficiencies enter the process of transformation and acquire a soul are 'psychostatic'. The summit of the psychostatic order of society is the external authority or leader.

All who are in process of transformation, who have committed themselves to the task of acquiring immortality, are 'psychokinetic'. This order of society consists of various grades: candidates, who aspire to transformation and have made a committment; specialists, who have developed some skill through which psychokinetic ideas and techniques can be transmitted; counsellors, who are able from long experience to guide others in their troubles on the hazardous path of transformation; and initiates, those who have entered into communication with the Demiurgic intelligence, though not in a permanent way.

The Masters themselves are 'psychoteleios', those who have completed the transformation and can communicate directly with the Demiurge and even with the Father Creator. The psychoteleios man has learned the secret of immortality in the *duraosha haroma,* 'from whom death flees'. This order includes saints and guides, who inspire groups seeking transformation; and prophets and messengers, those given a task 'from above'. The Messenger is an incarnation 'from Above'.*

To enable human societies to acquire this structure, there must be a division of functions. Outwardly, this results in a class society. The middle class arose when commerce and industry were established and when the city states required professional administrators. For brief periods, as at the time of Menes, the first king of united Egypt, Gudea of Lagash, Sargon the Great of Akkad and Brihadratha in India, the heroes were truly great men and something near to the ideal society was established for several generations. They were both kings and priests in direct association with Masters of Wisdom, some of whom we know by name, such as Imhotep the founder of Egyptian astronomy and medicine, Hammurabi the law-giver of Babylon and Manu the law-giver of India. I believe that we should add the enigmatic figure of Melchizedek of Lagash, whose name appears in such decisive places in the Jewish and Christian scriptures as the man who initiated Abraham the patriarch.

The Heroic age inaugurated civilization as we know it. This required sufficient visible authority to make an entire region accept a system of values regarded as mandatory. This is why the Masters of Wisdom appeared as law givers like Ikshvaku, Manu

---

* *Editor's note.* He originates from beyond the Creation and from beyond the Demiurge.

and Moses. Some of these belong to the highest rank of the
psychoteleios order – that is Messengers from the Father Creator.
Others were like Tiresias the prophet in Homer's *Odyssey* who
alone among the dead retained all his powers of perception and
action. He was greater than the heroes who seek his help.

All accounts of the Heroic epoch agree in presenting us with
the picture of men with a prodigious force of life, but with
uncontrollable passions and often lacking in commonsense. They
were quite distinct from the prophets and guides. We see the
picture in the stories of King Saul or Agamemnon.

It is particularly important for us to appreciate the total lack of
respect for human life and the indifference to suffering that runs
through all the literature and records of the epoch. We see
engraved on stone hero kings boasting of unthinkable atrocities.
We read in sacred books that 'God' commands us to destroy
man, woman, child, beast, every living thing in a conquered city.
We see that we are looking at an age that we cannot possibly
understand. We cannot grasp that three thousand years ago, only
heroes counted, ordinary people were animals and even less than
animals.

And yet in the Heroic epoch great things were achieved.
Science began its slow march of conquest over Nature and over
man himself. Trade routes by land and sea connected all parts of
the world. Great temples were built. This period includes the
megalithic art of Europe, the building of the pyramids and great
temples of Egypt. It covers the greater part of the Bronze Age
and the discovery of iron smelting by the Hittites. Mathematics
was established in Chaldea with astrology and medicine. The
catalogues of their achievements would make us respect the men
of the Heroic epoch, if we did not also remember their cruelty,
their childish vanity and their lust for power.

About the middle of the second millenium BC a remarkable
event occurred. This is commonly known as the 'destruction of
Atlantis' from the description given by Plato in the *Timaeus*. To
understand it we must look at the state of affairs in the countries
of the eastern Mediterranean. We know that Egypt had been
invaded by a mysterious people, the Hyksos, and was recovering
under the great pharaohs of the eighteenth dynasty. The little
island of Crete was the first empire to discover the power given
by command of the sea. She controlled all trade routes and built a
fleet of war vessels that enabled her to invade where she chose to

further and protect her commerce. The Cretans of the early Minoan period are credited with great technical achievements. They perfected navigation by the lodestone. They discovered the making and casting of bronze, the first dyeing of textiles and invented fire-throwing weapons that were the terror of the Mediterranean. We must believe Plato's story of the wickedness of Crete at the height of its power. Such wickedness was typical of the Heroic epoch in its time of degeneration, but does not account for the peculiar horror evoked by Minoan Crete. The explanation lies in the rejection of the entire system of values which sustained the epoch. The Cretan society was not heroic, it was an oligarchy of princes whose aim was material prosperity and the enjoyment of life. The sacred rituals of the Creator God and the Great Mother were turned into sporting occasions. Bullfights and athletic contests took the place of the worship of the Creator and the mysteries of the Mother Goddess. During their occupation of Egypt, the Hyksos had degraded the sacred priesthood, ridiculed the divine claims of the pharaoh.

The Masters of Wisdom foresaw the danger that a materialistic, hedonistic philosophy of life might take possession of men's minds, at a time when the capacity for independent judgment was almost totally lacking in the mass of the people. Only belief in a personal destiny after death, the happiness or misery of which depended on the way life had been lived, would stand up against the appeal of pleasure for its own sake that would take man back to his state in the first Adamic cycle. This was a threat that could not be met by force, because the Minoans combined love of pleasure with the possession of overwhelming naval power against which no land forces could prevail. Egypt was at the height of her own power. Thothmes III, like Napoleon, had pushed his conquests across Asia to the great rivers, but Crete like England, ruled the waves.

We can read of the Egyptian power in the *Torah*. Pharaoh was a cruel oppressor holding captive the Israelites whose extraordinary destiny was to unite the great cultures in a single religion. They had come to Egypt with the tradition of the Great Spirit and had been converted to the Creator God. They knew that they had come from Mesopotamia and that they were destined to return to the land promised to Abraham. But they were helpless, unarmed and enslaved.

Between the powers that threatened the world, there was no

human agency that could gain time for the Revelation that was to come. I cannot tell whether the Masters knew in advance what was going to happen or whether they may even have had powers to make it happen. However it may be, they were prepared.

On a fateful day in the year 1447 BC * the greatest natural catastrophe since the Siberian meteor destroyed the small island of Santorini; a prodigious submarine earthquake opened the bed of the sea and millions of tons of water rushed on to the white hot magma beneath. The resulting explosion set up a huge tidal wave which swept through the eastern Mediterranean. On its way it destroyed the entire Cretan fleet and the palaces of Knossos and Kato Zakro. It swept over the Peloponnese and Attica causing the flood known as Deucalion's in Greek literature. It poured into Egypt and caused the plagues so vividly described in *Exodus*. The entire might of Egypt was momentarily paralysed and Moses was able to lead the children of Israel out of captivity.

It is hardly conceivable that the exodus was unpremeditated. The Masters of Wisdom with whom Moses was closely connected must have been prepared. Moses himself was more than a Master. The story of his strength and his defects as recounted in *Exodus* show us that he was no ordinary man. He was the founder of the first true religion and, like all the founders, he had the support of the Masters of Wisdom.

If we agree in identifying Crete and Santorini with the large and small islands described in Plato's *Timaeus,* the story of the loss of Atlantis is clearly to be read. Plato could not explain just what the wickedness of the Minoans consisted in. They were no more ruthless than the heroes of Homer's *Iliad* or the Egyptian pharaohs. Their sin was against human destiny itself: it was the more grievous in that they had it in their power to open the whole world to the Revelations that were to come. Because of their failure its arrival in Europe and, perhaps, even America, was delayed for many centuries.

When the Masters of Wisdom had launched the concept of the Hero-king to provide a driving force to make man taste and use his creativity, these events were still in the distant future. By the

---

* I venture to cite the year by using the lapse of time quoted in *Kings II* between the Exodus and the building of Solomon's temple in Jerusalem. The approximate date is confirmed by the archaeologists who have reported on the Santorini earthquake.

beginning of the first millenium before Christ, the Hero had committed spiritual suicide. He had become a tyrant and not a hero. Instead of bringing his people to immortality, he made them slaves.

All this had been foreseen and provided for. History was about to move in an entirely unexpected direction. Before we come to this I must refer to an event which occurred about four thousand five hundred years ago when the Heroic age was at the height of its splendour. The temples in Egypt, Stonehenge in England, the great Ziggurats of Ur and Lagash were being built. Peace and prosperity were assured by strong priest-kings like Sargon the Great of Akkad. The Masters knew that the tide would turn and the momentum of the Heroic age would ebb and lose itself in the quicksands of human egoism. They decided to found a brotherhood that would be responsible for preserving the core of the teaching and make it the custodian of the special powers they possessed. This brotherhood was later called the Sarman Society from the Persian words meaning 'head' and 'pure'. It happens that *sarman* also means bee. The play on words so much loved in the East, conveys the two-fold responsibility. The society was to keep in its pure form the head-force of the Masters. This was called at that time *Hvareno* which meant the secret of success and associated with the halo that surrounds the Hero. The second duty was, like a bee, to collect and preserve the knowledge that had been acquired by the schools of Wisdom on different levels. This society sent its representatives to all the centres of Wisdom and was responsible for preparing the remarkable events to be recounted in the next chapter.

Chapter Three

The First Revelations

The end of the Heroic epoch was a time of great confusion and fear. The grand sweep of events had brought a new racial order. From the Atlantic to the Pacific oceans, there was a chain of settled communities controlled by tyrants who usurped the name of Demigod. The four cultures had not only met, but merged, so that there was an immense variety of beliefs and practices. But there was not yet, in the true sense, religion which would give men the assurance of being bound together in a common spiritual action. Outwardly the people of different regions had drawn closer together and travel was easier than ever before. The Assyrian power which dominated in western Asia was a bloodthirsty tyranny, but it had opened up trade routes by land and sea that brought China and India, Bactria and Arabia, Egypt and Europe into contact by trade and by culture. The age of bronze had created a demand for tin that sent ships all over the world in search of the precious metal. England, which had participated in the megalithic achievements, was now one of the chief sources of tin and other needed metals. The products of far distant countries found in sites of the period show how active trade had become.

Economic and technical progress was in sad contrast with social and moral degeneration. The unity of history had been lost. The heroic empires of China, India, central and south-west Asia, of Egypt and of Europe were running like a clock with all its wheels out of gear. We even have traces of the same disorder in central and south America. Only the nomads of the great plains preserved their ancient way of life in the northern latitudes of America and Asia. Elsewhere, the common pattern of human existence was the lust for conquest of the degenerated hero-kings, the self-interest of a debased priesthood and the sufferings of the common people.

Such were the consequences of implanting in man the master idea of the Superman who leads his people to an immortal heritage. Was the epoch to be accounted a failure because heroes failed to be heroic? We should look at it in a deeper perspective. The human mind was not ready to contemplate the mysteries of religion and the idea of the·divine king was only a step on the way. The king should have been a symbol of love as well as of grandeur; by his very failure he made plain that, without love, human life must always be wretched.

Between 600 and 500 BC a tremendous change came over the world. The Assyrian empire was crushed by Cyrus in 612 BC. The Achaemenid rulers no longer claimed semi-divine status, but rather called themselves humble servants of God. In Egypt, the wise rule of Psammeticlus restored prosperity and the rule of law. The Egyptian priesthood renewed its contact with the Masters of Wisdom, a contact that continued for a hundred years. The pharaoh no longer claimed a divine status. The same is true of Rome where Servius Tullius instituted the principle of equality of all Roman citizens including the ruler. In India rulers like Rasenadi of Kosala and the kings of Magadha totally abandoned the heroic claim. The same is true of the Ch'in rulers of China.

Such were the outward changes. They left the common man still without hope of a personal destiny. Not all were so deprived. Throughout the Heroic epoch, the *Way of Initiation* was opened. I have referred to the great Sarman Society. There were other brotherhoods into which initiation was possible for all who were capable of transformation. This was the way of the Mysteries. It was the means whereby the Masters of Wisdom could prepare and select those who were to be admitted to the great work.*

The 'new way' was to be open to all men and women and it could only be known by Revelation. The new message was to be openly proclaimed and it came almost simultaneously in all parts of the world. The Masters of Wisdom can see far ahead and they

---

* I have here followed Rudolf Steiner who emphasized the transition from initiation to worship that occurred at this time.

can look back far into the past. They were aware that a great experiment was going to be made: no less than an attempt to enable mankind, at the completion of the half-cycle that started ten thousand years before their time, to acquire the characteristic that would complete human evolution. This would allow the second half of the great cycle to be devoted to bringing about the unity of man and nature. Since love is the characteristic needed for this, it was necessary to make mankind aware that universal love is beyond creativity and that man must learn to love with the same impartial, unselfish love that Great Nature has for him.

It was first necessary to give men in general – not only the select few who were heroes or priests – confidence in their own destiny. This could not come so long as they were treated as beasts of the field by their rulers. Every man must be confident that he has within himself the seed of an immortal soul and be prepared to treat others with love and respect for the same seed in them. Up to this time, the Demiurge had been concerned with the evolution of the human *mind*. It was now necessary to look to the *soul* of man. Men had soul-stuff, even individuality, but they did not have the reality of love. The soul needs love as the mind needs creativity. The Demiurgic intelligences could not bring love into the soul themselves, but through the Masters of Wisdom they could establish appropriate conditions in the mind of man.

The event can be called the birth of religion. Man was to form an idea of God as a being that each individual could approach. During the previous epoch there were, no doubt, many thousands of men and women who were initiated into the mysteries, but they were veiled from the common man by the official rituals performed by heroes and priests with no participation on the part of the spectator. The new dispensation assured all people of their participation in the destiny of man.

The four cultures each made a distinctive contribution to the event.

The Mother Goddess was at the heart of the mysteries in Greece, Syria, Asia Minor and Egypt. The Phrygian Cybele opened her arms to all people about 600 BC. The mystical union with the Great Mother was transformed into the way by which man acquires his own soul. Unfortunately, due to the Minoan influence that overshadowed the eastern Mediterranean, the Masters of Wisdom could not bring Her into the concerted action that was taking place all through Asia. The result was to turn men's minds to a human rather than a religious interpretation of the message. We can see how they wrestled with the problems when we read Hesiod's *Works and Days* written in the seventh century BC. The outward manifestation can be seen in the Ionian philosophers and the time of Solon in Athens.

The great prophets of China, Lao Tzu (604–510 BC) and Kong Fu or Confucius (551–479 BC) represent two manifestations of the Great Spirit. Lao Tzu taught men to look upon *tao* as the source and end of the world and the core of their own being. Since *tao* is the same for all, there is no need for any intermediary. Man has only 'flexibly to follow the course of Nature' and put his trust in *tao* and all will go well with him. Confucius expressed the working of the Great Spirit as *jen* or goodness. Neither showed signs of being influenced by the other traditions. Both *tao* and *jen* express the new Revelation that every human being has the same spiritual nature. The 'Wise Ones of Old' knew this truth: now was the time for everyone to know it. Only in this way can human happiness be assured.

In India, the old Great Spirit culture of the Dravidians, who had entered the sub-continent four thousand years earlier, had been superseded by the Aryan Vedic tradition. The caste system with Kshatriyas and Brahmans in an impregnable position of authority had grown out of the heroic legends of the *Ramayana* and *Mahabharata*. The lower castes were as helpless here as in other parts of the world. We are accustomed to think of Buddhism as a movement of reform within the Vedic system. It was, in fact, a rejection of the caste system in favour of personal freedom to seek salvation. The preaching of the Buddha had much more in common with the Great Spirit tradition. The doctrine of liberation, *mukti,* and of right living as the path to it was so consistent with Chinese and other Great Spirit doctrines, that it is not surprising that Buddhism lost its foothold in India, but was accepted joyfully from Burma to China and Japan.

The important thing is, however, not the origin but the message of Buddhism. It is expressed in the last words of the Teacher: "Work out your own salvation with diligence!" The Buddhist fraternity, *sangha,* was open to all: noble or commoner, freeman or slave.

Mahāvīra Jain, a contemporary of the Buddha, was emphatic

in his message of limitless compassion towards all beings. Maskarin Gosala, another teacher of the same period, preached the gospel of universal liberation. The Way, *magga*, was open to all.

The true significance of the Saviour God who sacrifices himself to liberate the world from the dragon forces was not to appear for many centuries. Nevertheless, perhaps the greatest prophet of the Revelation was Zoroaster who came from the heart of the Aryan culture. He probably lived from 628 to 551 BC, the year when Confucius was born. He was twenty-four years older than Lao Tzu, so that he was probably both the first and the chief of those who proclaimed the right of every man to possess his own immortal soul.

Until this time men were expected to act rightly because it was God's commandment conveyed by the heroes and priests.* Now, for the first time, a reason was shown to them. The Vedic sacrifices were more than symbolic representations of the delivery of the world, they were man's contribution to the sacrifice made by the God. But outside the rites, the ordering of men's lives was prescribed by law: the laws of Manu or Gautama.** The common man lived as he was commanded to live, under the domination of the ruler and his priests. Zoroaster's message was a new Revelation. Ahura Mazda in the struggle with the evil spirit Angra Mainyu needed the help of all good men. Vohu Manah, the good mind, was there to help all men and women to live in such a way as to be on the right side of the conflict and to be rewarded by immortality. When the *saoshyans*, saviour, came, only those possessed of the Good Mind would recognize and join him. Moreover, the notion of service was given a new importance. The men and women who have been purified and transformed ensure the progress of the world and prepare the coming millenium.

The idea of the Creator God was brought to fruition in the Children of Israel who had a special role in bringing all the four streams together.

The Great Mother in the Jewish tradition was never represented as a Goddess like Ishtar or Cybele, but this does not

---

* We must except Moses who lived a thousand years earlier, but was a true Messenger.
** *n.b.* The law-giver, not Gautama Buddha who was a totally different person.

mean that she was not represented. Jerusalem was, and still is, the
Mother. She is represented again and again in the Hebrew
scriptures as the mother who bears and suffers for her children. In
one of the visions of Esdras (*Esdras II* 10) Jerusalem is seen as the
mother and the temple of Solomon as her son. There is nothing
strange in the transition. The Great Mother has always been
identified with places, as Ishtar with Babylon and Diana with
Ephesus.

The story of Abraham confirms his origin in a Great Spirit
culture. He came from the Euphrates with the tribal belief in a
Spirit Power that was sacred for his own race and not for others.
Then came the long sojourn in Egypt under the powerful
influence of the Creator God. The Israelites kept their identity by
combining the two cultures, remaining always closer to Egypt
than to the Aryans who invaded from the north. Five hundred
years passed and the prophets proclaimed the universal godship of
Jehovah as the Father of all men.

Another four hundred years later came the sack of Jerusalem
and the Babylonian captivity, when the Israelites became aware
of the mystery of the Saviour God. The Zoroastrian saoshyans
became the Messiah and they returned to Jerusalem filled with
the same eschatological hopes as the other oppressed people in
Babylon nourished, until the Assyrian rule was overthrown and
Nineveh was taken by Cyrus.

Under Cyrus' son Darius I, the Israelites were much favoured,
the temple was rebuilt and the new law (*Deuteronomy*)
promulgated. If we are to accept the *Book of Esdras* as authentic,
the Persian king did take counsel of the Masters of Wisdom and
Esdras himself was the mouthpiece of the Demiurgic inspiration.
It seems most likely that the whole of the Torah as then revealed
was powerfully influenced by all that Esdras had learned in
Babylon. The coming of the *saoshyans* as the Son of God was
explicitly announced. The Israelites were now in a unique
situation. They had the tremendous revelation that a Saviour was
to come. Prophets like Isaiah were aware of the implications and
knew that the Saviour must suffer. The ordinary people were
looking for a Saviour who would come in power.

According to Gurdjieff's account in chapter 24 of *Beelzebub's
Tales*, there occurred a great meeting of 'learned beings' in
Babylon. As he specifically connects this with the Persian king
who carried off the wise men from Egypt, we can date the event

at 525 BC when Cambyses invaded Egypt and established the Persian rule there for more than a hundred years. In Iamblichus' *Life of Pythagoras*, he specifically says that Pythagoras studied for many years with the Egyptian priests and then went to Babylon where he was initiated by Zoroaster. He stayed seven years in Babylon and learned all the wisdom of the Magi. Solon is also said to have studied with the Masters of Wisdom in Egypt and Persia. At that time Confucius was a young man but his Chinese biographers knew little of his early life. Prince Siddhāra, to become Gautama Buddha, was nine years older and the time coincides with his withdrawal from the companionship of his fellow-seekers. It is therefore possible that both could have been present in Babylon when the great conference is said to have occurred.

I do not think it necessary to assume that such a conference ever took place. Those who are in receipt of direct inspiration do not need to meet or even to know one another. They have complete faith in their own revelation and can be confident that whatever they do fits perfectly into the universal pattern, the Dharma which is the Great Work.

When once one has discerned throughout history the guiding hand of the Demiurge one cannot doubt that the events of the sixth century BC form one single whole and that the key to understanding them is to regard them as a preparation for a step forward in the destiny of man.

For nearly two centuries, all went well. This period includes the reigns of the Achaemenid kings from Cyrus to Xerxes II, and the Golden Age of Athens from Pericles to Socrates. It saw the rise of the Roman republic to the beginning of its splendour. India and China were digesting the results of the Revelation. Mencius (372–289 BC) in particular insisted upon the need to combine spirituality and practical goodness in everyday life. In India the new religions spread everywhere and the old Vedic rituals and sacrifices lost their significance for the ordinary castes: though the Brahman priesthood retained most of its privileges and practices.

In the latter part of the fourth century great changes came over the world. Alexander of Macedon destroyed the Persian and Egyptian powers and even invaded India. After his death in Babylon in 320 BC Alexander's generals divided the spoil. Chandragupta Maurya (reigned 321–296 BC) founded the great

Mauryan dynasty which was to produce King Asoka (reigned 264–228 BC) the greatest Indian ruler, a man close to the Masters of Wisdom. For three generations (about 250–175 BC) Buddhist missionaries were sent all over the world. Central Asia was largely converted and the Buddhist Noble Eightfold Path influenced even those who were not converted. It seems to me that at that time the Masters of Wisdom were concerned to counteract the ruthless cruelty of the Seleucid rulers in Babylon so terribly described in the book of the *Maccabees* and other Hebrew chronicles. The sufferings of the Jews are tersely described: "And there was very great wrath upon Israel" (*Maccabees I.* I:64). At this time, we first hear of the Essene Brotherhood. The Sarmān Society who had left Babylon before the arrival of Alexander and travelled up the Tigris, had made their headquarters in the abandoned capital of the Assyrian kings near where Mosul stands today. To this day, there remains a sanctuary that contains relics of the Sarmān Society guarded by the Yezidis who, in my personal opinion (unsupported I must say by any positive evidence) know more about it than they are prepared to admit. We have also the picture of Simon the high priest in Jerusalem who succeeded in making friends with both Rome and Babylon. He and his circle of friends were connected with the Essene Brotherhood and so with the Masters of their time. The rabbinical tradition that has given a hundred generations of Jews direct access to the spiritual powers, was established not long before this time.

With the fall of the Achaemenid empire, Zoroastrianism lost its official status. New cults such as Mithraism spread and reached the West. Buddhism supplanted Zoroastrianism in most of central Asia. Then, within a generation of the death of King Asoka, Buddhism too began to decline. The Mauryan dynasty in India was replaced by rulers hostile to Buddhism. Brahmanism was re-established and has dominated in India to this day.

In Egypt, the old religion had entirely collapsed by the third century. The Ptolemys with their Hellenistic leanings had little use for the priests and their ancient tradition.

By the second century Rome was already the greatest power in the western world. We cannot readily believe that the Gracchi or Cato were Masters of Wisdom. There was, however, a real struggle to establish the rights of the common man, *pleb,* against the nobility who controlled the Roman Senate. I have not done any research that would allow me to form an opinion as to whether there were Masters of Wisdom in any part of Europe before the time of Christ.

Such is the picture of Europe, Asia and Egypt in the first century before Christ. Of Africa and America, I know nothing except that the Zapotecas in Mexico were expecting the end of the world and were preparing to abandon their homes and temples and take to the mountains. The picture gives the impression that the wonderful Revelation of the sixth century had come to nothing. India and China had reverted to the old traditions. The western world, including Babylon and Egypt, was dominated by the Hellenistic way of life, which attached little importance to religion. Even the Jews had lapsed into dependence on the formal ritual. To preserve themselves from the Seleucid persecution, they had turned to Rome, but Rome had established itself as the dominant power and regarded Israel as a key point in its military plans for the future conquest of Asia. So began the terrible and wonderful century which ended with the destruction of Jerusalem in AD 70 and the dispersion of the Jews who survived the massacres.

Chapter Four

The Time of Christ

We have followed the slow emergence of human nature from its brutish origins through the two great transformations by which man was endowed first with consciousness and then with creativity. The history of the twelve thousand years since the end of the Ice Age has seen the partial transfer of responsibility for human progress from the Demiurge to man himself. This has led to great achievements but also to great disasters, for human nature when it acquired creative power became, at the same time, tainted with egoism. Man has used his creativity to dominate rather than to serve nature. Two thousand five hundred years ago the lust for power was in danger of poisoning the human race and the Great Revelation was set in motion to prepare man for the coming of the higher cosmic impulse of love, without which consciousness and creativity lead man to destroy his own birthright. We human beings have a deep awareness, deeper than egoism itself, of our kinship with nature. We feel that creativity without love is daemonic, but we are forced to recognise that love has no power to overcome egoism. Life on earth is threatened today, not by man's failure to love his fellow-man, but by his inability to love at all. Love untainted by egoism is to be found only in the rarest of the rare.

We have traced the consequences of the first Revelation and must now come to the Time of Christ. The preparations for the great event were continuous from the time of Zoroaster, but were concentrated particularly into the two centuries before and after the earthly life of Jesus. Our concern is with the role of the

Masters of Wisdom. We have followed the obscure indications of the role of the Sarmān Society, who at every stage have remained in the background. We have now to look at two societies that played a more visible but still misunderstood part. These are the Chaldean Magi and the Jewish Community of the Covenant known as the Essene Brotherhood.

The *Magi* were members of a caste or class that existed in central Asia from before the time of Zoroaster. They accepted Zoroaster when he came to the court of King Vishtaspa, the Bactrian king of Khorasmia. Two Magi were given the task of testing Zoroaster's credentials and found that his initiation went beyond anything they themselves knew of. The king was converted on their advice. Through the conquests of Cyrus, the Magi spread all through the Persian empire and reached Syria and Egypt. The Greeks looked upon the Magi as Masters of Wisdom. Porphyry in his book *On Abstinence* says that magus means 'one who is wise in the things of God and serves the divine.' The word *maga* meant the gift or 'grace' of God, by which men have the power to perform great works. This sacred power was the secret of the Magi. During the four hundred years that cover the time of Christ, the Zoroastrian religion had no royal devotees such as the Achaemenid kings before and the Sassanid kings after.* The Arsacids left no record of their religious beliefs, but the Magi retained their position and spread even more widely. They were experts in astrology and divination and it is in this capacity that they are mentioned in St. Matthew's gospel.

It seems to me that the Magi were divided into three castes or categories. The first was exoteric: in this capacity the Magi were priests, whose presence was necessary for any religious ceremony, even non-Zoroastrian. This role was very similar to that of the Brahman caste in India and of the Egyptian priests described by the Greek travellers. The second caste or order of Magians were those who preserved the sacred literature and who possessed special knowledge and powers. They were the 'magicians' of popular legend. The third order of the Magi were the true esoteric society who were aware of the significance of the great

---

* The Achaemenids ruled Persia from Cyrus 623 BC to the defeat of Darius III by Alexander 323 BC. The Sassanids ruled from AD 240 to the rise of Islām in AD 650.

event that was being prepared. They had a centre in Asia Minor that continued to work for three or four centuries after the time of Christ and transmitted its secrets to the Christian brotherhood in Cappadocia. They also played a part in the establishment of the Essene Brotherhood inaugurated in Judaea about two centuries before Christ.

There is no longer any doubt that the Essenes were connected with the central Revelation. Thanks to the Dead Sea Scrolls, we now can confirm what was written about them by Pliny the Younger and Josephus the Jewish historian. The Essenes were a brotherhood whose mode of life was very different from that of their Jewish compatriots. They were highly organised and very selective in admitting new members. They particularly revered the Teacher of Righteousness who lived about 150 BC and was himself a high priest. He was persecuted and murdered. Professor Dupont Somer identifies the Teacher of Righteousness with Onias the High Priest treacherously murdered at the instigation of Menelaus. The episode and the indignation it provoked caused repercussions beyond Israel.*

The connection between the Essenes and the Magi is proved above all by their belief in two opposing spirits of the Truth and the Lie, exactly as in the Zoroastrian Scriptures. The sacredness of Truth was a cardinal teaching of both the Magi and the Essenes. According to many legends the Essenes had the power to foretell the future. Josephus tells the story of the way the murder of Antigomes was foretold by Judas the Essene. Judas was renowned for the invariable accuracy of his predictions. One day, he saw a man named Antigomes passing through the temple and cried out to the circle of pupils whom he was instructing: "Ah! I had better die now, since truth has died before me. Here is Antigomes alive when he should have been dead today. He was fated to be killed at Straton's tower a hundred miles from here. It is now the fourth hour of the day, so that time has made a mockery of my prophecy." These were the words of the old man. Shortly afterwards, however, the news came that another Antigomes had perished in a subterranean place called Straton's tower. It was the identity of names that had disconcerted the seer. Another Essene, Menahem, foretold that a young boy would be king of Israel and when this boy unexpectedly came to the throne

---

* *Maccabees II*, 4:21–50.

as Herod the Great, he honoured the Essene Brotherhood.

Although the Essenes were described in glowing terms as an ideal society by both Greek and Jewish writers they are not once mentioned in the canonical books of the Old or New Testament. This is the more surprising as both Philo and Josephus state explicitly that there were three principal sects among the Jews: the Pharisees, the Sadducees and the Essenes. From the evidence of the Dead Sea Scrolls we can now confirm what Philo said about the Essenes: that they were represented in the chief cities of Israel, but had their principal settlement near the Dead Sea. This was at Qumran close to the caves where the scrolls were found.

The Essenes were not only influenced by Zoroastrianism and the Magi. They were also close to the Pythagoreans and knew the Pythagorean teaching about number and harmony which was incorporated into their liturgy. They were also in contact with the Buddhist missionaries whose teaching about the Noble Eightfold Path must have influenced the Rule of the Community of the Covenant. It seems probable that the great Teacher of Righteousness, whose title could equally be translated as Master of Wisdom, was responsible for combining the different traditions in a teaching and way of life that attracted the very finest spirits among the Jews, including many of the 'Sons of Zadok', the Sadducees before they divided into worldly and other-worldly branches.

The Essene way of life was based on mutual love and the sharing of all possessions and activities. In their rule it is written: "For all things shall be in common, *beyahad:* truth and virtuous humility and loyal love and the zeal for righteousness, each towards his fellow in the Holy Party and as sons of the Eternal Assembly. They shall eat communally, *yahad,* and bless communally and take counsel communally." We are not concerned with the strict conditions for admission, nor with their customs, except the great ritual acts performed daily. They rose before the sun and stood together to give thanks to the sun for all the gifts of nature. After working until the fifth hour they put on white garments after a purifying bath and ate a solemn meal which included the distribution of freshly baked bread and wine. The same ritual was repeated in the evening.

Now we must come to the heart of the matter. It seems clear that some at least of the Essenes were Masters of Wisdom. The Teacher of Righteousness and his immediate followers possessed great knowledge and supernormal powers. They were in contact with all the streams of spirituality of Asia and Egypt. They had strict methods of training and a long novitiate. Those who became elders were regarded with deep veneration and their word was law for all the ordinary members of the community.

There is a very ancient tradition that John the Baptist and Jesus Christ both received their first training with the Essene Brotherhood. Certainly John began baptising in Jordan very close to Qumran where the principal Essene community had been established for a hundred years. It is probable that John received a personal revelation that compelled him to separate himself from the brotherhood and take a more open stand against the hypocrisy of the ruling priesthood. *St. Matthew,* 3:7, tells us that John was taken aback when Pharisees and Sadducees came to his baptism. His message: "Repent ye, for the kingdom of heaven is at hand", was meant for the ordinary people, who had not the courage and singleness of mind needed to accept the severe discipline of the Essenes. The Pharisees also claimed to follow the law in all its purity, but had been involved in the persecution of the Essenes and were remembered in connection with the murder of the Teacher of Righteousness. This was the reason for John's outburst: "O generation of vipers, who hath warned you to flee from the wrath to come?"

Jesus was a Galilean and would not be expected to know about Qumran: but there were Essene groups not only in Galilee but even in Samaria. Much of Jesus' teaching, and especially the Sermon on the Mount, is so close to the Essenes' own doctrines that it is reasonable to suppose that in his early manhood he went through the full training and initiation of the brotherhood. They alone among the Jews could understand the meaning of: "except your righteousness exceed the righteousness of the scribes and Pharisees, ye shall in no wise enter the Kingdom of Heaven."

Some authorities believe that Joseph died when Jesus was in his middle twenties and that he returned to Nazareth to support his mother as a carpenter. The references to his brothers and sisters indicate that there were at least eight or nine in the family and that at some point Jesus left home and never returned. He was attracted by the preaching of John, a fellow-Essene, and accepted his baptism in the Jordan. Baptism played a great part in the Essenian ritual and was the preliminary to every act of initiation. In the moment of his baptism in Jordan, Jesus became aware that he was to preach a new gospel of the Fatherhood of God and the bond of love. There was, however, a transcendental mystery which the evangelists either did not understand or were forbidden to reveal. This was the secret of the way in which the Power of Love was to be transmitted to man. This is the secret which was known to the innermost circle of the Masters of Wisdom and we must try to unravel it, as far as it is permissible to do so, by looking at the account given in the four gospels.

The four gospels were compiled by four different schools of wisdom, each entrusted with a different task. St. Mark's gospel recounts the story of the event as it appeared to the uninitiated disciple. It could be recognised and confirmed by eye-witnesses or those who had had contact with them, such as their children and grandchildren. St. Luke's gospel was written to connect Christianity with the Great Mother tradition through the Virgin Mary. The Asian Christians for centuries venerated Mary to such a degree that she was virtually deified. St. John's gospel is an interpretation based on the Gnostic tradition. It expresses the true significance of the event in symbols and, of course, it emphasizes more than any other the need for full mutual acceptance and love between the disciples. St. Matthew's is pre-eminently the gospel of the Masters of Wisdom. It is a *legominism** carefully constructed according to the pattern that connects the three worlds.

There are three ways of interpreting the mission of Jesus as the Holy One of God. I shall not consider the picture of Jesus as a 'great and good man with an extraordinary power to arouse the devotion of his followers'. Such an image totally fails to account for the lasting change that came over the world from the Time of Christ. The three ways can be regarded as: exoteric, or for the world; mesoteric, or for the disciples, and esoteric, for the true initiates. The first is Pauline Christianity that presents Jesus as the Lamb of God sacrificed to propitiate God and obtain the forgiveness of sins. This interpretation encounters the serious objection that God could have forgiven sins without the need for the Incarnation of His Son and without the sacrifice of Calvary. The exaggeration of human sinfulness which is required to justify Anselm's *Cur Deus Homo*, "Why did God become Man?", is

---

* *Editor's note:* This term is introduced by Gurdjieff in *Beelzebub's Tales* to designate information intended for posterity and put into a work of art in such a way that its meaning can be deciphered only by initiates.

another objection. Man is not so much sinful as weak and ignorant. Modern psychology has thoroughly established the absurdity of holding man responsible for all the terrible things he has done and is still doing. Pauline Christianity has taken such a firm hold on the Roman world that very few theologians have attempted a radical revision without losing the deep significance of the Event.

The second, or mesoteric, picture is that of the small brotherhood of Judaean disciples led by James the brother of the Lord, who himself was put to death. It seems that this brotherhood to a great extent reverted to the way of life of the Essene community to which they had belonged and put their faith in the promised coming of the Son of Man in glory to redeem Israel and establish the reign of righteousness. This was apocalyptic Christianity as presented recently by Albert Schweitzer in *The Quest of the Historical Jesus*. The vision looked forward to great disasters which were to prepare for the coming of the Son of man, *Parousia*. The destruction of Jerusalem in AD 70 and the massacre of most of the members of the Judaean church was not followed by the expected *Parousia*, and the Judaean church lost the foundation of its faith. No more was heard of the Judaean Christians after they had retired to Pella. The great service rendered by this community was the preservation of authentic accounts of the acts and sayings of Jesus during the period between his baptism in Jordan and the resurrection.

These enable us to relate the event as a whole to the evolution of mankind and recognise the important part played by the Masters of Wisdom. I shall not attempt to justify in detail the interpretation that I believe to be the nearest approach we can now make to the esoteric truth. It was first suggested to me by my teacher Gurdjieff, who once said at a gathering of many of his pupils at his ritual evening meal: "One day Mr. Bennett will give a conference on the Last Supper, and many people will be thankful for what he will say".*

The one thing certain is that a tremendous event did occur and has left its mark on humanity for nearly two thousand years. I believe that we do not and cannot know what the event was in its full majesty, because it took place in a region that human

* This present chapter is based upon a talk I gave to the Third Basic Course at Sherborne House on Sunday, August 4th, 1974.

consciousness cannot reach. To grasp what this means, we need to have a clear picture of the 'other worlds' that are not perceived by our senses. To bring about great and dramatic changes in the visible world it is necessary to bring about an interaction between all the four worlds.* To bring absolute creativity into direct contact with absolute laws would create an impossible situation. Put in another way, there is perfect freedom and there is complete constraint. These two cannot be reconciled; but the ultimates are never reached, so there are regions whose reconciliation is almost, but not quite, impossible. We can say that God is not so free in His creativity as the Absolute Source, that is the Godhead, and that man is not so constrained to obey the laws as the material world in which he exists. Between God and man a reconciliation is possible, but it is still very difficult.

The Old Testament is to a very great extent occupied with telling us how hard this reconciliation is. It is very necessary to grasp this, because through misunderstanding it we are led either to deny God's Love or man's limitations. Man's repeated failure to respond to the destiny offered to him from Above is a common theme in all sacred writings but we do not so readily see what is done to redeem the failure.

The Christian message is greatly concerned with redemption, but the secret of its working has remained hidden. Non-Christians ask why, if God is all-merciful and all-powerful, it should be necessary for Him to be incarnated as a man and die on the cross to enable Him to forgive sins? This question has never been answered in convincing terms. The reason is that we attempt to make sense of the visible event as it was recorded in the memory of onlookers. We seek to interpret an action that is beyond the mind of man in terms that derive from our human experience of this visible world.

Job was asked if he could bind the sweet influences of the Pleiades or loose the bands of Orion to remind him that he had no conception of the working of the supra-terrestrial forces. We have forgotten their salutary lesson and seek to catch the heavenly Leviathan with an earthly hook.

After this parenthesis, I dare say no more than what I have come to understand for myself. I believe that the mission of Jesus was no less than an attempt to bring mankind to the next stage of

* *Editor's note.* The fourth is the absolute world of the unfathomable godhead, *lahū t.*

human evolution when love will be an inherent property of the human essence as creativity has been for the past thirty-five or forty thousand years. The experience of the Great Revelation of the sacredness of the human individual had shown that this would not help mankind to a better way of life unless men were capable of accepting and loving one another. Although the worst horrors of the Heroic epoch had been mitigated, men were no more capable of loving than they had been before.

Now, we have seen that the bringing of creativity was a prodigious step made possible only by the complete ascendancy gained by the Magicians over the Neanderthal tribesmen. Even so, the Magicians themselves could do nothing. It required the incarnation of the Demiurge in human bodies to enable creativity to be transmitted by way of sexual reproduction. The same expedient would not avail to bring love to mankind. There were several reasons for this. Men had grown independent and, moreover, had little confidence in their rulers and priests whose chief concern was to maintain their authority. Moreover, love cannot be transmitted either through body or mind, because it is an attribute or energy of the *will.* Love is an unconditioned energy and cannot be transmitted by any conditioning process, physical or mental. Therefore, it requires an action that is beyond body and mind. This action will influence both body and mind, but they are not the locus in which it takes place. Love can flourish only in freedom, that is in the third world.

None of this is obvious and to develop the theme in all the depth that it requires would be beyond the scope of this book. It is sufficient to say that only those whose perceptions have been opened to the worlds beyond form, *alam-i imkān,* could be witnesses of the event and they could not express their understanding in language that would be understood by those who had not shared the experience.

The third world is, in ordinary circumstances, able to act in the first, that is, the visible or material universe, only through the second, that is, through mind. When a break-through is made, the freedom of the third world manifests in this world as a miracle. Since the action is concerned with love, the miracles of healing and conversion fit into the picture. But they do not account for the action itself: we must turn to the gospels.

The first question that most people ask when they begin to study the first gospel, *Matthew,* is why the genealogy of Joseph is

traced back for forty two generations if he was not the father of
Jesus. The perplexity is increased by the abrupt transition to the
statement that Mary was with child of the Holy Ghost. Many
explanations are given but the true one is missed. Three groups of
fourteen generations are cited. From Abraham to David, the Jews
were connected with the Creator God tradition. From David,
Jerusalem and the Temple were the pivot of Judaism and, as I
have suggested, Jerusalem stood for the Great Mother. This is
strengthened by the association with Wisdom, the feminine
associate of Jahweh in the Creation. The third period specifically
mentions the Babylonian captivity when the children of Israel as-
similated the Saviour God tradition and the belief in the coming
Messiah. Having conveyed in this way the connection of Christ
with the three traditions, we find an immediate reference to the
Great Spirit as the direct progenitor of Jesus. The extreme
reverence shown by the authors of the first gospel to the Holy
Spirit is nowhere so strikingly manifested as in *Matthew* 12:31. in
the words of Jesus: "Wherefore I say unto you, All manner of sin
and blasphemy shall be forgiven unto men: but the blasphemy
against the Holy Spirit shall not be forgiven unto men". Thus, in
the very first chapter the gospel tells us that the events to be
described are concerned with integrating the four great traditions
into one Revelation.

The gospel starts with three incidents not recorded by the
other evangelists. The first is Joseph's intended repudiation of
Mary and the dream that reveals the working of the Holy Spirit.
The second is the coming of the Magi and the third is the flight
into Egypt with the strangely artificial explanation quoting *Hosea*
11:1: "Out of Egypt have I called my son". The significant part
occupied by the dreams of Joseph and the Magi in these incidents
tells us that we are concerned with the invisible worlds. Thus we
start with two clues to the interpretation. First, the Masters of
Wisdom are involved, the Magi and the Egyptian priests and
second, revelations are coming from the higher worlds.

We pass immediately to John the Baptist who is represented as
"more than a prophet". In John's gospel he is a "man sent from
God". He is also "Elias which was for to come". The Spirit of
God appears as prophesied in *Isaiah* 11 where He is specifically
associated with Wisdom and Power. The incident again serves to
prepare us for an action that will bring together the highest and
the lowest worlds. The role of the denying principle is brought

out immediately afterwards in the temptation in the desert. Jesus now endowed with wisdom and power starts upon his mission, the story of which is interrupted by the long digression of the Sermon on the Mount. The purpose is to show that those who were to participate in the mystery were no ordinary men. Again and again in this gospel, Jesus is represented as making a total distinction between those who are chosen and prepared and those who follow him because of his mighty work. The preaching of the Kingdom was for all and it was made public though veiled in parables. The action that was to bring the Kingdom was performed in secret and never made public at all.

When Jesus had been baptised by John, he accepted the task entrusted to him by His Father, which was to transmit to those able to receive it the direct action of Divine Love. This is the highest Cosmic Impulse that can enter the Creation. Beyond it is the Unfathomable Source of which nothing can be said or even imagined. When man is united with Love, he is God; but Divine Love can enter only into a soul that is utterly empty of itself and liberated from all taint of egoism. How then was Love to come to sinful man? This is a far greater mystery than that of the redemption. The Essene Teacher of Righteousness had led his followers by the path of self-denial and humble obedience to superiors. They had access to the power of Love in their ritual meal of bread and wine, which as we know required total purity and was open only to those who had undergone three years of rigorous training. John the Baptist remained an Essene in his ascetic discipline and in his demand for repentance and submission but he was not an Essene missionary, for he did not invite his penitents to join the brotherhood, but told them to return home and prepare for the imminent coming of the Kingdom. He did not yet understand what the 'Kingdom' meant.

Jesus knew that he had to work through prepared people and his first task was to attract, to select and to train his disciples. This part of his mission can be reconstructed from St. Matthew's gospel.

We learn from the gospel that the disciples were very rigorously trained. They had to be free from all attachments, able to accept persecution and be expert in all procedures for the transformation of energies. The Beatitudes are of special significance not only by their content, but even more by their arrangement in three groups of three. They can be represented on the enneagram* as follows.

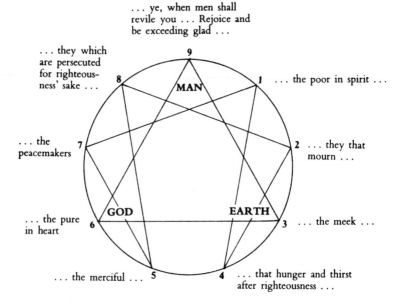

The points 3, 6, and 9 represent the three components of the action. This throws a new light upon the event, entirely different from the usual view that the Christian religion is concerned solely with the relationship between man and God. If the earth comes in as an equal partner then we must entirely change our way of thinking about religion. So the third beatitude raises a more serious question than anyone who has commented on the first gospel has yet supposed. Why should 'inheriting the earth' be brought into a spiritual and indeed other-worldly document? It is because man's very existence is justified only to the extent that he accepts his responsibility towards nature; but he must be *meek* in his attitude towards her.

* *Editor's note.* The symbol is Gurdjieff's. Mr. Bennett believed that it came from the Sarmān Society and incorporated knowledge of universal laws which is not to be found elsewhere. It was used in the construction of legominisms as Gurdjieff described in the chapter "Art" in *All and Everything* (*c.f.* J. G. Bennett, *Gurdjieff – Making a New World.* Appendix II).

There are two basic duties for man in this life; one is to serve nature and the other is to find God. The keys to fulfilling these duties are *meekness* and *purity of heart*. Our duty to ourselves is to achieve perfection – "Be ye therefore perfect as your Father in Heaven also is perfect" – and for this we must be ready to suffer. In Gurdjieff's language, we must accept conscious labour and intentional suffering. The blunt assertion in the ninth beatitude that persecution is the common lot of all who fill the role of prophet or apostle is followed by "rejoice and be exceeding glad" to make it clear that the suffering is positive and creative. The perfected man who accepts the role of apostle, the one who is sent out, has to bear an immense burden. He has to endure the tension between perfect freedom and total slavery that is felt when the third world acts directly on the first.

The remaining six Beatitudes depict the total action by which the perfection of manhood is achieved. It begins with the 'realisation of one's own nothingness' expressed by "poor in spirit". Spiritual poverty is apparent to oneself, not to others, whereas material poverty is of the visible world. From spiritual poverty arises the hunger and thirst, point 4, that leads to the awareness of the gulf that separates us from the glory of God, point 2. At this stage awareness of the true meaning of discipleship enters and the soul has glimpses of "theirs is the Kingdom of Heaven", point 8. The realisation of our common nothingness before the Glory of God opens the heart to mercy, point 5. We can love others as ourselves when we all stand in the presence of the Glory. We then can act effectively to create harmony in place of discord, to make peace and ensure it, point 7. Realising that whatever we achieve is not our own doing but the working of the power of God brings us back to our own nothingness, point 1. This brief excursion into the legominism may convince the reader that there is much to be learned from *St. Matthew's* gospel that does not appear on the surface.

The Sermon on the Mount is a further development of the so-called 'Manual of Discipline' of the Essene Brotherhood, which is perhaps the most valuable discovery among the Dead Sea Scrolls. It teaches humility and contempt for this world and confidence in the world of providence. It requires a very high standard of non-egoistic behaviour, the merit of which is not 'seen of men' but by the Heavenly Father. A remarkable feature of the Sermon on the Mount is its timelessness. There is not a precept that is less applicable today than it was two thousand years ago. The disciples were trained first of all in moral discipline and then were initiated into the arts of divination and healing. Jesus himself could heal on all levels from the psychic to the truly spiritual. The disciples acquired as much as was possible in the time available.

All this happened in Galilee, especially north of the Sea of Galilee in towns such as Capernaum, Chorazin and Bethsaida. Jesus himself taught also in the synagogues, mainly on the Sabbath day when his deep training in the Essenian interpretation of the scriptures enabled him to astonish the people by his wisdom and the authority with which he spoke.

I am sure that we can accept literally the greater part of the accounts of miraculous healing and even the raising from the dead of the daughter of Jairus. The sceptical and positivist philosophy that has dominated Western thought for two centuries has conditioned us to reject miracles as 'impossible'. We forget how many 'impossible' events occur round us every day. True miracles are the working of the spirit of God within the material world.* When Divine Love works in a self-free being it can work more miracles than we can imagine.

We now arrive at the critical moment when Jesus selected the twelve disciples with whom he intended to perform the greatest miracle of all: the transmission to them as sinful human beings of the power of Divine Love. The next step was to send them away from himself to test and confirm the transformation that had already taken place. "He gave them power against unclean spirits to cast them out and to heal all manner of sickness and all manner of disease". The instructions for their missionary journey described in *Matthew* 10 are reminiscent of the rule of the Essenes. They were to be without any personal possessions, without a home of their own, and they were to address themselves only to orthodox Jews whom they found worthy. They were to rely solely upon the Spirit of the Father to guide and support them.

The disciples were warned that they would be persecuted but were to remember that this had been the lot of the prophets before them. Jesus: "came not to send peace on earth, but a sword". The Kingdom of Heaven was so near that they would

---

* *Editor's note.* An action from the third world, *ālam-i imkān*, into the first world, *ālam-i ajsām*.

not have gone through all the cities of Israel before the great day came.

While the disciples were absent on their missionary journeys, Jesus himself continued to teach and to preach in the cities south of the lake. John the Baptist, who had been imprisoned by Herod, sent two of his own disciples all the way from Jerusalem to ask Jesus the question: "Art thou he that should come, or do we look for another?" In reply, Jesus points to his work of preaching the good news of the Kingdom, supported as it was by his acts of healing. The narrative makes it clear that John was not destined to know the real secret of Jesus' mission. "Verily I say unto you, among them that are born of women, there has not arisen a greater than John the Baptist: notwithstanding he that is least in the Kingdom of Heaven is greater than he". In other words, the Kingdom is not for the natural man born of woman, but for the supernatural man transformed through the power of Love. At this point, Jesus parts company from the Essenes in his saying: "I thank thee, O Father, Lord of Heaven and Earth, because thou hast hid these things from the wise and prudent and hast revealed them unto babes." The Great Teacher of Righteousness who had prepared his people by way of 'wisdom and prudence' had not penetrated into the final mystery of Love.

When the disciples return, the second act of the drama begins. Jesus deliberately provokes the Pharisees, who cannot understand why he does not join them. They know that the Essenes condemn their policy of compromise with the Roman occupying power; which falls, of course, far short of the open collaboration offered by the Sadducees. They regard Jesus as one of themselves: a pious man learned in the scriptures and a devout adherent of the law. He begins to do things that shock them, such as allowing his disciples to pluck the corn on the Sabbath day. He then attacks them openly and makes it clear that so far from joining them, he is going to rouse the people of Galilee against them. He repudiates his mother and his family whom he had been supporting by his own labour, (*Matthew* 12:47–50), an action that would be quite understandable if he were returning to the Essenes, but he is not doing this either. He rejects asceticism in terms reminiscent of the Buddha after his Enlightenment.

The parables of the Kingdom begin to emphasise the priceless value of the gift that he is to confer on those who can take up their cross and follow him. The multitude flock to him in such numbers that in order to be alone with his disciples he is obliged to go right outside Jewish territory into the heathen lands of Tyre and Sidon. Here the incident of the Syrophoenecian woman of Greek extraction, whose faith allowed her daughter to be healed, emphasises the universal character of the mission on which Jesus had been sent. It was no longer confined to the Jews. This enormous step makes the final break with the Essenes who accepted only Jews of pure descent into their brotherhood. One has only to read the translation of the Qumran documents to recognise that no Essene would have conversed with a non-Jewish woman. Far more important than their taboos was the bitter hatred towards non-Jews expressed in the 'Rules of Warfare for the Community of the Covenant' which was so important a document that fragments of seven or eight different copies were found among the Dead Sea Scrolls. The Essenes were awaiting the great war which was to last ten years and end in triumph for the Jewish cause. The 'Kittim', thought by most authorities to be the Seleucids, were the cruel oppressors who were to be utterly wiped out. Jesus could see the folly of such dreams and no doubt the Masters of Wisdom knew it also: but they could not know precisely what a task he was preparing to accomplish.

Jesus was now alone and was entering regions where even the Masters of Wisdom could no longer follow him. He celebrated the New Dispensation with the miraculous feast that is reported twice over. Although in its outward form it reproduces the love feast of the Essenes, there is no mention of preliminary purification. The feast was not confined to the disciples, but was open to all who were so strongly drawn to Jesus that they followed him into the wilderness, *Mark* 8:1 and *Matthew* 15:32. As soon as the feast was ended the multitude was sent away and Jesus took ship and went north again with his closest disciples. He once again moved into pagan country: the region called Caesarea Philippi, forty miles north of the lake. Now comes the great test. He asks the disciples: "Who say ye that I am?" Peter answers: "Thou art the Christ" (*Mark* 8:29) that is, the Anointed One of God who was foretold by the prophets. Jesus begins to explain that so far from triumph he was to undergo humiliation (*Matthew* 16:23) and Peter rebukes him privately. Then comes the most significant saying: "Get thee behind me, Satan, for thou savourest not the things that be of God, but those that be of men".

This makes it perfectly clear that none of the disciples yet understood the true mission of Jesus. He called the people together with his disciples and said openly to all of them: "whosoever will come after me, let him deny himself, and take up his cross and follow me", *Mark* 8:34 and *Matthew* 17:24. The enigmatic saying that is reported only by Matthew: "Verily I say unto you, there be some standing here which shall not taste of death till they see the Son of Man coming in his kingdom" appears to be a false prophecy and many attempts have been made to explain it away. The truth is very simple. Six days later, Jesus takes three of those who were standing there: James and John, the sons of Zebedee, and Peter up into a high mountain apart, *Matthew* 17:1.

We have now to part company with nearly every account of the Transfiguration. This stupendous event occupies nine verses in *Matthew* and *Luke* and seven in Mark's gospel. It is not mentioned at all in the fourth gospel; sure evidence that its true significance had been lost by the time it was compiled. All that is recorded in the synoptic gospels is the change in the appearance of Jesus, the apparition of Moses and Elias and the 'voice out of the cloud'. This is all the three witnesses were entitled to mention to their fellow disciples.

It was not intended that the true nature of the incident should be understood for this would have distracted attention from the final drama. Not only could the body of believers not understand, but the disciples were also at sea, as is shown by the immediately following incident of the lunatic child whom they could not cure.

The key to understanding the Transfiguration is the transmission of Divine Love. If we recognise that this, and not the redemption of mankind from sin as St. Paul supposed, was the mission undertaken by Jesus we see the event in its true perspective. The obstacle to this vision is our false conception of love as a polar force of attraction, similar to the attraction between two bodies carrying opposite electric charges, or between the poles of a magnet. Attraction implies repulsion. As unlike charges attract, like charges repel. If the love between man and God were of such a character, it would imply that man and God stood at opposite poles and could never be united without losing their love for one another. Divine Love does not derive its power from separation but from union. It is not fullness but emptiness, not Being but the Void.

The Transfiguration was an action that embraced all worlds. The three disciples belonged to the natural world, but they had already been initiated, with the rest of the twelve, into the spirit world. Moses and Elias unite the world of spirit and the world of creativity. Moses represents the covenant made by the giving of the Law, and especially the covenant of Love between Jahweh and his people (*Deuteromony* 27–30) and brought up-to-date in the covenant of the Essenes. Elias stands for the creative power that works miracles. Jesus goes beyond all the limitations of time and space and is in direct communication with the Father, represented by the Voice from the Cloud. I believe that there was a seventh person present, but as no such suggestion appears anywhere in the scriptures, I shall not mention his name at this stage.

From this moment, the character of the narrative changes. We see a drama enacted in which each participant has a precise role to play. As the last passion approaches, the tension grows. We must here remember that the gospels all, without exception, were edited to make them acceptable to Rome. Very little is said of the contact with the East. The Magi are never again mentioned. Even more remarkable is the absence of reference to the Essenes although we are told that at least one disciple, Simon belonged to the Zealots, committed to the liberation of Jerusalem from foreign rule. The truth is that the Romans were seriously concerned with the danger of a mass rising of the Jews under a new Messiah. The people were in a state of ferment and the Jewish authorities were above all anxious to avoid provoking reprisals from the Romans which might include the closing of the temple.

The intense emotional energy generated was a necessary element in the drama. The secret action had been completed and it was now necessary to release the force of Love by an explosion of hate. *Matthew* 23 purports to be an account of Jesus' deliberate provocation of the scribes and Pharisees. It is irrelevant to the narrative and to the readers of the gospel fifty or a hundred years later, it could have little or no significance. It is inserted to illustrate the process by which the scene was set for the final drama. The Jewish leaders were sufficiently occupied with the delicate task of maintaining a balance between Herod, the nominal ruler of the country, and the Roman delegate who held the effective power. They had no wish to be involved in the extraordinary movement initiated by Jesus. They had nothing to gain from a fresh wave of revolt against the Roman army of occupation. Herod himself was a superstitious man, half inclined to believe that Jesus was John the Baptist risen from the dead. It was necessary to close the event that had been consummated on the mount of Transfiguration.

The Transfiguration was the making of the New Covenant of Love and the Revelation was that this covenant requires from man humiliation or abasement, which alone can liberate him from the egoism which keeps him prisoner of the worlds of time and death. We must remember that according to the Books of *Exodus* and *Kings,* both Moses and Elijah spoke with God and were transformed, so that they were no longer men like the rest of mankind. A similar transformation was wrought in the disciples with Jesus on the mountain. They were made aware of the presence of God and this burned up their egoism and left them completely empty. This was the very core of the mission of Jesus. Once it was accomplished what subsequently happened was the process of opening the channel of Divine Love to the other disciples and eventually to all who were capable of receiving it.

Abasement and humiliation are spontaneous when finite man finds himself in the immediate presence of the Unfathomable Truth. But it is also necessary to live through humiliation here in this world in order to be established in Love. The gospel story, from the Transfiguration on, is concerned with humiliation.

The first to be humiliated were the sons of Zebedee. They ask Jesus to grant that they may sit on his right and left hand in his glory, and are rebuked for their lack of understanding, *Mark* 10:35–42. In Matthew's gospel they are represented as bringing their mother to ask for this privilege. The gospel adds that: "when the ten heard it they began to be much displeased with James and John". Only those who have been in similar situations can know the bitterness of being despised and rejected by one's closest friends on account of a real or fancied ambition to occupy the highest place. James and John were so completely discredited that we hear little of them again. The incident is not reported by Luke, who puts in its place a dispute among all the disciples as to the place they would occupy in the Kingdom. It seems that James and John deliberately allowed themselves to be disgraced, in order to eradicate the last traces of egoism that haunted them from the vision of the mount of Transfiguration. In the Acts of the Apostles, John is shown as humbly following Peter, who performs the miracles of healing and boldly addresses the Sanhedrin.*

The second humiliation is that of Peter. The story of Peter's denial appears in all four gospels and clearly made a profound impression on the disciples. Because of the tremendous achievements of Peter, we are inclined to treat the threefold denial as a momentary aberration or as evidence that the disciples did not receive the Holy Ghost until after the resurrection. The truth is that the denying of his Master was a betrayal that could have had as disastrous consequences as the betrayal of Judas. If Peter had boldly entered and taken Jesus' part before the High Priest, it might have been impossible to convict him. We must have a picture of the weakness of the Jewish authorities in complete subjection to the Roman legate, to realise how much might have turned upon Peter's loyalty.

How could Peter have done it? This question has tormented every reader of the gospel. It can be answered only if we understand the need for total humiliation in those who had been initiated into the Power of Love. Peter had to descend to the hardest perfidy in order to extinguish in him the subjective and personal attachment to Jesus that was inseparable from his own self-love. In order to become the perfected instrument of Divine Love, Peter had to accept the humiliating experience of seeing the falsity of his imagined love of Jesus exposed to himself and the world. I do not mean by this that Peter was play-acting. He could not help denying Jesus because his egoism had not yet expired.

The true significance of the Last Supper was the transmission to the disciples of the power that had descended upon Jesus at the Transfiguration. All the humiliation suffered by those directly involved was necessary to neutralize the negative forces released by the action. Jesus had plainly said: "He that exalteth himself shall be abased and he that abaseth himself shall be exalted."

* I should make it clear that I believe both St. Luke's gospel and the Acts of the Apostles were written in ignorance of the real character of Christ's mission. They are regarded by scholars as literary rather than historical works. Even so, the subordinate role of James and John is in striking contrast to their earlier pre-eminence.

We must picture the scene in Jerusalem on the eve of the Passover. The Roman army was not overwhelmingly strong in the city and was on the alert to crush by a drastic move – possibly wholesale massacre – any sign of a popular uprising. The multitude saw in Jesus a new Maccabaeus* armed with miraculous powers and was ready to follow him in a desperate venture. The Jewish authorities above all wanted to avoid open conflict with the Romans. Herod was alarmed at the threat to his hereditary role as 'King of the Jews'. Rumours and counter-rumours were everywhere. Roman patrols were all over the city and no one knew where they might strike.

In this strained atmosphere, the Jews were celebrating the Passover in memory of the night when the first-born of Egypt were slain by the angel of the Lord. The scene with Jesus and his disciples was far removed from such memories. They were looking into the future and making the final preparations for the entry of Divine Love into the human nature. This was done by a transfusion of substance. This action was possible because three of those present had already been transformed on the mount of Transfiguration. The gospel of St. John refers to the washing of feet, *John* 13:4–17. This version contains memories of the ceremony but leaves out any reference to the sharing of bread and wine. Jesus says: "a new commandment I give unto you, that ye love one another even as I have loved you" (*ibid* vv 31–35). This makes no sense unless it is part of a special action connected with the transmission of the *power to love* as Jesus loved.

We now come to a very hard task: that of understanding the betrayal of Judas. The humiliation of Judas was total. Unlike Peter he has never been pardoned in the eyes of Christendom. Many people have seen that we are before an impossible story. If Judas was really a traitor and yet Jesus chose him to be one of the twelve, either Jesus was a poor judge of men or else he allowed Judas to fall into the cruellest trap and this would be to impute lack of compassion to the Lord of Love. There was no need for Jesus to be betrayed: he could have spared Judas by allowing himself to be discovered. None of the usual explanations make sense. Some like to think of Judas as a misguided busybody who thought he knew better than Jesus and would force him to show

---

* Judas Maccabaeus, the freedom fighter who brought Jewish independence from Greek cultural dominance in 167–165 BC. Jewish independence lasted for a further century, to 63 BC.

thought he knew better than Jesus and would force him to show his power and bring in the Kingdom. This again is to belittle Jesus and make nonsense of the terrible sequence of events.

It happens that the truth is unmistakably indicated in the gospels and especially the fourth. Jesus tells his disciples that one of them is to betray him and they all begin to question among themselves which of them it was to be. This shows that the betrayal was an agonising duty that someone had to perform, but most of them did not understand. "Jesus says: 'He it is to whom I shall give a sop* when I have dipped it.' And when he had dipped the piece of bread, he gave it to Judas Iscariot, the son of Simon. And after the piece of bread, Satan entered into him. Then Jesus said to him: 'What you have to do: do at once.' Now no man at the table knew for what intent he said this to him." *John* 13:26–28.

We cannot understand this unless we remember first that the betrayal and crucifixion of Jesus were not necessary for the forgiveness of sins. Jesus had declared, when he cured the man sick of the palsy, that they should know that the "Son of Man hath power upon earth to forgive sins", *Matthew* 9:6. The arrest and condemnation of Jesus could happen at any moment that he permitted himself to be found. It follows that both the betrayal and the crucifixion have another and profounder reason. The highest possible reason for any action in this world is to allow Divine Love to penetrate. Love cannot enter where there are egoism, hate and envy. These are represented by Satan.

It was necessary for the transmission of Love to the disciples that Satan should be expelled. This was the task undertaken by Judas. John's gospel states it in plain terms. Jesus gave Judas the piece of bread and "after the sop, Satan entered into him". He had to leave the room at once so that no satanic action should occur.

Why should Judas be charged with this most odious task? He was close to Jesus. Unlike the remaining disciples who were Galileans, Judas was a Judaean and more highly cultured than the rest. He was probably an Essene initiate who had joined Jesus because he recognised that the Essenes, for all their self-discipline and obedience, were still trapped in pride of race and hatred of

---

* The Greek word *psomion* is the diminutive of *psomos* – bread. It is used currently in modern Greek to mean bread.

the oppressor.* Judas was more fully aware than any of the disciples of the magnitude of the step that was to be taken. This is why I believe that he was the seventh present at the Transfiguration. His name was suppressed when he had carried out his mission and accepted the entire blame for the betrayal of Jesus. I was led to this conclusion by conversations I had with Mr. Gurdjieff in 1949 shortly before he died. He said, in the presence of many of his pupils, that Judas was of all the disciples the closest to Jesus and the only one who knew all his secrets. He insisted upon my replying without equivocation to the question he put to me: "Do *you* believe that what I say about Judas is the truth?" I could only answer at that time, that there was no other explanation that made sense.

It was only very recently that the whole truth became apparent to me. Judas was the one into whom Divine Love had most completely entered, and therefore he was the one whose abasement and humiliation had to be the most complete. He alone was strong enough to allow Satan to take possession of him without losing his own soul. The words: "Satan entered into him" are among the most terrifying in the four gospels. When we pause to reflect, we can see that Judas was himself the lamb of God that took away the sins of the world.

I have never been able to accept that Jesus, who was sinless, could take sins upon himself. Anyone who aims at perfection knows that suffering comes from our own sins, not the sins of others. We must know that we ourselves are sinners in order to have true compassion for others. By making himself the greatest sinner of all, Judas could undergo the greatest humiliation; not only in the eyes of others, but in his own also. When the dreadful thing had been done and Satan left him, he could not be sure if the betrayal was his own act or the consequence of taking on the 'sins of the world'. When he hanged himself, it was not play-acting but the inevitable consequence of having allowed Satan to enter him; even though he did so consciously and even at the command of Jesus himself.

The humiliation of Judas was complete and irredeemable in this world. He has remained in the eyes of Christendom the very

* The saying: "Render unto Caesar the things that are Caesar's" would shock not only the Essenes, but even the Pharisees, who paid tribute only under duress. This is why, for a time, the Sadducees thought he might side with them in their policy of 'collaboration' with the Roman power.

symbol of wickedness. But the gospel gives us the assurance that
he was one of the initiates. He was the first of the disciples to
receive the sacramental bread from the hands of Jesus. He could
see for himself the miracle that was being enacted. And yet he
could continue to doubt and to condemn himself for the part he
had played in it. Is this not the true psychology of a saint?

If this is the deep, esoteric, significance of Judas' betrayal we
must also take account of the visible event. All Jerusalem was in a
state of excitement. Jesus had aroused the wildest expectations by
his onslaught on the money changers in the temple. The Romans
were on edge because they feared an uprising led by the Zealots,
who had separated from the Essenes because they would not wait
for the 'great and dreadful day of the Lord' foretold by Malachi,
Malachi 4:5. On all sides Jesus was under suspicion, and he and the
disciples were in imminent danger of arrest by the Romans,
whereas the drama required that the Jewish authorities should
also be involved. Judas would ensure that the Sanhedrin would
act before the Romans. He knew that the Sadducees were willing
to sacrifice Jesus. In the words of Caiaphas: "It is expedient that
one man should die for the people, and that the whole nation
perish not." *John* 11:50. Since it suited the Romans to deflect the
anger of the people – which they had good reason to fear – from
themselves and the Jewish authorities, Judas' action enabled the
drama to proceed according to Destiny.*

We now come to the act known as the Last Supper. All
authorities agree that it was an initiation by which the disciples
were enabled to transmit the blessing. The Pauline idea of a
'redemptive sacrifice' distorted the significance of the *agape,* or
Act of Love, as it was certainly understood by the first disciples,
and continued to be understood by the Judaean church. The Last
Supper was not on the same Divine Plane as the Transfiguration.
There was no 'Voice out of the Clouds', nor the appearance of
other sacred beings. The giving of bread and wine is not
mentioned at all in the fourth gospel. In the three synoptic
gospels, it is repeated in much the same words in seven to nine
verses. It is hard to believe that this action had the central
importance that is attributed to it by most Christian churches

---

* I have put this in because it is the explanation given by Gurdjieff (*c.f.*
Beelzebub's Tales p. 740–2). I think it is valid, but not the crux of the matter.
This is why Gurdjieff said that I would some day have to give the true
explanation.

today. It is so like the miraculous feeding of the four and seven thousand that it seems to be rather a connection with the second phase of Jesus' teaching than the consummation of his mission. Furthermore, the liturgic action is clearly derived from the Zoroastrian tradition through the Essenes. It was given its present form and importance in Cappadocia at a time when the Magi had an important centre there. In short, I think that the sharing of bread and wine – the Eucharistic Feast – was not the central act of the Last Supper. The long homily in St. John's gospel, *John* 13–17, gives us the clue. The central theme here is Divine Love. "A new commandment I give unto you, that ye love one another; as I have loved you, that ye also love one another. By this shall all men know that ye are my disciples, if ye have love to one another". *John* 13:34–5. These two verses appear out of context because in the next verse Peter takes up from verse 33 ignoring what his Master has just said.

We have here the vestige of a very strong tradition that something *essentially new* took place. Why a new commandment? Because something new had just happened. They had been endowed with the *Power of Love* and therefore they were set apart from ordinary men and women, whose egoism made them incapable of participating in the Divine Love. Soon after, Jesus adds the famous saying: "Greater love hath no man than this, that a man lay down his life for his friend" (*John* 15:13). The disciples are no longer "of this world", *John* 15:19. They have been initiated into the world where Love is the only law.

The communion of substance by which the transformation was effected was repeated in the act of sharing the bread and wine. The disciples had entered the Kingdom of Heaven and were beyond life and death. They had shared the spiritual body of Christ, and now they knew who He was.

But the price was still not fully paid. The humiliation of Judas was to be followed and consummated by the ultimate humiliation of the rejection of the Son of Man, his crucifixion and abandonment. Peter had to complete his own humiliation. His egoism was finally extirpated as he saw his proud boast that he would die with Jesus rather than deny him trampled in the dust as the cock crew.

Once the full tragedy of despair and humiliation was complete, the resurrection became possible. The 'resurrection body' is perceptible only to those who are able to love. From time to time, saints have visions of Jesus in his resurrection body, but they cannot approach him, as could the disciples who had been transformed into the resurrection world. This is where Paul fell into error. His vision of Jesus was not the same as the awareness of immediate presence that was possible for the disciples who had been initiated at the Last Supper. Paul saw himself as redeemed and assumed that Christ was crucified to redeem mankind. This is of course true, but not in the sense of Pauline Christianity which makes redemption necessary to *restore* man to his pre-existing sinless state in readiness for some future action that would usher in the Kingdom of Heaven. The disciples, with Peter at their head, knew that the Kingdom had already been entered; but they did not yet understand that it was an Universal Kingdom open to all people of all times. This was partly revealed to Peter in the vision in Joppa which sent him to Caesaria to baptise the Centurion Cornelius. It is significant that in describing the Resurrection, Peter said God showed Jesus: "Not to all the people, but unto witnesses chosen by God, even to us, who did eat and drink with him after he arose from the dead". *Acts* 10:41.

In short, the Essenes and the Pharisees followed the way of Gnosis and power, whereas the first Christians went by the way of Love and humiliation. We might even venture to say that the God of the Old Testament was the Demiurge, whereas Jesus looked beyond to the source of Divine Love. We shall have to see in later chapters which of the paths was taken by the Masters of Wisdom.

Chapter Five

A Thousand Years of Love

Whether or not you accept the account I have given of the life and passion of Jesus Christ, and whether or not you believe that He was the only-begotten Son of God, you cannot dispute the central place that Love held in his mission. More than any other prophet or teacher, he both preached and exemplified the pre-eminence of Love. His epitome of the commandments: "Thou shalt love the Lord thy God with all thy heart and with all thy mind and with all thy strength and thou shalt love thy neighbour as thyself", was taken from the Hebrew Scriptures, but it is his message to mankind and everyone has recognised it as his.

I scarcely need to produce evidence of the extent to which the message has been rejected, not least by the church founded in his name. This book is about the Masters of Wisdom and not a history of religion; nevertheless, I must face the contradiction between belief that Divine Love is the highest energy and the most needed for human evolution, and the recognition that it has disastrously failed to establish itself in human nature. I have already made my own convictions plain enough: Love requires humiliation, which is its protection from destructive reaction. Without humiliation, Love, when it enters the conditioned world, gets caught into the polarity of love and hate and finishes as its own opposite.

This truth was taught by Jesus to his closest disciples and it was understood by the early Christians, particularly of the Judaean Church. It was understood and practised by the Essenes, but those

MAP OF NEAR EAST

who refused to follow Jesus fell into the trap of accepting humiliation within the community, and holding on to the arrogance of moral superiority to those outside it. The influence of St. Paul was very great among the early Christians outside Judaea. He was aware of the secret of Love and humiliation; but I do not believe that he received the initiation himself. He accepted humiliation, because in doing so he knew that he was following in the steps of Jesus, but he could not *communicate* the power of Love to his churches. This can be seen from his epistles where he preaches charity as a quality superior to faith and hope, but still accessible to man if he wishes for it. Humility is treated as a consequence, rather than a condition, of Love and this apparently minor error has been responsible for endless disaster. Had St. Paul been one of those directly initiated by Jesus, he would not have made such a mistake.

I do not pretend to the scholarship that would be needed to decide whether the Gnostic brotherhoods that had their chief centres in Egypt between the first and fourth centuries preserved any better record than the Catholic Church of the true mission of Jesus. One important difference is that they believed that after the resurrection Jesus continued to teach a small group of disciples, men and women, and only during this time revealed the deepest mysteries of the spiritual world. In the *Pistis Sophia*,* the principal woman disciple is Mary Magdalene who represents perfect love for her Master and who asks a great series of questions that lead to the revelation of the "First Mystery" which is that Jesus is the incarnation of the Divine Love. Jesus says to Mary: "This will I tell you when I have explained to you the expansion of the universe. For this cause, therefore, I have rent myself asunder and have brought the mysteries into the world, because all are under sin and all are in need of the *gift of the mysteries*".** All the Gnostic documents I have seen agree that the crucifixion of Jesus was to allow the Mystery of Love to be enacted and that it was not a sacrifice made for sin. The Gnostics could see that, notwithstanding the coming of Jesus, sin remained in the world and that sin could be cancelled only by humiliation. This is probably why they assigned so lofty a role to Mary Magdalene as representing the sinner who is redeemed by humiliation and Love.

* trans. G. R. S. Mead: Watkins, 2nd Edn. 1921.
** *loc. cit.* pp. 292–293. *Editor's note:* the italics are Bennett's.

It remains true, however, that St. Peter was one of the four great initiates. With James and John he did possess the power to transmit Love through the laying on of hands and to renew the transmission through the Love Feast or *agápe*. This is the foundation of the Apostolic Succession upon which the claims of the Catholic Church are based. We are, therefore, still left with the dreadful mystery of the disappearance of the very core of the Revelation. I can, in one chapter, do no more than look for signs that mankind had not been deserted by the higher powers.

The first millenium after the time of Christ falls into three periods, so far as concerns the great area from China and India to Morocco and Europe. The first to AD 321 saw the slow rise of Christianity carrying the hopes of the world. The second, from the adoption of Christianity by the Roman Empire, was that of the degeneration of Christianity and the rise of Zoroastrianism. The third was from the flight of Muhammad, the Prophet of Islam, AD 622, from Mecca to Medina. The next three hundred years saw the rise of Islam and the degeneration of Zoroastrianism. By the end of the millenium, mankind had three times denied the great gift of Love and had put in its place the worship of power.

The rise of the Christian Church in Judaea was rudely interrupted by the Jewish war of AD 68–70. Until then the Christians had accepted humiliation and persecution as the welcome price of the love they enjoyed for God and for one another. There were very few martyrs during this time, chiefly because the Christians made no attempt to assert themselves and were content to find their converts among humble people, including slaves. At one time, I was inclined to attribute the prodigious concentration of energy that, within three centuries, carried the Christian faith from Spain and England as far as China and India, to the persecution of the church and the sufferings of martyrs. This would lead to the conclusion that suffering itself is good and hence to ascetic practices and puritan morals.

I now see how very wrong such a conclusion is and how much trouble it has caused. So long as the early Christians were ready to follow the way of life laid down in the Sermon on the Mount, they had no need to submit themselves to artificial suffering. Those who could not accept humility and plain self-discipline accepted "Christ without the Cross". Those who wanted the

Cross thought they could find it by retiring to the solitary life of a hermit in the desert* or, later, in ascetic communities harsher than those of the Essenes.** In both cases, humility was lost and with humility, Love went also.

The earliest Christians understood that they could not grasp the true nature of Christ. They had no doubt that God had intervened in an unique and direct way in human affairs; but they did not think of Jesus as God. The evangelists who compiled the synoptic Gospels knew that Jesus was "more than a prophet" and that he was the "One who was for to come". They knew that they themselves had been transformed by an action that they could not and did not wish to understand. They trusted the disciples and especially those who had been with Jesus on the mount of Transfiguration and they did not dare to ask what had been revealed. They could see for themselves that the disciples had been totally humbled; that *egoism* had died in them and they themselves hoped to participate more and more in the experience of Divine Love.

The early fathers Papius, Irenius and Jerome all agreed that there was an early Syriac gospel which was the treasure of the Judaean Christians, who were called Ebionites, to mark their belief in holy poverty. They were not concerned with asking whether Jesus was God or Man but with the hope of being transformed by the Love which still emanated from those who had been initiated by Him. This Divine Love came to be known as the Holy Spirit and it was understood by all Christians to be the centre of their initiation. It was renewed weekly in the Eucharist or *agápe*. For this the personal presence of one of the original initiates was regarded as very important though not indispensable. Moreover, all Christians in Judaea accepted the need for the personal discipline laid down in the teaching later to be known as the Sermon on the Mount. This was the core of the

---

* The father of the ascetic life was St. Antony, an illiterate Egyptian peasant who lived to be a hundred and five and was during his life time honoured throughout the Christian world. Emperors sent to him for advice whether or not to go to war. After a long and painful novitiate among the tombs, he finally settled near the Red Sea. Before he died more than five thousand hermits and monks had followed his example.

** Pachomius who was one of the founders of the cenobitic life — that of a community of monks or nuns vowed to celibacy and poverty — was particularly insistent on the importance of obedience and prayer. These do concentrate energy, but they are not sufficient to open man's nature to Love.

Syriac gospel and all true Christians learned it by heart. When it was replaced by the Greek testament that became the canonical scripture, whatever obviously contradicted the new ideas about the nature of Christ was suppressed.

These profound changes came after AD70; the churches were now composed of men and women scarcely any of whom had seen or heard an apostle. There had been a false expectation that the horrors of the Jewish war would usher in the Millenium and that Christ would come in glory to rule on the earth. The Christians who did not understand that the Kingdom had already come to them in the form of Divine Love, were led, chiefly by the Pauline theory of redemption, to believe that the significance of Jesus was that he was the Dying God of the Promise. For this, Jesus had to be God, and two centuries of anxious enquiry on the part of some, and bitter controversy on the part of others, destroyed the unity of Christendom and prepared the way for still worse things to come.

The saddest feature of the Christological disputes is that they totally distracted men's attention from the sublime event which had occurred. In the eyes of nearly all the disputants 'God' meant the creator of the world – the autocratic power that commands obedience – the same creator before whom the Jews had trembled in the days of Moses. For the Greeks, 'God' was either Zeus the Father and king of the gods, or Aristotle's First Cause or Prime Mover. To endow such a 'God' with a Son was either a "foolishness" or a "stumbling block" as Paul himself had declared. Among the Gnostics, Valentinus saw this clearly for himself, or else he was aware of the Great Initiation or at least an important stage of it. He may have known that Jesus was sent to the earth from an infinitely higher level than that of the creative power; but his teaching was encompassed in such a fog of speculation that only his personal disciples could penetrate to the real meaning. His enemies, and they included the greatest writers of the Catholic Church, were concerned to show the absurdity of doctrines ascribed to him and so to reject everything that he taught.

I do not doubt that a School of Wisdom existed in Egypt both before and after the time of Christ. The Gnostics were ardent lovers of Jesus and had no doubt of his Divine Mission. It is not easy to see why they should have been so relentlessly combatted and finally suppressed by the orthodox church, unless they possessed secrets that might have undermined the doctrines about the nature of Christ and the Deity that were the pretext for power-seeking adventures of the bishops who surrounded the Roman emperors from Constantine to Justinian. This suspicion is strengthened by the zeal with which the sacred books of the Gnostics were sought out and destroyed.

One thing is certain: from AD 321 onwards Christianity ceased to be the religion of Divine Love and became a cult of power and persecution. All Christians, whether the old Judaean or of the churches in Persia and central and southern Asia, or those in the Roman empire, were until AD 321 a weak and sometimes persecuted minority. The humiliation so necessary for the Spirit of Love was imposed on them by circumstances. Now this is not how it should be: it is personal rather than communal humiliation that allows us to love.

Gurdjieff makes a decisively important distinction between *voluntary* suffering and *intentional* suffering.* Humiliation that we attract through our opposition to society was condemned by Jesus as exposing us to the sin of pride.** The pagan world of Greece and Rome regarded religion as inferior to philosophy. Since it is the task of philosophy to question all assumptions and to reject nothing on any ground but that of demonstrable falsehood, the pagan world was tolerant to the most diverse beliefs. The Christians with their high moral principles would have been accepted if they had not thought it their sacred duty to adhere to the same intolerance that had made the Jews notorious throughout the ancient world. It was the Jews who introduced intolerance as a way of life and it was totally unnecessary that the Christians should follow them.

The Christians rejected the religious institutions of the Roman Empire which unfortunately were regarded by the Emperor and Senate as the guarantee of the stability of the state. I refer to this because we have to see something that Gibbon and other historians could not see. All intolerance is pride, and pride destroys love. The Christians had the obligation to proclaim the Gospel of Love, but no obligation to create trouble. They set themselves deliberately to flout the symbols of Roman culture

---

* *c.f.* J. G. Bennett, *Gurdjieff – Making a New World* p. 174
** *c.f. Matthew.* "Judge not that ye be not judged . . ." and his approving quotation from Isaiah: "He shall not strive nor cry nor shall his voice be heard in the street"; perhaps most of all: "Resist not evil".

that for the Romans themselves were time-honoured rituals, not to be taken very seriously, but for which they nevertheless demanded respect. The attitude of the Christians to 'idol worship' was always irritating and sometimes infuriating. The seven famous 'persecutions' from Nero to Diocletian seldom lasted long, and in two hundred years probably fewer than 40,000 were martyred. If we compare this with the persecutions by Christian kings and bishops of other Christians who sincerely held different beliefs as to the nature of Christ, the contrast is appalling. Under St. Cyril, the defender of the Nicene creed, more than 200,000 Christians were massacred in Damascus alone in the space of a few months.

It is painful and disgusting to read the contemporary accounts of cruelties committed, but we must form a true picture of the extent to which the mission of Jesus was befouled and betrayed as soon as Christianity became the dominant religion of the Roman Empire. I am obliged for this reason to recount the story of Hypatia, the authenticity of which is vouched for in several independent accounts.* Hypatia was the daughter of Theon the mathematician and initiated into her father's studies. She extended the brilliant work of Diophantus, the greatest mathematician of his age. In the bloom of her beauty and in the maturity of wisdom she refused her lovers and instructed her disciples. Cyril as Patriarch of Alexandria was in deadly rivalry with Orestes the Imperial Praefect. Hypatia was a friend of Orestes and enormously popular with the people of Alexandria. A rumour was spread among the Christians that Hypatia stood in the way of reconciliation. On a fatal day in the holy season of Lent, Hypatia was torn from her chariot, stripped naked, dragged to the church and inhumanly butchered at the hands of Peter the reader and a troop of savage and merciless fanatics. Her flesh was scraped from her bones with sharp oyster shells, and her quivering limbs were delivered to the flames. The first process of enquiry and punishment was stopped by seasonable gifts; but the murder of Hypatia has imprinted – says Gibbon – an indelible stain on the character and religion of Cyril of Alexandria, later to be canonized as St. Cyril, the defender of the Catholic faith.

* I have used Gibbon's *Decline and Fall*, Chapter XLVII, which takes the details from Socrates and Baronius, who were contemporaries and both tried to present Cyril under a favourable light.

One might conclude from this and so many other dreadful happenings that the Christian Church had totally betrayed its origin and had lost contact with the power of Love. Subsequent events have proved that this did not happen. The "Apostolic Succession" continued to transmit the grace of the sacraments, even through totally unworthy and depraved bishops and priests. Of this I have no doubt, but I do not conclude from it that the Christian Church has fulfilled the high purpose of its foundation or is ever likely to do so. The transmission of Divine Love was the *high purpose*, the forgiveness of sin and communion with the Sacred Image of Christ were not the aim, but the means of attaining the aim of bringing Love into the world. The third and most essential means, that of abasement and humiliation, was recognised only by very few. St. John Chrysostom who was persecuted by the same Cyril of Alexandria, driven from the patriarchal throne and ended his days in humble exile, was one of a series of wise men from Asia Minor who knew far more than they revealed. Another, Origen, had been a pupil of Ammonius Saccas, the head of a school of Masters who preserved the Pythagorean and Egyptian traditions and he could have done much to restore Christianity to its truly sacred mission.

In the sixth century Justinian, the last of the great Byzantine emperors, under the influence of his fanatical wife Theodora, closed the Academy and other schools of Athens which for nine hundred years had been centres of wisdom open to all the world. In Athens, scholars from India, Egypt or Persia could meet with scholars from Spain, England or Ireland. An immense moderating influence and a means of sharing the learning of many different cultures was thus suppressed from motives of avarice and petty jealousy. The very last of the great Greek philosophers was Prochlus (AD 412–485). We can tell from his writings and from those of his immediate disciples that they were influenced by Zoroastrian ideas. The connection is confirmed by the fact that when the schools in Athens were closed, seven philosophers were invited by the great Persian king Chosroes I (r. 531–579) to a conference that was held in Ctesiphon.*
According to Gurdjieff, the Sarman Society at this time had its

---

* *Editor's note.* The gathering of philosophers by Chosroes I is well-attested. The notion of a conference is Bennett's own interpretation. Rudolf Steiner also made much of this gathering, c.f. *The Redemption of Thinking.*

headquarters near Mosul or possibly in Edessa, and was represented at the gathering of the Masters of Wisdom.

The Masters of Wisdom had means of discerning the pattern of future events and knew that great calamities threatened. In September 531, a comet was seen for twenty days in the west. Eight years later another comet appeared and grew enormously, its head in the east and its tail to the west, and was visible for forty days. This was the fifth appearance of what we now call Halley's comet.* Several observers agreed that the sun grew pale, not at the time of the appearance of the comet, but some time later.

The earth itself was severely shaken at this time. Between AD 540 and 590 there were more great earthquakes than at any time in recorded history. One great earthquake lasted for forty days and was felt all over the Roman world and as far as Persia and India. There were great tidal waves that destroyed a great part of the world's shipping. The mountains of Lebanon were split and an entire mountain hurled into the sea at Botrys in Phoenicia. Two hundred and fifty thousand people died in two days in Antioch where a great concourse of people had assembled for the feast of the Ascension. Equally great catastrophes were recorded in Japan and the Pacific ocean.

However terrifying comets and earthquakes may be, and however great the material destruction caused by the latter, neither could decimate human life like plague. The greatest recorded epidemic of plague occurred during the reign of Justinian and spread all over the world. It appears to have started in north-east Africa, probably in Egypt. At one time ten thousand people a day were dying in Constantinople alone. The plague continued to come year after year for fifty-two years, spreading from the ports. As the nature of the infection was not understood, no attempt was made to restrict the flow of people and goods. Many cities were completely depopulated. Harvests and vintage withered on the ground for lack of reapers, and famine was added to pestilence. The years of plague were grimly

* The previous appearances of 1767 BC, 1193 BC, 618 BC, 44 BC, are all recorded as being connected with great historical events, such as the founding of the Persian Empire and the assassination of Julius Caesar. The tradition, preserved by Varro, that in 1767 BC the planet Venus changed her colour, size, and even her orbit, has been examined by Velikovski who believes that a catastrophe affecting the entire solar system did in fact then occur.

recorded by Procopius, an eye-witness, who estimated that more than a hundred million people perished in the Mediterranean countries alone. The total death-roll throughout the world may have been two hundred million, one third of the entire population. It was many centuries before mankind recovered and could again make progress. We cannot readily picture to ourselves the conditions of life during the Dark Ages.

As if these horrors were not enough, the end of the sixth century was marked by perpetual wars between the Romans, the Scythians and the Persians. No human agency could save mankind. Ignorance and hatred had exposed the human race to destruction and the very nature of the planet and the forces of the solar system seemed to conspire to make an end of the race that had so betrayed the supreme gift of Divine Love offered to it five hundred years before.

To discern, at this time, the role of the Masters of Wisdom, we must look to the Persian empire. The Sassanid dynasty which ruled from AD 225 to 640 was strictly Zoroastrian, but for a long time was tolerant of Christianity which spread and flourished even beyond the boundaries of the empire. The Magi, who had retained their identity through centuries of Parthian rule, gained greater and greater authority, and no Persian king could disregard their rulings on religious and sometimes even on social matters.

The Magi were a hereditary caste like the Brahmans in India, but they accepted candidates for initiation from the other castes. Within the Magi, there were special societies who maintained particular traditions and jealously guarded their own secrets. It is probable that the Sarman Society was connected with the Zurvanite band of the Magian tradition. In Gurdjieff's *Beelzebub's Tales to His Grandson,* the role of the "Merciless Heropass" corresponds more closely to that of Zurvan than to any other tradition, eastern or western. Gurdjieff very often refers to the "Persian dualism" and says that it led to false notions of "good and evil" as forces external to ourselves. Zoroastrianism as it finally emerged as a world religion was uncompromisingly dualist. There are two spiritual powers: Ahura Mazda, the Good Spirit, and Ahriman, the Spirit of the Lie. Ahura Mazda became Ohrmazd in Sassanid times and Ahriman, Aremanios; but they remained two independent and eternally irreconcilable powers. There are reasons for believing that this was not the original teaching of Zoroaster, because in one of the authentic hymns of the Avesta it is said that Ahura and Ahriman were twins.

An essential element in the Zoroastrian teaching is that Ahura, the Good Spirit, is limited. He has no dominion in the realm of Darkness in which Ahriman holds sway, nor can he destroy or even conquer Ahriman so long as the latter has the Dark World in which to take refuge. The complete independence of the Spirit of Evil makes it unnecessary for the Zoroastrians to worry about the origin of sin and suffering. Evil is a fact that is independent of the Good Spirit. As the Jews and the Christians regarded God as the creator and source of all, they were bound to regard Satan as a creature and so were faced with the impossible task of reconciling the infinite goodness of God with the fact of evil and suffering. Everyone who has wrestled with this problem knows in his heart of hearts that Hume was right in saying that it is impossible to conceive an All-loving and All-powerful God who has created the world and man and allowed them to get into the disastrous situations that have arisen. The Zoroastrians rejected Christianity precisely because it affirms that God is Almighty and yet permits evil.

Nevertheless, the Magi were sensitive to the objection that the dualism of Ahura and Ahriman is itself an absurdity. Where did the two opposing spirits come from? About AD 300 there arose a very powerful teaching which said that beyond good and evil is Zurvan the Unfathomable Source. Zurvan is not the 'father' of the twin spirits, as in Greek mythology Chronos is the father of Zeus and the Titans. Zurvan is the totally impersonal source of the laws of existence, one of which is that in the existing world everything is confronted with its own opposite. By this law the Truth must be balanced by the Lie and the Spirit of Truth, Ahura Mazda, must be in eternal conflict with the Spirit of Falsehood, Ahriman. The Good Spirit is intelligent and is the manifestation of Perfect Love. The Evil Spirit is filled with hate and its nature is blind aggression.

Although the two spirits are equal in force, the superior intelligence of Ahura allows Him to conceive a master plan to neutralize the destructive power of Ahriman. He creates the existing world within the *Vay*, void, that separates the worlds of Light and Darkness. Ahriman hates this creation and rushes recklessly in to destroy it, but he is trapped by his own aggression. He can no longer return to the safety of the Outer

Darkness where Ahura is helpless. Once trapped in the existing world, Ahriman is subject to time and must sooner or later face the final show-down with the forces of Good. In this, man has an essential role to play.

After the various elements of the natural world were brought into existence, Ahura specially created the primal "sole-created Bull" and the first man Gayomart. Gayomart is hermaphrodite and very like the primal man of Plato's *Symposium*. In him, Ahura placed his hope for the final overthrow of Ahriman, but when the Evil Spirit erupts into the creation, he kills the primal Bull and afflicts Gayomart so that in thirty years he also dies. Meanwhile, he has been seduced by Ahriman's ally, the whore, representing the negative principal in its evil aspect and from his seed a race of man arose whose nature was mixed and in whom the conflict of Good and Evil became an hereditary characteristic that will persist to the end of time. Nevertheless, Ahura continues to love mankind and sends messengers to incarnate in human form to help men to liberate themselves from their own spirit of evil.

Orthodox Zoroastrianism, as it was established at the time of Chosroes I accepted this account and its followers believed that nine thousand years after the first creation, a saviour, the Saoshyans, would come and fulfill the promise of Gayomart. Ahriman will be finally rendered impotent and cast into the Outer Darkness with no possibility of ever again attacking the Realms of Light.

Zurvanism was rejected as a heresy and it is hard from the existing sacred books of the Parsees to reconstruct the doctrine as it was originally taught. It is probable that groups of Zurvanites remained as secret societies and preserved knowledge of the true significance of Zurvan. Those who have studied Gurdjieff will certainly recognise the many points of contact, and will probably agree that Zurvan is the origin of the Merciless Heropass, whom, by the way, Gurdjieff never represents as an evil or lying spirit. On the contrary, he often writes of the "lawful commands of the Merciless Heropass".

It is also clear that *Vay*, the void, is the same as Gurdjieff's Etherokrilno and that it also represents the Third or Reconciling Force by which the Merciless Heropass is overcome. I believe that Zurvanism contained the true message of the prophet and that it was rejected in the reign of Shapur II (AD 307–79) under the influence of a leading dualist magus called Adhurbadh. He was a friend of the king and was supported by the aristocracy, so it is not surprising that he rejected the doctrine of humiliation that had kept Zoroastrianism together through the Arsacid period of the Parthian kings. Adhurbadh was influenced by Aristotelian ideas and emphasised the importance of the mean or middle way. The nearest he came to the teaching of Jesus was in such sayings as: "wherever you sit at a banquet, do not sit in the highest seat, lest you be moved away and made to sit in a lower one." For him, *Khrat,* Wisdom, meant moderation in thought, speech and action. The love between man and the Good Spirit that inspires the Avestan hymns is replaced by common sense and the avoidance of extremes.

Zoroastrianism reached its highest peak under the reigns of Chosroes I and his son and grandson. For a time, it spread from India to Egypt and far into central Asia. I must briefly mention the Manichaean cult which was an off-shoot of Zoroastrianism, but totally different in its attitude to life. For Mani the world itself is the evil principle. The dualism is not that of Truth and the Lie, but of Spirit and Matter. This leads to rejection of life and the exaltation of asceticism and self-denial. For the Zoroastrian, the world is the beneficent creation of the Good Spirit and it is good in its very essence. We can see a reflection of this attitude in the first chapter of Genesis: "God looked upon His work and saw that it was good".

Zoroastrianism had the immense advantage of being able to affirm the absolute goodness of God and to reject any connection between God and the evil and suffering that pervades the world. Its followers were encouraged to enjoy the good things of life. They had a religion with its own ritual and sacraments that brought them the sense of an intimate communion between man and God. Unfortunately, as the religion came to be universally accepted, the principal Magi insisted on a rigid orthodoxy. They persecuted not only Jews and Christians but also followers of what, by then, was the Zurvanite "heresy".

By the end of the sixth century, Persia, like the rest of the world, suffered from earthquakes and plague and yet the Sassanid kings remained bent on conquest. The last bitter struggle between Chosroes II and the Byzantine emperor Heraclius was decided in favour of Byzantium by the control of the sea; but Rome and Persia were exhausted by the generations of plague and devastation and by the madness of war. The time had come for a new star to rise.

The brief period from AD 632–642 saw the collapse of the Sassanid empire and the loss of Egypt, Syria and most of Asia Minor by the Byzantine empire. Islām appeared and conquered by the force of conviction: but it was confronted by empires weakened by famine, pestilence and war, led by weak kings and incompetent generals, so that the victories of Umar were less astonishing than if they had occurred a hundred years earlier. In fact, it is pretty clear that the Prophet of Islām appeared at the one moment in history when the Arabs, inexperienced in large scale warfare and strangely ignorant of the world around them, had any chance of overcoming both the Persians and the Romans and creating a new power in the world.

There is, however, one aspect of the advance of Islām that no authority I have studied has been able to explain. This is the collapse of the Zoroastrian religion and the disappearance of the Magi. For at least twelve hundred years, the Magi were a coherent and usually a very powerful caste or society that had an immense influence in Persia and the surrounding countries. They reached the height of their power in the reign of Chosroes I when they were represented in Egypt, Syria, Asia Minor and the Caucasus, right through Persia into Afghanistan and Turkestan. One can understand their disappearance from countries recently conquered by Persia; but something very extraordinary must have happened within Persia itself.

By contrast, the Christian churches in the countries conquered by Islām were left in peace. It is well-known that the Caliph Umar, after signing the capitulation of Jerusalem, personally supervised the entry of the victorious Arabs to make sure that no church was desecrated or Christian molested. He even stood with the patriarch in the Church of the Resurrection and paid his respects to the Risen Lord of the Christian faith. His example was followed by the Caliphs for three centuries until the coming of the Saljuk Turks began a period of persecution of non-Muslims.

The Assyrian church came to terms with the Caliphs. The patriarch and bishops were allowed privileges they had never enjoyed under the Sassanid kings. Christians occupied honourable posts – many were physicians to the Commander of the Faithful – and they grew wealthy, though always regarded as inferior in status to 'true believers'. One of the patriarchs, remembered as Timothy the Great, was able to hold a council of his twenty-seven archbishops and seven hundred bishops and had the privilege of being able to go directly into the presence of the Caliph Harūn ar-Rashīd. The privileged position of the Christians was partly due to their superior education. The illiterate Arab conquerors went to school and learned from their Christian subjects. As time went on, these advantages disappeared, but still the two Christian churches* retained their position.

The same tolerance was not shown to the Zoroastrians; chiefly because theirs was the religion of the Persian empire and the Muslims were suspicious of revolts. Even so, there is no record of forcible conversions, of massacres or of the desecration of Zoroastrian temples. They were even accepted as 'People of the Book', that is one of the peoples who possessed a revealed scripture like the Torah or the Gospels. How then are we to account for the disappearance of the Magi?

They did not totally disappear. As late as the ninth century, there were devout Zoroastrians who were responsible for collecting and preserving the sacred books and for making new compilations such as the *Bundahishn,* the *Denkart* and the *Shikand Gumani Vazar.*** But these activities only serve to demonstrate the weakness of the Magi. They were written to convince the Muslims that they, too, should receive the toleration accorded to People of the Book.

This is by no means the strangest feature of the situation. The Arabs conquered, but never colonized Persia as they did Iraq. Within a century of the death of Harūn ar-Rashīd, the great Abbasid Caliph of Baghdad, Persia was again virtually independent. On all previous occasions since Cyrus the Great re-established Persian sovereignty in 650 BC, the Zoroastrian religion had been the rallying point. It was in the name of Ahura Mazda and with the support of the Magi that the Sassanids drove out the Parthian usurpers. The same could easily have happened in the eighth century AD when the Persians set themselves free

---

* One was the so-called Nestorian or Assyrian church which believed that the Son was subordinate to the Father, and the other were the Monophysites who believed that Christ had only one divine nature.
** *c.f.* R. C. Zaehner, *The Teachings of the Magi,* London 1956; *Zurvan, A Zoroastrian Dilemma,* Oxford 1955; *The Dawn & Twilight of Zoroastrianism,* Oxford 1961.

from Arab domination. Instead of restoring their ancient religion, they generally accepted Islām, perhaps initially for economic and social reasons. They brought to it many elements from their own culture, particularly a tendency towards the mystical, which led in some instances to a preference for Shiism. But why should the Persians choose to develop a mystical form of Islām rather than revert to their own ancient religion?

I believe that the solution of this riddle is to be found in the role of Salmān, the Persian famous as a Magian personally converted to Islām by the Prophet himself, whose close companion he became. If we combine this with the legend of the conference of Persians, Greeks and Indians convened by Chosroes, I believe we can recognise the hand of the Masters of Wisdom. An important difference between the Shiahs and the orthodox Sunnī Muslims is the insistence of the latter upon the Unity, *wahdat,* of God, and of the former upon Divine Love, *ishq.* Persian mystical literature is dominated by the conviction that a bond of Love unites man and God. When we read the Quran with the eyes of a Persian, we see how it starts by proclaiming the Love and Mercy of God: *Bismillāh ar–Rahmān ar–Rahīm,* in the name of God the Merciful, the Compassionate. The Love of God and his intimate closeness to the heart of man is combined in Islām with insistence on God as Spirit, entirely different from anything that our senses can perceive or our minds think of.

The critical moment was when the Arab Caliphate of Damascus, the Ummayads, was overthrown by the more Persian influenced Caliphate of Baghdad, the Abbasids. By the year 750, the Abbasids, represented by Abū Muslim, had gained complete control and were supported by the Magi who saw in them the hope of the return of Persian rule. Not all the Magi acquiesced. At Nishapur a Zoroastrian reformer Māh Afarīd called on the people to restore the pure Zoroastrian dualism.* It was Abū Muslim who supported the Magian hierarchy, who in return took an active part in the adaptation of the Islamic creed to Persian sensitivities.

It seems most probable that the majority of Magi decided to embrace Islām and through it express what had been lost in Zoroastrianism and what they could not find in Assyrian Christianity. This is the notion of the transformation of man

* *c.f.* W. Barthold – *Turkestan down to the Mongol Invasion,* London 1958 p. 194.

through the power of Love. We shall find that the belief in transformation is to occupy an increasingly important place in our search for the work and teaching of the Masters of Wisdom.

The Muslim historians refer to the conversion of famous Magi, whereas there are no similar records in the annals of the Assyrian Church. There were secret societies or sects who outwardly professed the Islamic faith, but within their communities preserved and practised their traditional customs. I have myself come across two such societies in Persia: the Yezīdīs and the Ahl-i Haqq. The former are called 'devil worshippers' because they retain the Zoroastrian dualism and believe that we are now in the Dark Age when Ahriman has power over the lives of men. The Ahl-i Haqq, People of the Truth, date their foundation more than a thousand years back, but their society has been reformed and renewed several times since the tenth century. My personal impression of both these societies was extremely positive. I went to Shaikh Adi, the chief sanctuary of the Yezīdīs, and could recognise many evidences of their Zoroastrian origins both in their respect for all forms of life, especially trees, and in their sacred symbols. Whenever one approaches a Yezīdī settlement one sees ahead a valley full of trees and rich vegetation, in happy contrast to the Muslim and Christian villages where the trees have been cut down and barren rock surrounds the cultivated areas. The Yezīdīs are totally committed to the dualistic belief that the Good and Evil Spirits are independent powers that will never cease from strife until the end of the world. The silver peacock concealed from all but the priests is the symbol of the Spirit of Truth and the black serpent, who appears at the entrance of the outermost court, is the symbol of Ahriman, the Spirit of the Lie.

I was particularly drawn to the region extending from Zākho at the foot of the Kurdish highlands to Karind and Hamadān in the south and from Mosul and Nineveh to Tabriz in the north, by the feeling that the Masters of Wisdom had for many centuries possessed an important centre in this area. Many sects and societies besides the Yezīdīs, the Ahl-i Haqq and the remnants of the Assyrian Christians are still located in the region; and at sites like Mar Behmen one can see evidence of more than two thousand years of recognition as a 'Holy Place'.

I must make it clear that what I am about to write is no more than a vision that at least does not contradict any facts I am aware of and does fit in with the widely held belief that the region to which I refer has for thousands of years occupied a special place in the esoteric tradition. In fact, as I was many times assured by those who there, at the centre of the region below the ravine of Rawāndiz was the site of the Garden of Eden in which Adam discovered the secret of good and evil.

In the sixth century the great conference of wise men took place with the authority of Chosroes the Great. The Persian king set his seal on the event, as is shown by his insistence in his treaty with Justinian that the seven Greek philosophers who came from Athens should be given a safe conduct, and guaranteed against the vengeance of the Christians. He also encouraged the participation of Christians chosen for their learning rather than their ecclesiastical eminence. There were also Buddhists from the Uighurs of Turkestan, known as 'Bakkshis' from the Sanskrit word *Bhikshu* meaning a member of the Buddhist Brotherhood. The Magi of both the orthodox and the Zurvanite tradition were represented, but those selected belonged to the inner brotherhood that stood apart from the sectarian disputes.

The conference lasted for three years to give time for astrological readings to be obtained from different parts of the world. I have already mentioned the expectation of the appalling catastrophes that were about to descend upon the world. I believe that the coming of Islām was also foreseen and that it was agreed that it would give the best hope of reconciliation between the warring nations and religions. Let us turn to the actual fate of Islām.

When Muhammad did come and received his Revelation on Mount Hira, he certainly strove hard to gain agreement between Jews, Christians, Zoroastrians and the Arabian polytheists on the basis of the simple formula: "There is only One God and He is entirely loving and merciful towards all creatures". When this message failed to gain acceptance from the Jews and the Christians, but was accepted by some of the Magi through Salmān the Persian, the great mission of Muhammad had already partially failed. He persisted, and through his immediate successors Abū Bakr and Umar the spirit of reconciliation was maintained.

By the ninth century, Islām was already degenerating. The Caliphate of Baghdad had fallen under the domination of the Turkish Beys who formed the body-guard of the Commander of the Faithful. In Spain, there was still a strong tradition which eventually found expression in the great sufi Abd ar-Rahmān ibn al-Arabī, who came to the east and died in Damascus. In Egypt, Islām was to lose its vitality under the Fatimid Caliphs. Strangely enough the living stream of the Islamic faith was flowing far to the north in Turkestan, and the Turks who paid nominal allegiance to the Abbasid Caliph in Baghdad knew that some of the deeper secrets of Islām were preserved by their own saints and sages.

At that time, the balance between Christianity and Islām in Turkestan was evenly held. In the eighth century Christianity made its way successfully into China under the Tsung dynasty (AD 500–900). The famous Si-an monument, still preserved tells how the Emperor Tsai gave greeting to: "Olopen the first teacher of this excellent, mysterious and pacific religion." The Emperor Hsan Tsung issued a formal edict recognizing the Christian Church as one of the state religions. The Chinese Archbishop George was given the right to bear the insignia of one of the highest grades of Mandarins. One might well have expected that the Christian religion would have prevailed in other areas not directly under Arab dominion.

This did not occur. On the contrary western Turkestan became one of the most vital centres of Islām, even though the Saljuk Turks, who poured south and west in wave after wave of invasion, destroyed every Arab city and even massacred their co-religionists. I believe that the Masters of Wisdom had their centre in the region between Mosul and Hamadān and that they sent missionaries into Turkestan to prepare for a move to the north where they were to remain for five centuries. Islām was no longer a living religion in the country of its origin. Mecca and Medina were neglected and religion had suffered the inevitable consequence of gaining political domination and accumulating the riches of this world. This danger was particularly great in Islām where the political and religious leadership was united in the person of the Caliph.

The Shiahs alone rejected this identification. According to them, the Caliphate terminated with the "four Just Caliphs" Abū Bakr, Umar, Uthmān and Alī. After the martyrdom of Husain at Karbala, there came the 'Twelve Imāms', the last of whom was veiled from the people. Thus the leadership of religion disappeared from sight and the doctrine of humiliation could be preserved. In the next chapter we shall see how this doctrine came again into the open in the teaching of the Khwājagān, the first society to be officially known to their contemporaries and to posterity as Masters of Wisdom.

Chapter Six

The Return of the Masters

The seventh century, which saw the collapse of the Persian and Byzantine empires, was for Europe the start of the Dark Ages when the devastation left by the plague was aggravated by the waves of invasion by Goths and Huns. In this grim situation, Christian monasticism underwent a revival and renewal in the hands of St. Benedict and his successors. I am not aware of any evidence that the father of European monasticism was ever in personal contact with a school of Wisdom; but he certainly penetrated more deeply into the true significance of the Christian message than the leaders of the Church. He recognised that poverty, humility and love are inseparable and established a rule that remained a valid way of life for hundreds of thousands of men and women throughout the world to this day. The monasteries converted the invaders to the Catholic faith and taught them to read and write in Latin. They restored agriculture in abandoned areas and facilitated travelling by providing shelter reasonably safe from the gangs of robbers that infested all parts of Europe. They were a great civilizing influence; but unfortunately, they grew strong and wealthy. The abbots were like feudal lords and within three centuries the monasteries had become a burden rather than a support for the common people. Nevertheless, I believe that between the time of St. Benedict and that of Pope Gregory the Great, there were schools of Wisdom in several centres in Europe.

My main concern in this chapter will be to reconstruct the history of the Masters of Wisdom in central Asia, and for this, we must return to the events in Persia. The Arabs always had a great admiration for the Sassanid kings of Persia. The great epic poem of Ferdausī, the *Shāhnāma,* recounts the exploits of Chosroes, Nushirvan and the other great kings of the pre-Islamic period. The Abbasid Caliphs modelled their administration on that of the Sassanids, and the famous dynasty of Grand Wazīrs, the Barmakids, even regarded themselves as direct successors of the great Magi who advised the Persian monarchs. Whereas the Christians were able to exercise their talents in professional capacities as school teachers and physicians, the Magi rose to very responsible positions in the state, thanks to the admiration felt by the Caliphs and their subjects for the administrative system of the Sassanids. This same admiration resulted in a return to the system of satrapies by which the governors of outlying provinces enjoyed a high degree of autonomy so long as they kept the frontiers safe and sent the tribute money required for maintaining the Caliph and his capital. The defect of this system is its dependence upon the high prestige and military prowess of the ruler and the army under his control. As soon as the centre weakens, the provincial governors throw off their allegiance and usually begin to neglect the frontier guard. This happened with the Achaemenids and Sassanids and it happened again when the great Abbasid Caliphs were succeeded by weaklings and lost, into the bargain, the Barmakids who had created the administration and made sure that it operated successfully.

I must pause here to describe the region in which the Masters of Wisdom were to make their appearance. From time immemorial – by which I mean perhaps the eight thousand years since the great migrations described in Chapter Two – the nomads and the settled populations had been divided by two great rivers running east and west. These were called by the Greeks the Oxus and the Jaxartes, and in the times we are speaking of, the Amu Darya and the Syr Darya. These rivers rise in the great mountains north of Tibet, the Altai and the Hindu Kush. The Oxus formerly flowed into the Caspian Sea a thousand miles away to the west. Now, both empty into the Aral sea and water the immense plains and valleys of Turkestan. The Amu Darya is known throughout central Asia as 'The River', *an-Hahr,* and the region to the north is called 'beyond the river', *Mā warā an-Nahr.* Persia lies to the south of the river and Turkestan to the north. For thousands of years the river was the

frontier that restrained the nomads from penetrating southward
except at such times as they could gather great hordes and find a
bold leader to lead them on adventures of conquest and pillage.

In the eighth century the Arabs, after the conquest of Persia,
were able to penetrate far to the north and east and even, at one
moment, to contemplate the invasion of China. By the ninth
century, the tide had turned. The Persians had regained their
independence and the Turkish kingdoms of Transoxania were in
open revolt against the Caliph. Turkestan was finally established
as Muslim territory, but it was free from Arab or Persian
domination. In spite of wars and civil wars, and the break
between Baghdad and Bukharā, Turkestan kept its importance
both by virtue of its natural wealth and as a link between China,
India, Persia and the Roman empire.

Although Islām was dominant, there was still a strong Assyrian
Christian church. Christianity was strong in China and was in
some way allied to Buddhism, at least in the eyes of the rulers of
China and Turkestan. There were flourishing Buddhist
monasteries in Balkh and other cities of eastern Turkestan.
Further north, the nomad tribes of Turks and Mongols kept to
the Great Spirit worship and the guidance of their shamans. The
Zoroastrian tradition was by no means dead and we find
references in the Islamic histories to the temples of the
'fire-worshippers'. In short, Turkestan was a meeting point of
many traditions and many races. It was also threatened, though
few could have known it, by the great wave of invasions that
was, within two centuries, to destroy the old world and
inaugurate a new cycle.

The Masters of Wisdom undertook an extraordinary task, the
significance of which I hope to show in this and the next chapter.
It was to demonstrate the power of humility and weakness, and
from that demonstration to lead men back to Love. I must first
make a distinction between Sufism as generally understood, and
the teaching of the Masters who are often described as Sufis. We
can separate the Sufis of Arabia, Mesopotamia, Syria, Africa and
Spain – that is the 'southern Sufis' – from those of Persia,
Turkestan, Afghanistan and the Caucasus – that is the 'northern
Sufis'. The Sufis of Turkey were between the two and shared
some of the ideals of both. The southern Sufis came mostly from
countries which had been Christian and they adopted the
Christian concept of God as Love and made union in Love with

God the highest aim of the spiritual path. In this, of course, they agreed with the aspirations of the Christian saints. The northern Sufis understood the human situation more profoundly and knew that the secret of Love is in the death of self by way of humiliation and abandonment. In this, they were closer to the Assyrian Christians for whom death with Christ was the necessary condition of resurrection. The notion of the *void* which was shared by the Buddhists and the Zoroastrians was expressed in the doctrine of annihilation *mahw wa fanā*. They even adopted the term *itlāq*, liberation, from the Buddhist idea of the *Arahant*, liberated man.

Such ideas were already being expressed by Muslim teachers in Baghdad such as Bāyazīd Bīstāmi and Junaid before the tenth century, but they remained within the orthodox tradition according to which salvation is assured to everyone who accepts belief in the Unity of God and the prophetic status of Muhammad with no further obligation than to carry out the religious duties and conform to the moral precepts of the Quran.

Although there were great saints among the southern Sufis, there was not the true doctrine of transformation that I have referred to as the great innovation introduced by the Khwājagān. Transformation was, of course, not new to the Masters: but it had formerly been esoteric and reserved for those initiated into the mysteries of a particular way. The early Christians understood the need for transformation and knew what was meant by death with Christ and rebirth, but this knowledge was lost when salvation was rigidly linked in men's minds to orthodox beliefs and the observance of rules.

The tenth century was a period of relative peace and prosperity for central Asia. This was mainly due to the wise administration of the Sāmānid dynasty which dominated the region from Ferghāna and Balkh to the east and Merv and Khiva to the west. At that time, Samarkand began to acquire fame as a centre of culture which made its name known throughout the world. Samarkand paper makers learned from the Chinese with whom there was a very active trade, but they developed their own methods of manufacture which later spread to Europe. It also seems that under the Sāmānids coal was first used for smelting iron in Ferghāna, eight hundred years before it was rediscovered in England. The silk and cotton fabrics of Turkestan were prized from Cairo and Baghdad to India and China. The Sāmānids

ruled on the principle that the glory of a monarch is to increase
the prosperity of his people, to build roads and bridges and to
erect fine mosques and schools in every city. I must add that there
were plenty of troubles also: civil wars, wars of succession and
the need to be on guard against raids from the Turkish nomads
north of the Syr Darya and even, sometimes, the threat of
invasion from China. Nevertheless, compared with earlier and
later times, the century of Sāmānid rule in Turkestan was
remembered as a period of general well-being. The Sāmānids
were orthodox Muslims; they had great respect for the regular
priesthood who were in conflict with teachers with new ideas
who were gaining influence with the people. One of these was
the great philosopher Ibn Sīna, who became known to European
students as Avicenna. When the Saljuk Turks became powerful
and the Sāmānid dynasty collapsed, the Turkish Khāns, though
very pious Muslims, were strongly drawn to the ideas of
transformation that were being spread. There is a story of the
Turkish Shaikh Abū Saīd* meeting with Avicenna at the end of
which the Shaikh said: "That which I *see*, he knows." The
philosopher said of his companion: "That which I know, he
sees." There are many stories of the humility shown by the great
Tamgāch–Khān Ibrāhīm. Once a preacher, Abū Shujā, a
descendant of Alī, said in a sermon before him: "Thou art not
worthy to be a king". The Khān closed the doors of his palace
and decided to relinquish the throne, but such was the love felt
for him by the people of Bukhārā, that they would not leave his
side until he accepted their assurance that the preacher had been
mistaken.

We can see in such stories that the teaching of Love and
Abasement was already beginning to spread in Turkestan. It was
about this time that the first of the Masters of Wisdom appeared.
He was Abū Yaqūb Khwāja Yūsuf of Hamadān. Yūsuf was born
in 1048 and died at the age of ninety-five in 1143. At the time of
his birth, Hamadān was within the domain of the Saljuk King
Tughrul, who dominated Persia to the south of the Amu Darya
and even invaded Armenia. In the very year that Yūsuf was born
the Saljuks won the decisive battle of Dandānqān that destroyed
forever the power of the Ghaznavids south of the river. Tughrul

---

* The story is given in Hamdallāh Qazwīnī's history quoted in Barthold *loc.
cit.* p. 311.

was acclaimed as the Amīr of Khurasān. This was the start of Saljuk domination that continued for three hundred years, moving finally westward to Asia Minor. I mention this historical event because it accounts for Yūsuf's connection with the ancient centre of the Masters of Wisdom north of Mosul. His third successor wrote a biography* in which he refers to his connection with Christians and Magi as well as with "teachers of other religions".

At the comparatively early age of thirty-five, Yūsuf was already recognised as a teacher and he was the first to receive the title of Khwāja which under the Sassanid kings had been resumed for the Wazīr, the chief counsellor of the monarch. From the time of Yūsuf the Khwājagan** seldom took any part in the affairs of state, but they had a great influence with the rulers and with the people. According to his biographer, Yūsuf was tall, slender with a fair complexion and yellow hair. He was pock-marked, but always gay and smiling. He wore a patched woollen cloak.

By the year 1080, Yūsuf had formed a group of initiates with whom he moved from Hamadān to Bukhārā nine hundred miles to the north east beyond the Amu Darya. At that time, the Karakhānid rulers in Turkestan were men of great piety and there were many teachers outside the orthodox priesthood. The Sultan Shams al-Mulk, like his father, enjoyed the reputation of a just sovereign. He retained the nomadic customs of his forebears and came to Bukhārā for the winter only. Nevertheless, he was responsible for many fine buildings including the cathedral mosque of Bukhārā. He was not in favour with the orthodox priesthood because of his encouragement of unorthodox teachers. This was no doubt a factor in deciding Yūsuf to make the long journey into a country where he could not even speak the language. He always taught in Persian, although he had a majority of Turkish pupils.

Eleven men went with Yūsuf from Hamadān to Bukhārā.

---

* Abd al-Khāliq Ghujduwānī, *The Mission of Yūsuf Hamadānī* cited in Hasan Lutfi Şuşud's *Islam Tasavvufunda Hacegan Hanedani*, Istanbul 1958, p. 9.
** Khwāja originally meant 'possessed of superior learning'. The word was of Persian origin and never used in Arab countries. The chief Wazīr of the Sāmānid kings was called the *Khwāja-i Buzurg* and his insignia of office was an inkstand. The Khwājas under the Sāmānid kings occupied much the same position as the chancellors of the Plantagenet kings of England. They were intended to be, and some times in fact were, 'Masters of Wisdom'.

They included the first of the Turkish Masters, Ahmad Yasawī, and others who had a profound influence in the vast area from China to Constantinople. According to his biographer, Yūsuf inherited the turban and the walking stick, *asa,* of Salmān the Persian which came to him through the Imām Zain al-Abidīn, who was the teacher of Husain the grandson of the prophet, martyred at Karbāla. The precious relics passed to the Imāms Muhammad Bāqir, Jaafar as-Sadīq, Chancellor to Harūn ar-Rashīd, Bāyazīd Bistāmī the great sufi of Baghdad, and then to Abū Hasan of Kharaqān. From Abū Hasan the teaching was transmitted to Shaikh Abū Alī Farmadi who was Yūsuf's teacher and his link with the Masters of Wisdom who remained in obscurity in Khurasān.

So we see Yūsuf installed in Bukhārā where for nearly sixty years he is to fill the role of the Grand Master. Until the last years of his life, he kept aloof from public affairs and avoided contact with the ruling classes. The latter were divided into the military leaders, the great landowners and the rich international merchants and the orthodox Muslim priesthood. Whatever money came his way was distributed to the needy and he accepted no personal presents for himself. He was courteous to all and had great compassion for anyone in trouble. Whether walking or sitting, he constantly recited the Quran. His biographer says that he often would stand facing towards distant Hamadān with tears pouring down his cheeks.

His attitude towards religious orthodoxy was simple. He told his disciples that religion was a mystery which could not be explained and that the study of theology was a waste of time. The mind of man cannot penetrate the mystery and was not intended to try.

He was impartial towards all religions and his love was universal and felt by everyone who approached him. There were still Magi in Bukhārā at that time – they used to visit him regularly. He said: "All men know that Love is the Supreme Power that unites Man and God, but no one who is not free from self is capable of Love." The technical term for freedom from self is *itlāq.* God is always referred to as *Haqq,* the Truth, thereby strongly suggesting a connection with Ahura Mazda the Spirit of Truth. To find God is to find the Truth, *tahqīq,* which is practically synonymous with *itlāq.* I use the word 'transformation' to signify that which happens when a man attains to freedom from self and realizes the Truth.

The Khwājagān were above all insistent upon the importance of method. The seeker requires someone to show him the way. This is called *irshād* and the one who shows the way is *murshid*. An important distinction between the Masters and the southern Sufis is to be seen in the teacher-pupil relationship. The southern Sufis were possibly influenced by the idea of the guru in India and by the insistence upon complete obedience to the superior in the Christian monasteries. The shaikh accepted complete responsibility for the spiritual welfare of his *murīd* – the word *murīd* means one who is under obedience – and in return the disciple gave up all his possessions and set himself to conform as perfectly as possible to the way of life shown by the shaikh. The extinction of self was to come through submission and obedience. It was called *fanā fi'l-shaikh,* which means totally to lose oneself in one's teacher. When this was attained the next step was *fanā fi'l-rasūl* or self-extinction in the Prophet of God, leading finally to *fanā fillāh* or extinction in God. The Masters of Wisdom entirely rejected this path. They would never allow their pupils to show them personal reverence and they insisted that Muhammad rejected every suggestion that he himself was the way by which others could reach God.

In the time of the Masters the spiritual life of central Asia was extraordinarily free. Again and again they showed by their example that all ways and all teachings are to be respected because they all have something good from which we can learn. I have studied the history of the spiritual search of many periods and places and always, always, have found a record of doctrinal disputes, sectarianism, the rejection and persecution of heretics. Each teacher or spiritual leader insists upon the superiority of his own way and his followers regard it as an obligation to show their loyalty by enobling their own teacher and belittling others. The history of the Khwājagān is almost unique in its freedom from references to any such disputes and rivalries. This, more than anything else, attracted me to study the lives of the Masters and to write the present book. In my own experience, the really great teachers know that rivalry and divisions are essentially unspiritual. It is only in the lower nature of men – that selfish nature from which we seek liberation – that: "I am right and if you disagree, you must be wrong" has any place.

The Khwājagān are represented as strict Muslims, fulfilling

their religious duties and treating the Quran as the revealed word of God; but they would not follow the orthodox theologians of the Abbasid Caliphate who were much influenced by Aristotelian philosophy and developed a rationalist tradition completely opposed to the idea of transformation. Here, I should note that the influence of Greek philosophy which was so powerful after the Dark Ages came indirectly from Islam through Spain and the Ummayad Caliphate. I have always felt that the main reason why the Masters of Wisdom were obliged to abandon the region from Spain through Byzantium and Baghdad and even India was that Greek rationalism largely disregards the need for transformation. Central Asia, including Persia, was never so deeply infected with rationalistic prejudices and was therefore more fertile ground for implanting the new seeds.

We must return to the story of Yusuf Hamadanī. Like all the Masters, he kept himself and his family by his own work. He never accepted gifts from wealthy supporters. There is a revealing story of one of his closest disciples and second successors – *Khalīfa* or Caliph – Khwaja Hasan Andakī who was one of the eleven who came with him from Hamadan to Bukhara. When Hasan was initiated into the Method, he plunged into it so wholeheartedly that in a short time he reached such a state that he neglected his essential duties and ceased to provide for his wives and children. One day, Khwaja Yusuf spoke to him about it: "You are in a bad state and idle fantasy has taken possession of you. We all have the obligation to take care of our bodily existence and be responsible for our dependents." Hasan replied: "I know this, but my state is such that however much I try to work, I remain helpless." That same night, Khwaja Yusuf had a vision in which the voice of God spoke to him and said: "O Yusuf, I have given you the eye of wisdom; but to Hasan I have given both the eye of wisdom and the eye of the heart." After this Yusuf kept Hasan very close to him and saw to it that no earthly duties were prescribed for him.

We must have a picture of Bukhara at this time. The Saljuk Sultan Sanjar was the sovereign of all the countries north and south of the Amu Darya. For twenty-one years from 1109 to 1130 Bukhara was governed by Arslan Khan, the head of the Karakhans. During his reign, he adorned Bukhara with many fine buildings; he invited poets and learned men to his court. Due to the fame of Baghdad the rulers who wanted to demonstrate their independence of the now decayed Caliphate were ostentatious in their liberality and in the freedom given to teachers of different religions and cults. There were Buddhist temples, Christian churches and the old Zoroastrian religion was still practised by the Magi.

The Saljuk rulers in the west and south were more powerful and their Sultan Sanjar was a great admirer of Yusuf and his school. He persuaded him to send teachers into Khurasan and as far as Mosul. In the year 1114, Sultan Sanjar sent a considerable sum in gold coins by the hand of Qasim Jarhi to enable Yusuf to transfer from Bukhara to Merv and set up there a school and living quarters for the large number of dervishes who came to him for training. Yusuf moved to Merv and remained there till his death, though he travelled a great deal. In 1121, at the age of 72, he went to Baghdad and lectured at the Theological Academy. A well-known theologian, Ibn as-Saqa, ventured to question his orthodoxy. In reply Yusuf said: "Sit down: an infidel smell comes from you. I can see that you will not die without betraying the religion of Islam." This warning was verified. Not long afterwards, Ibn as-Saqa went to Constantinople with the Byzantine ambassador and in order to marry the Emperor's daughter, was converted to Christianity.

Khwaja Yusuf's influence extended from Mesopotamia as far as eastern Turkestan. His eleven disciples established the tradition of the Masters firmly among the people, though the orthodox priesthood for the most part remained aloof. Although Yusuf and his disciples were devout Muslims and never questioned the Divine origin of the Quran, their interpretation was a shattering blow to the complacency of those who accepted the easy rationalism of the Abbasid theologians.

I must make this as clear as I can because it is the very core of the wisdom of the Khwajagan. They took various passages of the Quran to show that man is asleep and that he can pass his life in a dream from which he does not awaken after death. The famous saying *mutu qablan tamutu,* die before you die, was interpreted to mean: unless you die to your self before you die to your body, you will not awaken from your illusions but carry them with you after death. The orthodox view divides reality into two worlds, the 'present' and the 'future'. The future world is eternal and for true believers it is a state of eternal bliss that differs from the present world only by the absence of evil and suffering and death. The wicked are punished, but not eternally, because Allah is merciful and wishes all his creatures to enjoy His Paradise. This simple creed had satisfied the illiterate Arabs; and, with the addition that even the worst sinner goes straight to Paradise if he dies in battle against the unbelievers, had carried the banner of Islam from Spain to India. The Abbasid Caliphs with their Persian background and their leaning to Greek philosophers were too sophisticated to accept the two-world doctrine in its naive form. Under the Caliph Mamun, the *Mutazilite* theologians who propounded a rationalistic and 'this-worldly' interpretation of Islam, established an ascendancy that in the end undermined the very basis of the faith and led to the downfall of the Abbasid Caliphate. In opposition to the rationalists were more mystical teachers such as the great Bayazīd Bīstāmī who pictured a more intellectual Paradise for those who were capable of understanding the secret of Unity with Allah. This is how southern Sufism developed, but its adherents did not see that they were still working for a dream world. The startling innovation of the Masters was to proclaim the possibility for man to go 'beyond paradise' and enter the World of Truth: but only on condition of awakening from his dream state and freeing himself from egoism which is the source of his dreams. This introduces a new division into the world between those who are content to remain in the dream state and those who are determined to awaken and find the Truth. By identifying the Truth, *Haqq,* with God, *Allah,* the Khwajagān could claim that they were acting wholly within the framework laid down in the Quran. They differed from the orthodox priesthood in their insistence upon the need for more than religious observance if man is to reach the Truth.

If we identify the World of Truth with the Kingdom of God as preached by John the Baptist and Jesus, we can apply to the Masters the saying from the Sermon on the Mount: "Except your righteousness exceed the righteousness of the scribes and Pharisees, ye shall in no wise enter the Kingdom of heaven". We must also take into account the spiritual powers, *Karāmat,* attributed by all authorities to the Khwajagān. They were able to foretell the future, to cure disease, to communicate with one another at a distance and to transmit their powers to their initiated disciples. Their influence with sultans and khāns was due not only to the esteem in which they were held by the people, but to the universal belief that they were not ordinary men.

The science of breath has always been regarded in Asia as the means for developing special powers. The Indian yogis practised it long before the Masters of Wisdom appeared in central Asia, but there were important differences of method. The Buddhist meditation which was certainly practised by the Uigur *bhikshus* made use of sacred syllables; and the Masters of Wisdom used the *zikr* or repetition of the names of God or words of praise and thanksgiving. The Masters also practised fasting, basing themselves on the tradition that the Prophet regarded fasting as the best means of purification. Different Masters had special ways of carrying out the exercises, but the three basic techniques were the same all through: breath control, repetition and fasting. These all concern the transformation of energies. They do not in themselves lead to the death of the ego, that is the *fana* which is the key to transformation. The methods used for the attainment of *fana* will appear as we study more closely the Acts of the Masters as they appear in the numerous books written by their pupils.

I believe that Yusuf Hamadani was himself not so much an innovator as a man chosen by the inner circle of Masters on account of his exceptional spiritual qualities. He was, above all, a very good man, humble and unpretentious and with an unlimited love for his fellow-men. Even if his successors attained to higher degrees of transformation, he has a place that is unique in the history of the Masters of Wisdom. He came out into the open to be seen and heard by ordinary people. He had no position in the official hierarchy, as might have been the case if he had been an arch magus five hundred years earlier or a Christian patriarch like the great Timothy, or one of the great Muslim *Faqihs* or theologians who occupied very high official positions at court. Even in the last ten years of his life at Merv, when his school was famous throughout Persia and Turkestan and pupils were coming to him from Egypt and even Spain, Yusuf continued to live as a poor man by the work of his own hands and would not let his own pupils bow to him as was the custom with all teachers. To the end of his life, he practised his spiritual exercise. It was said that his breath control was so severe that his body would be covered with sweat. Like many others, he attributed his long life and abundant energy to the *zikr* and *habs-i nafas,* breath control.

Several of the great dervish brotherhoods that have survived to our time trace their origin back to Khwaja Yusuf. In 1205, Shaikh Awhad ad-din of Kirman communicated his method to Ibn al-Arabi in Damascus. Nevertheless, the method of the Masters did not find the same response in the west as in central Asia. Here the great figure was Khwaja Ahmad Yasawi. His native town Yasi is better known as Tashkent, the name it received after the Mongol invasions. He is regarded as the father of Turkish spirituality. He lived to be 120 years old and died in Tashkent in 1166. According to the *Rashahat ain al-Hayat** Khwaja Ahmad was possessed of great spiritual gifts of healing and prophesy. In his youth, he studied alchemy with the famous alchemist and magician Baba Arslan. Baba Arslan was told in a vision by the Prophet that he was to undertake personally the training of Ahmad and teach him all his secrets. So long as Baba Arslan lived, Ahmad remained with him. When the Baba saw his death approaching, he advised him to go to Bukhara and complete his training with Khwaja Yusuf Hamadani. His transformation was completed and he became the first Khwaja trained in Turkestan – the remaining eleven having come from Hamadan with Yusuf.

Khwaja Ahmad's father, Shaikh Ibrahim, was one of the spiritual leaders of Chinese Turkestan and his mother was Aisha Khatun, the daughter of one of his father's initiates. His father and mother died when he was seven years old and he was brought up by his only sister Jawhar Shahnaz Khatun. His father foretold that he would become the "Shaikh of Shaikhs, the *Qutb* of Turkestan."

Soon after his final initiation, he returned to Tashkent and opened a school where he taught the way of the Masters in the Turkish language. He differed from the other initiates of Yusuf Hamadani in his interest in music and the sacred dance. For many centuries, Tashkent was a centre for the *sama* tradition which was

* This is the principal and the most reliable source of information about the lives and acts of the Masters of Wisdom. It was written in Persian by Fakhr ad-din Ali Husain al-Waiz Kashifi. It was translated into Turkish in the sixteenth century. I was fortunate to find a beautiful manuscript in an old bookshop in Istanbul. It is a book of 520 pages filled with instructive anecdotes and the biographies of the Khwajagan from Yusuf Hamadani to Mulla Jami. It has not been translated into any European language. My copy has copious marginal notes by a practising Sufi.

much older than Islam. Ahmad Yasawī had very friendly contact with the Buddhist monks of the region and shared with them the secrets of the Masters. I have been told, but have not been able to verify the connection, that Zen Buddhism was brought to China from Turkestan by the patriarch Bodhidharma who had been an associate of Ahmad Yasawī.

When Yūsuf Hamadānī died, he had wanted Ahmad Yasawī to follow him, but did not want to bring him away from the wonderful work he was doing in the east. He was therefore followed by the saintly Khwāja Hasan Andakī who is said to have astonished his pupils by the gentle meek way in which he revealed mysteries that no ordinary man could speak of. He lived himself very austerely but did not expect his pupils to follow him. He accompanied Khwāja Yūsuf on his visit to Baghdad. He died in 1059 at the age of ninety and no one dared to follow him. All the Masters agreed to ask Ahmad Yasawī to come to Bukhārā where the surviving disciples had moved from Merv. He remained for three years and then handed the leadership of the Masters over to one of the very greatest – Khwāja Abd al-Khāliq Ghujduwānī – and returned to Tashkent where he remained for the rest of his life.

According to the *Rashahāt*, Yasawi decided at the age of sixty-three to abandon all possessions and live in a cell which he constructed with his own hands. He continued to teach for fifty years, keeping to the central theme of transformation by way of self-discipline and humiliation. He left behind him the image of a man who radiated love and was able to perform miracles. Three hundred years after his death the great conqueror Tamerlane conceived a special veneration for Khwāja Ahmad as result of a vision of the Master on the occasion of a visit to his tomb in Tashkent. In his autobiography, Tamerlane asserts that the Master appeared to him and told him to learn by heart a verse from his book of poems adding: "Whenever you meet with difficulty, *mushkil*, repeat this verse."

Shebiyelda shemi shebistan itgan
Bir lakzada alem ni gulistan itgan
Bes müshkil isim tüshüpdir asan itgil
Ey barche ni müskilümi asan itgan

Upon the longest night light a candle in the dark
In a flash the world becomes a rose garden

However hard the task take hold and it will go
The galley itself makes the rower's labour light

Many years later in the critical encounter with the army of the
Turkish Sultan Bāyazīd the Thunderer, he repeated this verse
seventy times as his cavalry charged and he gained the decisive
victory.

Khwāja Ahmad followed the rule of all the Masters never to
accept personal gifts. He made his living by carving wooden
spoons. According to a legend, he used to put his spoons in a
pannier on the back of his ox, which used to wander through the
street. If anyone took a spoon, the ox would not move until the
price was put in the pannier. At night, the ox returned to his
master who took from the pannier what he needed to buy food
for the next day.

In spite of his retired life, Ahmad Yasawī had an immense
influence throughout Turkestan*. The Khwājagān had to
maintain a balance between the four elements of the population:
the rulers (at that time, the Khwarazmshāh dynasty), the Turkish
mercenary army, the orthodox Muslim priesthood and the
population of agriculturalists and merchants. Yūsuf Hamadānī
gave the simple advice: "Be loyal to the authority and maintain
the same behaviour and language to all four castes. If everyone
knows that you always speak the truth, no-one will touch you."
Only one of the shaikhs lost his life – this was Majd ad-dīn, a
young shaikh, pupil of the great Najm ad-dīn Kubrā, founder of
one of the great dervish orders – but it is notable that although a
pupil of Yūsuf Hamadānī, Najm ad-dīn Kubrā was never
initiated into the circle of the Masters of Wisdom – that is the
Khwājagān. The Masters never, in four hundred years,
compromised their position as completely independent of all
factions and personalities. The secret of their success was their
consistent avoidance of positions of wealth and power and the
practice of humiliation. All accounts agree that their influence
was based on the love which they inspired in all who met them.
Even the orthodox priesthood, who were bound to be jealous

* *c.f.* W. Barthold *loc. cit.* p. 376. "Both the founder (Yūsuf Hamadānī) and
the adherents of the school he founded are rarely mentioned in historical
works, but they undoubtedly had great influence over the population; among
its active members were saints who are highly revered by the people down to
the present day, such as Hakīm Atā and Ahmad Yasawī."

and also disturbed by their lack of respect for book learning and theological disputes, very seldom opposed the Khwājagān openly.

Several important dervish orders trace their origin back to Ahmad Yasawī. His fourth successor Hakīm Atā was invited to the west and his school established a section near the Caspian sea among the Turks of the Volga. This school remained in the Caucasus until the end of the nineteenth century. I have already referred to the influence of the Masters in China and the rise of Zen. Ahmad Yasawī's central school in Tashkent and Zaravshan is of special interest to followers of Gurdjieff's ideas because it was the main repository of the science of vibrations expressed partly through dance and music and partly through the sacred ritual that came from the Magi. This science distinguished the Yasawīs from the main tradition of the Masters which recommended, as I have said, the use of breath control, the *zikr* and fasting, together with the acquisition of practical skills, for achieving the second stage of liberation: that is freedom from the forces working in the physical body.

Yūsuf Hamadānī's fourth and greatest successor Khwāja Abd al-Khāliq Ghujduwānī represented the main tradition. He is described in the *Rashahāt* as the: "Grand Master of the central group of the Masters and the chief custodian of the Tradition". He was the greatest Master of the twelfth century. His influence extended throughout Turkestan and beyond. He was one of the eleven who went with Yūsuf from Hamadān to Bukhārā. Towards the end of the twelfth century Turkestan and Persia were in a state of unrest. The prosperity of the tenth and eleventh centuries was destroyed by the struggle for power between the Khwarazmshah of west Turkestan and the non-Muslim Kara Khitays of east Turkestan. The ancient Persian culture felt itself seriously threatened, but few could foresee the devastation that was to come with the Mongol invasions of the thirteenth century. The virtual collapse of the Abbasid Caliphate, and the eclipse of Baghdad as a centre of religion and learning, meant that cities like Bukhārā and Samarkand that had risen to their first period of splendour under the Sāmānid kings, no longer looked to the south for inspiration. We no longer hear of the Khwājagān going to Baghdad as Yūsuf Hamadānī had done.

The dismal ending of the Crusades had left a vacuum in Syria and many looked towards Turkestan for guidance. It is not easy

for us, who are accustomed to think of Europe as the centre of
culture in the Middle Ages, to realise how much European art
and learning owed to the East. The Assyrian and Armenian
Christians did much to promote the exchange. We must
remember that although the Masters were strictly orthodox
Muslims, they were completely open to other religions and were
ready to accept Jews, Christians and Buddhists in their groups.

Abd al-Khaliq Ghujduwani himself had connections with the
west. His father, Abd al-Jamil came from Malatya in Asia Minor
and his grandmother was a Saljuk princess. Abd al-Jamil was
regarded as a great saint and was reputed to receive guidance and
teaching direct from the Prophet Khidr, the immortal messenger
of God who was adopted by Islam from the Zoroastrian
tradition. He is associated with the coming of summer and his
'feast' is celebrated on the sixth of May. Abd al-Jamil himself
asserted that it was on the instruction of Khidr that he emigrated
from Asia Minor to Turkestan and settled at Ghujduwan a few
miles from Bukhara where his son Abd al-Khaliq was born. Abd
al-Khaliq is reported in the *Rashahat* as saying: "When I was
twenty years old the Teacher of the Masters and the Awakener of
Souls, the Prophet Khidr, recommended me to Grand Master
Yusuf Hamadani who accepted me in his old age and initiated me
into the Khwajagan. As he at that time was in Turkestan, I
decided to follow and serve him wherever he went."

When Yusuf Hamadani returned to Khurasan, Khwaja Abd
al-Khaliq adopted a severely ascetic mode of life, but hid this
from his friends and pupils. Through his ascetic practices, he
acquired unusual spiritual powers and was visited from far and
wide. A group of his followers was formed in Damascus. It was
through this group that Jalal ad-din Rumi made his first contact
with the Masters of Wisdom. The School in Damascus survived
until the time of the Ottoman Turks.

Khwaja Abd al-Khaliq was the first of the Masters to
formulate a 'system'. He divided the stages of transformation into
'right behaviour', 'the way' and 'completion'. A 'Counsel'
written for his second successor refers to the pattern of behaviour
recommended for a candidate for initiation.

"Your overall state should be founded upon know-how, self-
discipline and piety. Study the works of your predecessors. Learn
the principles laid down by the Prophet of Islam and avoid the
society of ignorant Sufis. Always do your prayers with the

congregation, but never undertake the call to prayer, *azan*, or lead the prayer yourself, *Imam*.

"Do not seek for fame, for in fame lies calamity.

"Do not meddle in the affairs of others. Never become intimate with kings and princes.

"Don't make a permanent home for yourself and don't settle down in any place.

"Do not engage too much in music and the sacred dance for excess of these destroys the feelings. But do not reject the sacred dance for many are devoted to it and rely upon it.

"Speak little, eat little, sleep little. Keep away from the crowd and learn to value your own solitude. Do not enter into discussion with young people, with women, with rich or with worldly folk. Eat pure food and avoid doubtful food. Postpone marriage as long as you can, for marriage arouses desire for this world and if you are attached to this world, your religion is vain.

"Don't laugh uproariously, for too much hilarity destroys the sensitivity of the heart. Nevertheless, you must always be cheerful and ready to rejoice with others. Never despise anyone on any pretext.

"Do not embellish your outer person, for ornament is a mark of inner poverty.

"Never quarrel with people and never ask favours from anyone. Be sure that you are a burden to no-one.

"Put no confidence in the world or in worldly people.

"Let your heart be filled with abasement and humility, let your body suffer, your eyes weep. Let your actions be straightforward and your prayers sincere. Wear old clothes and choose a poor man for your companion. Let your home be a house of prayer and let the highest truth, *Haqq Taala*, be your guide."

In appraising the significance of the Masters of Wisdom, we must never forget that all accounts agree that they demanded of themselves and their pupils the standards of behaviour that are expressed in this Counsel! Khwaja Abd al-Khaliq composed a series of aphorisms that were accepted by his successors as a true expression of the "Way of the Masters."

1. *hosh dar dam*. This can be translated 'breathe consciously'. The Persian word *hosh* is almost the same as the Greek *nepsis* – in Latin *sobrietas* – used eight centuries earlier by the Masters of the

Syrian desert and which appears very often in the *Philokalia*, a work that Ouspensky attributed to the Masters of Wisdom. He regarded this term as equivalent to Gurdjieff's 'self-remembering'. As used by the Khwajagan, it is always connected with breathing. According to their teaching the air we breathe provides us with food for the second or spirit body, called by Gurdjieff the *kesdjan* body from two Persian words meaning the 'vessel of the spirit'. The Masters of Wisdom have always possessed the secret of breath. The longevity of the early Masters is attributable mainly to the *zikr* with breath control.

Hosh dar dam, conscious breathing, was regarded as the primary technique for self-development. The *Rashahāt* says that the meaning of *hosh dar dam* is that breathing is the nourishment of the inner man. As we breathe, we should place our attention on each successive breath and be aware of our own presence. For this, it is necessary to be in the right state because if the breath is taken inattentively, it will not go to the right place. Mawlāna Saad ad-dın Kashgharı explained that *hosh dar dam* requires that from one breath to another we should keep our attention open to our goal. Inattention is what separates us from God. He further said that in the way of the Masters, great importance is attached to learning how to retain the breath, because in retaining the breath, our attention is sharpened and it enters into us more deeply.

Khwaja Baha ad-dın Naqshbandı said: "In this path, the foundation is built upon breathing. The more that one is able to be conscious of one's breathing, the stronger is one's inner life." He added that it is particularly important to keep awareness of the change from in-breathing to the out-breathing.

These directions for breath control are supplemented by detailed explanation of the way in which the *zikr* is to be performed. These were added by later scribes for the benefit of members of the Naqshbandı dervishes. Whereas the earlier Masters regarded *hosh dar dam* as the basic technique for nourishing the inner bodies of man, teachers outside the Khwajagan such as Najm ad-dın Kubra gave it a more mystical significance; he connected it with the syllable *Hū* which is the universal name of God that is pronounced consciously or unconsciously with every breath from the moment we are born until we die. Mawlāna Jamı, the great poet of central Asia, said that *hosh dar dam* is the absolute moment when personal identity is merged into the One. This, he said, is the ultimate secret of breath. *Ghayb-i huwiyyat* is a technical term used by the Khwājagān to signify the annihilation of self and union with the absolute being which is the final goal of liberation.

2. *nazar bar qadam.* Watch your step! *Qadam* means foot or step and also luck or fortune. It derives from the root *q-d-m* which expresses source or origin. The aphorism can be interpreted to mean: "Remember where you came from and where you are going. Keep your attention on the step you are taking at this moment." This aphorism is the basis of an important spiritual exercise used by the dervishes who trace their tradition back to the Masters of Wisdom.

3. *safar dar watan.* The journey home. This is interpreted to mean the transformation that brings man out of the world of unrealised potential, *alam-i arvāh,* to the world of will, *alam-i wujūb,* where man becomes aware of his destiny and is given the power to fulfil it. The *alam-i wujūb* corresponds to the Kingdom of Heaven in the Gospels. The Khwājagān taught that man can neither know nor realise his own destiny so long as he remains in the subjective dream state – *khayālāt.*

4. *khalwat dar anjuman.* Solitude in the crowd. This aphorism is perhaps the most often quoted of the sayings of the Masters. There are many commentaries and explanations. In its simplest expression, it is what Gurdjieff calls "non-identification": to be able to enter fully into the life of the external world without losing one's own inner freedom. When asked for a short statement of the method of the Khwājagān, Baha ad-dīn Naqshbandi replied: "*Khalvat dar anjuman,* that is, outwardly to be with the people and inwardly to be with God". Khwāja Awliyā said that it means: "to be so deeply occupied with one's own *zikr* that one can walk through the market place and not be aware of a sound."

5. *yād kard.* Remembrance. The explanation given in the *Rashahāt* is that one must learn to keep contact between the tongue and the heart, especially in the *zikr* – what we feel we should say and what we say, we should feel. Saad ad-din Kāshgharī commenting on this aphorism says that when the *shaikh* is initiating the *murīd,* he should make the declaration of faith "*la ilaha ilallāh wa Muhammad ar-rasūl allāh*" in his heart, and the *murīd* should feel it present in his own breast. Sitting in front of the *shaikh* he should hold himself, his eyes, his lips, his tongue

and his mind, firmly fixed on the *shaikh.* Keeping his teeth firmly locked together, he should hold his breath and with full awareness he should, with all his heart, join himself to the *shaikh.* By this means the power of the *zikr* will be transferred to the pupil in such a way that his lips and his heart will remain united. After this, the pupil must patiently continue to repeat the *zikr* three times over. At the end of each triplet, he repeats the holding of his breath. The *Rashahāt* goes on to give quite detailed instructions, which are amplified in the commentary, on the way in which the *shaikh* is to verify the transmission of the *zikr;* he must be sure that his pupil learns how to be aware of his feelings at the same time as he is speaking.

6. *bāz gasht.* Return, travel one way; be single-minded. Ubaidallah Ahrar interpreted this aphorism as meaning that we have within us the goal of our striving. The seeds of transformation are sown in us from above and we have to treasure them above all possessions. Where there is only one fruit-bearing tree, all else is weed and must be removed.

7. *nigāh dāsht.* Watchfulness. Be aware of what catches your attention. Learn to withdraw your attention from undesirable objects. This is interpreted as: "be vigilant in thought and remember yourself", *khawātir murāqaba.* I think that *nigāh dāsht* is the same as Gurdjieff's 'self-remembering'.

8. *yād dāsht.* Recollection. This is explained as the last stage before transformation is completed. The seeker becomes aware that his loss of 'self' will be compensated by objective Love, *hubb-i zātī.* The humiliation that leads to this stage ceases to touch the seeker for he discovers before him the unlimited joy that the Truth will bring him.

According to the *Rashahāt,* Khwaja Bahā ad-dīn Naqshbandī introduced three further technical terms:

9. *wuqūf-i zamāñ.* Awareness of time.* To keep an account of one's temporal states. To distinguish presence, *huzūr,* from absence, *ghaflat.* Khwaja Naqshbandī described this as 'self-possession' or 'mindfulness'. He added the significant advice that one must always remember to be thankful when one returns to a state of 'presence'.

---

* *Editor's note:* The word *wuqūf* also means 'checking', 'pausing' and it is taken in this sense by Trimingham, *The Sufi Orders in Islām,* p. 203. In the reality of the psychological experience of these last three techniques, however, both meanings coalesce.

10. *wuqūf-i adadī*. Awareness of number. Khwāja Ala ad-dīn Attar said: "The number of times you repeat the *zikr* is not so important. What matters is whether you do it with presence and awareness." Bahā ad-dīn Naqshbandī held that *wuqūf-i adadī* is the first stage of entry into the spiritual world. This stage is marked by the cessation of verbal mentation and the beginning of a direct perception that does not require words.

11. *wuqūf-i qalbī*. Awareness of the heart. This is the same as *yād dāsht*. It marks the awakening of Divine Love. The individual becomes aware that his own existence is an obstacle to his final transformation and he no longer fears to sacrifice it, because he sees for himself that he will gain infinitely more than he loses.

The poet Mulla Jamī in his book *Nafahāt al–Uns* says that Abd al–Khāliq was able to keep a good relationship with all classes and all parties. At that time, life was very difficult in Turkestan. The Sultan Muhammad Khwarazmshāh was on bad terms with the priesthood who were supported by his mother Turkān Khatūn. Power was divided between the Muslims and the infidel Kara Khitay whose ruler, the Gurkhān, was paramount. The people were no longer protected as they had been under the Būyid and Samanid rulers; and the Khwājagān, by their completely impartial attitude, were often able to prevent gross injustice and even massacres. When the Sultan's son-in-law Uthmān refused to impose penal taxes in Samarkand and Bukharā, Muhammad beseiged and sacked Samarkand. According to one historian, Ibn al-Athīr, 200,000 people were massacred; and to another, Juwainī, 10,000. It was due to the intervention of the Khwājagān that Muhammad ordered the massacre to cease.

The *Nafahāt al-Uns* goes on to say that Abd al-Khāliq was the first of the Masters to introduce the prayer of the heart, *zikr-i qalbī*, which had been revealed to him by the Prophet Khidr. He also made it clear that the way of the Masters was that of complete transformation from the subjective or dream state of ordinary man to the objective consciousness of the liberated man. There are four stages of liberation, *fanā*, and until all these have been completed a man is not free from the forces of sensuality and egoism.

We have now come to the beginning of the thirteenth century, the history of which is dominated by Chinghis Khān, to whom the next chapter will be devoted.

Chapter Seven

Chinghis Khān

The story of the Masters of Wisdom in central Asia must be seen against the background of the devastation caused by the invasions of nomads from the north. The decisive event was the destruction of the Muslim power by Chinghis Khān and his conquest of China and much of India. Chinghis Khān for fifty years of his life was known as Temujin and even the word 'Mongol' was his own invention. He was born in 1157 and belonged to an unimportant tribe of nomads on the border of northern China. He died in 1227 having conquered a greater empire than Alexander the Great and one that was to endure for much longer. He was, to the end of his life, illiterate and a stranger to the life of agricultural and urban cultures. Yet, he was not only a great military leader, but also a great administrator. His greatest power, which perhaps no-one before or after him has excelled, lay in his ability to judge men and to choose the right person for any position. All who met him agreed that he had complete self-control. He never acted impulsively even when insulted or betrayed.

At an early age, he saw that the nomad tribes could never hold their own with the Chinese unless they had competent leaders, and he formed a troop, each member of which was recruited by him personally from the aristocrats of the steppes. His patience may be judged from the fact that he was fifty years old before he felt ready to move towards the domination of Mongolia. With his guard of a thousand men, he overcame the Keraits and the

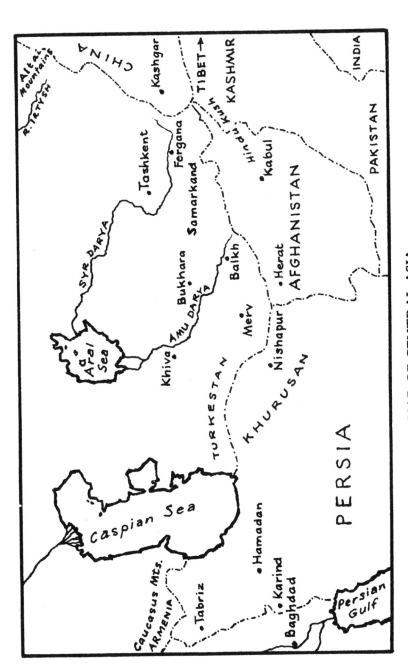

MAP OF CENTRAL ASIA

Tatars and adopted for his followers the name Mongol*. Chinghis Khan did not regard the term Mongol as designating a tribe and still less a race, but rather as a distinctive name for his own horde. At the age of fifty-one, when he had subjugated all the nomad tribes: "he set up a standard with nine white tails and took his seat as Khan of all the tribes of Mongolia with the title of Chinghis Khan."

His personal guard of a thousand bahādūrs, heroes, was built upon his chosen group and all of its members were personally known to him. His generals were nearly all selected from the bahādūrs who, whether generals or ordinary horsemen, had extraordinary privileges. Chinghis himself was unusually tall with a powerful head and hypnotic grey eyes. He completely dominated his own family, his generals and all who had dealings with him. The loyalty of his generals and soldiers even when they were meeting with triumph in some distant part of the empire was something totally unknown in the long history of central Asia. This was due not only to his wonderful judgement of men, but also to the long and patient training that preceded the campaigns that occupied the last twenty years of his life.

No great conqueror has aroused such conflicting feelings. Most accounts reached Europe from Muslim historians who hated him as the destroyer of their power and the enemy of their religion. It was not until the end of the nineteenth century that the Chinese records became available and gave a very different picture. The common belief that Chinghis Khan was totally indifferent to the welfare and the very lives of conquered people, that every city the Mongols captured was sacked and the inhabitants massacred, is certainly not true. It is true, however, that Chinghis Khan, as a deliberate act of policy, destroyed and massacred cities that resisted his arms, and spared those that surrendered without fighting. Historians rely upon official documents, such as the history of the Wazīr Rashīd ad-dīn, compiled on the orders of Ghazan Khan who ruled in Persia and the *Yuan-shih,* which was written in China after the fall of the Yuan — that is Mongolian — dynasty. No-one has seen the famous *Golden Book* which was secretly preserved by the personal descendants of Chinghis Khan and contained their own account of the rise of the Mongol empire.

* Until then, Mongol was a Chinese word which Temujin adopted to connect himself with another great leader, Kutula-Kaghan, famous for his victories over the Chinese in the early part of the twelfth century.

In this chapter, I want to look at the Mongol story from quite a different point of view: that of the Masters of Wisdom as it is preserved in their own private histories such as the *Rashahāt Ain al-Hayāt* and the *Nafahāt al-Uns*. These books, written in Persian in the fourteenth and fifteenth centuries, make few references to historical events in the thirteenth century, but they show how important was the role of the Khwājagān in restoring tolerable conditions of existence after the devastation of the Mongol conquest.

We must not think of the Mongols as descending upon a peaceful and prosperous society on either side of the Amu Darya. Peace and prosperity ended with the downfall of the Tāhirid dynasty in Iraq and Khurasān and the Sāmānids in Turkestan. These two dynasties genuinely accepted the duty of the ruler to ensure the welfare of his people. They maintained mercenary armies mainly composed of Turks. The Tāhirids were on good terms with their nominal suzerain, the commander of the Faithful, the Abbasid Caliph in Baghdad. The Sāmānids claimed independence. But both the rulers and their subjects were devout Muslims and were on good terms with the orthodox priesthood. The Tāharids ruled from 821–873 when they were overthrown by the Saljuk Turks. The rule of the Sā ˉnids continued till 899. The Saffārids (867–903) rose to power through the dissident and heretical sects of the Shiahs, Ismailis and Kharijites. With them came civil war and the rise of despots claiming absolute power. Finally, the whole region was brought under the domination – though not effective control – of the Khwarazmshāh rulers (1077–1231) the last of whom, Sultan Muhammad, was mainly responsible for the disasters that were to end the Muslim power.

Sultan Muhammad appears in the history of the Khwājagān as the murderer of Majd ad-dīn a pupil of Najim ad-dīn Kubrā, a member of the school of Yūsuf Hamadānī. Majd ad-dīn disregarded Khwaja Abd al-Khāliq's warning to avoid intimacy with kings and princes. According to several accounts, the Sultan suspected him of a love affair with his mother – an unlikely tale, as she was a great-grandmother at the time – and he is said to have ordered his death in a moment of anger of which he afterwards repented. Nevertheless, the story serves to show the extreme caution with which the true Masters exercised the influence they possessed with all classes of the population.

During the time of the Mongol invasion, the Khwājagān were

collected in Bukhārā and it is noteworthy that unlike Samarkand and Balkh, the city was not destroyed and there was no massacre of the inhabitants. A rather doubtful story by the Persian historian Juwainī asserts that Chinghis Khān assembled the people of Bukhārā in the cathedral mosque as if for festival prayers, himself ascended the pulpit and made a speech in which he called himself the: "scourge of God sent to punish the nation for its sins". Even if this story must be dismissed as a fabrication, it remains true that the people of Bukhārā knew that Chinghis Khān's action in demanding a huge ransom had justice on its side.

To understand this, we must make an excursion into the well-authenticated history of the events which led Chinghis Khān to invade Turkestan*.

In 1215, China was overrun and Pekin captured by the Mongols. Chinghis Khān now dominated from Semiryeche to the Pacific ocean. At the very same time, the Khwarazmshāh Muhammad had defeated the Kara Khitays and his power stretched from the Caspian sea to the Hindu Kush and even across the Indus to India. He dreamed of invading China and so "conquering the world". Rumours forestalled him. In order to verify this rumour and gain accurate information, he decided to send an embassy to the Mongol conqueror. The leader was Bahā ad-dīn Rāzī. The envoys arrived when Pekin had already fallen, but Chinghis Khān was still in China with his army. Signs of terrible devastation were everywhere visible, the bones of the slaughtered formed whole mountains and the soil was greasy with human fat. At the gate of Pekin lay a vast heap of bones.

Chinghis Khān received the envoys graciously and told them to give the Khwarazmshāh the message that he considered him the ruler of the west, as he himself was ruler of the east. He desired that there should be peace and friendship between them and that merchants should be free to travel from one territory to another. There is no reason to doubt his sincerity. Chinghis Khān was accustomed to saying plainly what he thought and his generals and soldiers knew that they could always rely on his word. It is very unlikely that at that time he had begun to think of world dominion. The immense booty gained in Chinawas

---

* The following account is based on W. Barthold's classical work *Turkestan down to the Mongol Invasion* and Sir Dennison Ross *Heart of Asia*. The original source is Juzjānī's *Tabaqāt–i Nāsirī*.

more than enough to satisfy the Mongol horde.* On previous occasions when the nomads were united under one leader they had always invaded China. The hordes that went west did so only because they were forced out by internal pressures. The nomads required trade. They produced nothing for themselves and had only to offer "the skins of foxes, wolves, beavers and other merchandise." Trade was mainly in the hands of Buddhist Uighur and Muslim Turkish merchants who were on good terms with the Mongols. On the other hand, Khwarazmshāh Muhammad was on bad terms with the merchants in his own territory because of the extortionate taxes levied to finance his wars of conquest. He had not sent the embassy to open trade but to spy upon Chinghis Khān and seek to divine his intentions. The mission was accompanied by a caravan which brought the finest cloths of Bukhāra and Samarkand. Chinghis Khān was angered by the exhorbitant prices asked for their wares but was mollified when they offered them at whatever price he decreed.

In reply to the Khwarazmshāh embassy, Chinghis Khān sent envoys and among the gifts intended for the Sultan was a nugget of gold from the Mountains of China "as large as a camel's hump", lumps of jade and horns of the khutuw** which was believed to cure all kinds of disease.

The envoys were received by the Khwarazmshāh in Bukhāra and told him that Chinghis Khān offered to make a treaty of peace and: "place him on the level with the dearest of his sons". Although infuriated by this suggestion of vassalship, Muhammad agreed to make a treaty of peace, but no mention was made of trade relations.

Chinghis Khān was very pleased with the treaty and relying upon assurances given by the envoys, authorised the dispatch of a caravan to Bukhāra***. There were in all four hundred and fifty men in the caravan, all of them Muslims and with them about five hundred camels laden with merchandise consisting of gold,

* The word horde comes from the Turkish — and Mongol — word *urchi* which means the entire army at the disposal of a commander. A division, *alay*, was composed of ten thousand horsemen.

** Readers of Gurdjieff's *Beelzebub's Tales to his Grandson* will recognise here the *pir maral* which was hunted in this part of the world.

*** One report, that of Nasawī, states that the caravan carried a safe-conduct with the personal seal of the Khwarzmshāh. It is more likely that the caravan started earlier, that is in the year 1217.

silver, Chinese silk, targhu stuffs, beaver skins and sables. All these merchants were detained in Utrār as spies by the order of the governor Inaljik who was a cousin of the Sultan. He informed Muhammad that he suspected the caravan of spying and was authorised to detain it. Apparently on his own initiative and acting solely from greed, Inaljik ordered all four hundred and fifty men to be massacred and seized the entire wealth of the caravan. As the governor was a member of the military party and under the protection of the Sultan's mother Turkān Khātūn, the Sultan was obliged to condone his action. The Sultan was certainly not blameless, as he ordered the camels to be sent on to Bukhara where the merchandise was sold to the local merchants. According to Juwainí, at least one man, a camel-driver, escaped the massacre and carried the terrible news to Chinghis Khān, who once again showed his invariable restraint and self-control.

Ibn Kafrāj Bughra accompanied by two Tatars was sent to the Khwarazmshāh to convey a protest at the treachery and demanded the surrender of Inaljik. The Sultan not only refused to meet the demand, but ordered the envoy to be killed and his two companions to be released after their heads had been shaved.

This made the invasion of Turkestan inevitable. Chinghis Khan was unaware of the internal weakness of the western empire and had not completed the subjugation of China or of Kashgaria and Semiryechye where the Kara Khitay ruler Kuchluk had retreated after his defeat by Muhammad in Ferghana. Chinghis Khān sent Jebe, his ablest general, who, appearing as liberator of the oppressed Muslim population, took possession of Kashgaria almost without fighting. Chinghis Khān himself prepared very carefully for the campaign against the Khwarazmshah. He spent the summer of 1219 on the Irtysh and in the autumn advanced towards the Syr Darya which was frozen over and easy to cross. He had an army of one hundred and fifty thousand of which about half consisted of highly-trained Mongol cavalry. The Khwarazmshāh had a much more numerous army, but there were quarrels among his generals, none of whom fully trusted him. Worse still, he had no strategic plan and wavered between holding out on the Syr Darya, fighting in Transoxania and even retreating right back into India. He was completely out-manoeuvred by Chinghis Khān and only a few cities were able to hold out for any length of time. Within twelve months, Muhammad died a fugitive on an island in the Caspian Sea, deserted by all but a handful of personal servants. His mother, Turkān Khātūn, abandoned Bukhara after drowning all the princes of the dynasty – mostly her sons and grandsons – in the Amu Darya. She was captured in Mazandaran far away to the west. Her grandson Jalāl ad-dīn fought on for two years, even winning a great battle against the Mongols at Parwan in Afghanistan. Chinghis Khān kept his usual composure, saying of the defeated general: "Shiki Qutuqu has got the habit of victory and so far never experienced the cruelty of fate. Now that he has felt it, he will be more cautious." Chinghis himself took over the campaign. In the siege of Bamiyan – near Kabul – his favourite grandson Mutugen lost his life. For this reason, orders were given that every living thing in the town should be killed. The decisive battle of the Indus took place on November 24th, 1221. With the defeat of Jalāl ad-dīn's main army, all India was now open to the Mongols.

Within the short space of two years, Chinghis Khān had established his ascendency from the Caspian sea to India and China. No such conqueror had been seen since Alexander the Great. The ruthless massacre of all populations who resisted the Mongols and the generous treatment of those who went over to their side, created such a profound impression on the entire civilized world that no-one felt safe. Chinghis Khān was now sixty-seven years old and still at the height of his powers. He planned to go through India and return to China by way of Burma, but was advised against it by his shaman who said that it would not be propitious to enter India until much later.

Here we must stop to look at the attitude of the Mongols towards 'holy men'. As the shamans had no 'revealed' tradition and therefore no theology, they could accept all holy men as equal. The Great Spirit culture has always been marked by tolerance and the shamans certainly made no attempt to impose their ideas on conquered people. The Mongols looked upon the shamans both as mediators with the Spirit Powers and as magicians who could foretell the future and even influence the course of events. Chinghis Khān remained faihful to his own teacher, the shaman Kokchu, and was prepared to accept the holy men of Islām as equally gifted and worthy of honour. This explains the tendency of the Mongols to turn more towards the Khwajagān who were reputed by the people to have spiritual powers rather than to the orthodox priesthood who were linked with the ruling dynasty.

During the first half of the thirteenth century, the Masters of Wisdom collected in Bukhārā and its environs. When he was dying, Khwāja Abd al-Khāliq sent for two of his initiates, Khwāja Awliyā and Arif Rıwgarawı, and told them to invite all the Khwājagān to come to Bukhārā which was to be their centre for two hundred years.

Khwāja Awliyā, by his own account, was still a student in the theological academy when he saw Khwāja Abd al-Khāliq Ghudjuwanı buying provisions in the market. On an impulse he offered to carry his parcels home for him. Abd al-Khāliq invited him to stay for a meal and then and there accepted him as his son and personally undertook his training. After Abd al–Khāliq died, Awliyā built himself a contemplation cell alongside the mosque at the gate of the moneychangers. This cell was preserved for more than two centuries and was visited by all the Masters. The term 'contemplation cell' was explained by Ubaidallāh Ahrār: "Contemplation cell does not mean a place where absolutely no thoughts come into the mind, but rather one where no outer thought takes precedence over the inner state. It is like a river whose flow is not impeded by sticks and straws floating on the surface."

Khwāja Awliyā's son Gharıb became a Khwāja and was a close friend of Najm ad-dın Kubrā. At that time, a famous traveller Shaikh Hasan al-Bulgharı came to Bukhārā from Russia and met all the Masters and many other teachers. He afterwards said that in his travels which had taken him all over the Muslim world, he had met no teacher to equal Khwāja Gharıb.

At the time of the Mongol invasion, the Grand Master was Khwāja Arif Rıwgarawı.* Rıwgara was a village about twenty miles from Bukhārā. According to a popular legend Chinghis Khān stopped in Rıwgara before beginning the siege of Bukhārā. Most of the population had fled, but Khwāja Arif remained and was seen working at a loom of his own invention. Chinghis Khān was impressed by his tranquil demeanour and by the skill with which he worked. He asked through an interpreter for an explanation. Khwāja Arif replied: "My outer attention is on my work and my inner attention is on the Truth; I have no time to

---

* A very short summary of his life is given in the *Semerat el-fuad,* an account of the Masters of Wisdom from the standpoint of the Mevlevi dervishes, compiled by Sari Abdullah Effendi.

notice what is happening in the world around me." Chinghis Khan was so pleased with this reply that he ordered that the inhabitants of Rīwgara should be left in peace and invited Arif to go with him to Bukhārā to advise him as to whom he should trust.

The siege of Bukhārā was over in a week and the Mongols entered the city on the 10th February 1220. The citadel held out for another twelve days and all the defenders were killed. Apart from this, there was no massacre. The merchants who had bought goods from the ill-fated caravan of Utrār had all their property confiscated, but others were not treated harshly. The entire population was ordered to evacuate the city which was given over to plunder. Owing to the severe winter, there was much suffering. It is said that Arif pleaded with Chinghis Khan to let them return, foretelling that an act of clemency at that moment would facilitate his victory over the Khwarazmshah. Apparently, Chinghis Khan accepted this just as he would have taken advice from his shaman and allowed the population to return within a few days. Because of this, Bukhārā recovered more rapidly than other cities. I do not know what credence we should place on the story already quoted that when the population returned Chinghis Khan made his "scourge of God" speech in the mosque. However it may be, there is little doubt that the Khwājagān in Bukhārā were instrumental in saving the lives of tens of thousands of people.

We must now pass to the end of Chinghis Khan's life. After his immense conquests, he returned to his own country and laid down the rules for the administration of his enterprise. His great organising ability deserves all the more admiration in that, to the end of his life, he spoke no language but Mongolian and learned solely from his observation and experience of people. He saw that if the Mongols were to profit from their marvellous military qualities, they had to take account of the needs of agriculture and industry and could not hope to administer a settled population without the help of the educated intellectuals. He was, however, both for himself and for his people always a nomad, a true adherent of the Great Spirit culture. This is one reason why the Mongol Yuan dynasty in China was able to assimilate the ancient culture of the Chinese and under his grandson, Kubilai Khan, to create the distinguished environment which so deeply impressed Marco Polo. Both Christian and Muslim historians write of the

Mongols as uncultured*. A similar mistake was made by the
early settlers in north America who could not appreciate the
refinements of the Indian nomad culture until they had almost
destroyed it. Chinghis Khān for all his self-control and his
ruthless destruction of all that resisted him, was found by those
who met him – such as the famous Chinese hermit Ch'ang Ch'un
– to be a sensitive man with a lively sense of humour: but he was
a great deal more than this. He had a creative vision of a world in
which the freedom of the nomad life would be preserved and
enriched by drawing on the wealth of settled populations. He
regarded the nomad as a superior being able to communicate
with the Great Spirit, *Tengri,* in the immense spaces of the north.
He did not leave, as did the founder of the Osmanli dynasty, the
precept to his people: "Wander, always wander and never settle
down", but there is no doubt he would have approved it. His
Yasa, Commands, were addressed to nomads and continued to be
quoted as articles of faith among the Mongols for at least two
centuries.

It must be recognised that Chinghis' vision – to unify the
wandering life of the nomad with high intellectual culture – was
incapable of realisation. If we cast our minds back nearly two
thousand years, we can recognise the same dilemma in the time
of Zoroaster who threw the entire weight of his influence on the
side of agriculture and the settled population. During all that
time, life on the steppes had changed very little; the Mongol
hordes rode the same horses and used much the same weapons as
their ancestors the Turanians of the seventh century BC; but this
time the nomads had a leader of outstanding genius, not merely
as a military leader, but as a leader of men. We can see a very
significant connection with the Khwājagān, who were not at all
concerned with religious leadership but were consummate
leaders of men. Among the nomads, human qualities counted far
more than they do in settled communities where institutions can
continue to work by momentum, even when human qualities are
lacking. This is what had happened to the Christian Church
between the fourth and seventh centuries and had happened to
the Magi and once again to Islām under the Abbasids. The
Roman empire as an institution was a poor substitute for the
human qualities of the republic.

* W. Barthold *loc. cit.* p. 46 for example, says that: "Chinghis Khān to the end
of his life remained a stranger to all culture".

Chinghis Khan did not institutionalise his empire, but carefully selected the men who were to rule it. He had three sons, Tuluy, Chagatay and Uguday. Of these, Tuluy inherited much of his father's genius. Chagatay had his unbending sense of purpose and severity. Uguday by his magnanimous and gentle character, won all hearts. When he knew that he was dying, Chinghis Khan collected his sons and grandsons and told them that Uguday was to be his successor and that the family should show to all the nations that they accepted his famous counsel: "Let Mongol never fight with Mongol".

So strong was the sense of discipline he had instilled into his family and his generals that all accepted Uguday. He proved to be a great ruler, not so much by the intellectual pre-eminence which he certainly possessed, as by his goodness and fearless honesty. He was, like his father, a good judge of men. The members of his family and the generals he appointed to positions of responsibility were well-chosen. Perhaps his greatest military achievement was the conquest of Russia which, for two hundred and fifty years, remained under Mongol domination.

The history of Turkestan after the death of Chinghis Khan was unlike that of other great conquerors. Alexander, Julius Caesar, Constantine, Attila, left behind them a legacy of wars of succession. In Turkestan the horrible practice of murdering all princes who might challenge the one who seized power, had been so consistently followed that few expected that the successor of Chinghis Khan would tolerate possible rivals. The revulsion and terror caused by the ruthless massacre of hundreds of thousands of Chinese, Persians, Turks, Arabs and Indians, soon gave place to admiration for the ability of the Mongols to provide secure conditions of life for the conquered peoples. The recovery was rapid and by 1250, only those not yet brought under Mongol dominion had reason to fear for their lives and possessions.

Chapter Eight

The Mongol Era

Chinghis Khān and his successor Uguday were both shamanists and adhered faithfully to the shaman principle that all spiritual men are holy. This led them to show equal tolerance to the three world religions, Buddhism, Christianity and Islām which were strongly represented in the conquered territories. Buddhist monks, *bhikshus,* Christian priests and Muslim *imāms* and *qādīs* were exempted from taxation. Only Jewish rabbis were excluded from this privilege because they participated in commerce. The great Khāns made no attempt to convert their subjects to shamanism. Such an idea would never occur to men who regarded spirituality as a spontaneous manifestation of the Great Spirit. The shamans were dedicated men who trained themselves rigorously to increase their capacity for responding to the guidance of the spirit. They made use of spiritual exercises, fasting and also breath control. It is even possible, though I have been able to find no written evidence, that the retention of breath as practised by the Masters of Wisdom came from the shamans and not from India as most scholars suppose.

Anthropologists present us with a picture of shamanism that is based on the present degenerated practices. They connect modern shamans with prehistoric times and follow their invariable custom of underestimating the level of culture of ancient peoples. In chapter two, I gave reasons for concluding that the Great Spirit culture of central Asia was on a very high level. It was the source of Taoism and, in fact, of Buddhism also. Among the Masters, Khwāja Ahmad Yasawī certainly had contacts with shamanism and derived from it much of his knowledge of the sacred dance. The shamans at the time of Chinghis Khān practised and taught the sacred dance, though in a more spontaneous form than the Yasawīs.

There is no doubt that both Chinghis and Uguday were satisfied with shamanism for themselves, but they had no conception of religion based upon a body of beliefs that people would be expected to accept. We associate spirituality with creeds and commandments and cannot easily put ourselves in the position of people who accept the reality of the Great Spirit but do not associate with it anything like our idea of a personal God. For a shamanist, the working of the Great Spirit is wholly from within. "The Spirit bloweth where it listeth" and no one can teach another person anything about it. The shaman receives his call from within and all he learns from others are the techniques for increasing his sensitivity. I think that the shamanist conception of the Great Spirit was much closer to that of the Demiurge as we developed it in Chapter One. The shaman was concerned to live himself, and to help others to live, in harmony with nature. He could put himself in tune with the pattern of history on the demiurgic level and so could predict events and give advice that was proved by results. This was not all he had to offer, for he knew a great deal about energies and their concentration in people and places.

It is not surprising that the Mongols were not anxious to share their shamans with other tribes; and there is no doubt that Chinghis Khān did have the conviction that he was leading a 'chosen people'. His policy throughout was directed to establishing the supremacy of the Mongols, but not of enforcing their spirituality or way of life.

So it continued until the death of Uguday on the 11th December, 1241. The authority of Chinghis Khān passed to his widow Toregene with the consent of the Khāns, each of whom became more or less independent in his own domain. In 1251, Mongke was elected as the Great Khān. During the following twenty years, the history of the world was in the balance. Mongke was strongly influenced by his Christian mother and two wives to adopt Christianity as the religion of the empire. He was aware of the weakness of the Byzantine rulers in Constantinople and saw the possibility of taking over all the Muslim territories as far as Morocco. Asia Minor and Syria were invaded. Baghdad was helpless; Egypt was in disorder.

At the time of Mongke's death in 1259, the Mongols in Turkestan were assimilating the culture, and preparing to adopt the religion, of the Muslim population. It seems that here the influence of the Khwajagan was mainly responsible for the prudent attitude of the Muslim priesthood. The Masters of Wisdom were on good terms with all races and religions. They alone would understand the significance of shamanism and Buddhism. It is even possible that they were interested in Christian unity.* From 1260 they resumed their public activity. Masters such as Khwaja Arif Riwgarawi acquired a high reputation among all classes in Bukhara. In the *Nafahat al-Uns,* it is said that he retired from the position of Grand Master, because his public reputation conflicted with the principle of 'avoiding fame' laid down by Abd al-Khaliq his teacher. He handed over to Khwaja Mahmud Faghnawi, who lived in the little village of Faghna about twelve miles from Bukhara. Mahmud refused to allow the notables of Bukhara to visit him and kept strictly to the task of training his successors, one of whom was to become one of the very great Masters. He was a carpenter and supported himself and his family exclusively by the exercise of his trade. In the history of the Masters, he is particularly remembered for his comprehensive grasp of methods. For example, he taught, for the first time, the 'present moment exercise' *zikr-i alaniyya.* When asked why he introduced an innovation he replied: "People are living in a dream, this is to wake them up".

The present moment exercise belongs to the second state of transformation that leads to *fana-i afal.* To understand this, we have to examine the basic nature of the Way of the Masters which is expressed in an aphorism I learned many years ago from the Court Chamberlain of Sultan Abdul Hamid: *"Def-i mefasid jelb-i menafiden evladir"* − the removal of the undesirable must precede the acquisition of the desirable. This is directed against the deceptive belief that one can be filled with the Spirit before one is emptied of self. There are four stages in the elimination of egoism.

First Stage. *fana−i ahkam.* This is not a true elimination or *fana* because it refers to the external world rather than the self. It is

* *Editor's note.* Bennett is referring to the contacts made between Christian Europe and the Christians in Mongol territory up to the end of Mongke's reign (1259).

disillusionment with the visible world – or the world of bodies. Our egoism is closely bound up with our dependence on the external world. Egoism is the fundamental illusion that we possess something – our 'ego' – that is our own. According to the teaching of the Masters, the ego is the 'great lie' by which man is cut off from his destiny. Since there is no ego 'within', man turns to the outer world – the world of bodies, *alam-i ajsam* – which being 'outside' allows him to feel that in some way he exists 'inside'. When he 'awakens', he becomes aware that the world of bodies supports his own body but does nothing for his ego. This is the 'first liberation'. It brings him face to face with the need to find within himself the 'reality' that he cannot find outside.

Second Stage. *fana-i afal.* This is the great and awful step that not many are able to make. It comes with the realisation that the 'inner life' is no more than a dream world – *alam-i arwah*. *Arwah* is the plural of *ruh*, meaning spirit. The *alam-i arwah* is the world of spirits, that is, of ghosts. People mistakenly call it the spiritual world and believe that it is the 'other world' promised by religion. According to the Masters, the world of spirits is here and now. We live in it because we exist in a dream state with rare moments of awakening. The dream state is the second stronghold of egoism. It is exceedingly hard to accept that we are no more 'real persons' in our waking state than in our sleep state. This acceptance comes only with repeated experience of "waking and seeing". This is why Mahmūd Faghnawī's 'present moment zikr' has been so valuable as a training exercise.

Students of Gurdjieff's ideas will recognise his: "Man is asleep; he has no 'I' and he can know nothing until he wakes up". This, and other ideas, demonstrate how closely connected Gurdjieff must have been with the tradition of the Khwajagān. Nevertheless, it still remains true that few seekers do arrive at the *fana-i afal* and see that they are ghosts living in a ghost world.

Third Stage. *fana–i sifat.* This again is a very great step because it opens the way into the real world – the *alam-i imkan*. This is the world where free acts of will are possible. It is the true 'inner world' that we lose contact with when we believe in our dreams.

All spiritual paths must lead to this step; but, because it takes us beyond the mind, no words can adequately describe it. In the sayings of the Masters, we find again and again the warning that liberation cannot be uttered. Mahmūd Faghnawī's great successor Khwaja Azīzān Ah Ramitānī was a weaver, *nassaj.* He was

known everywhere as one of the greatest of the Masters. It is said
that he was largely responsible for one of the most important
events in history: the conversion of the Mongol Khans to Islam.
His influence in Bukhara enabled the Khwajagan to teach openly
without compromising the rule to avoid intimacy with the rich
and powerful. His reputation reached Damascus and Konya
where Jalal ad-din Rumi wrote: "If inner state, *hal*, were not
beyond speech, *qa*, would the notables of Bukhara have become
the slaves of Khwaja Nassaj?"

Those who reach the third stage of *fana* cannot convey their
inner state, *hal*, to others, but all who meet them are aware of
being in the presence of real being.

After Mahmud Faghnawi, a change came over the Masters.
They were recognised by the ordinary people as having a special
role to play. Khwajas were invited to Samarkand and Balkh
where new cities were arising from the ruins of the old. Many
teachers appeared throughout Turkestan, Kashgaria and as far
west as Iraq. Nevertheless, the Khwajagan retained their unique
position because of their understanding of transformation. This is
apparent if we come to the fourth stage of liberation.

Fourth Stage. *fana-i zat.* This is the complete liberation from
self that enables Divine Love to take possession of the soul. All
separateness is overcome and the creature becomes the Creator.
Here, we must recall the distinction made in chapter six between
the southern Sufis and the Masters of Wisdom. The former also
speak of *fana*, but interpret this in a personal sense. There are also
four stages.

> *fana fil-shaikh*
> *fana fil-pir*
> *fana fi'l-rasul*
> *fana fillah*

In this path the *murid*, pupil, learns to create a mental image of
his *shaikh*, teacher, and holds on to it until he is able to feel that
the *shaikh* is really present. He represents his teachers as possessing
all the qualities to which he aspires and models his behaviour on
him. When the *shaikh* perceives that the power of creating a
mental image has been acquired, he directs the attention of the
murid to the *pir*, that is the founder of the brotherhood to which
they both belong. Thus a mawlawi will form a mental image of
Jalal ad-din Rumi, a bektashi of Hajji Bektash Veli, a ku-
brawi of Najm ad-din Kubra. When I met the last of the

mawlawī *chelebi* in Aleppo, he told me that he was constantly aware of the image of Jalal ad-dīn Rūmī who had promised to meet all his faithful dervishes at the moment of death and bring them into the presence of God. It was evident that this was a tangible reality for him: but I could see also that it prevented him from going further. He had, indeed, experienced the third stage *fana fi'l rasūl,* losing oneself in the Messenger of God, *rasūl,* but this had occurred only once and he did not look for its return.

The fourth and last stage is *fana fillāh,* which is reached only by the fewest of the few. This stage is the same as the *fana-i zāt* of the Masters, but it is interpreted as union with God and realisation that God is the sole substance, *wahdat-i wujūd.* This way can lead to pantheism and loss of contact with the Supreme Will. The danger attending this path is that it does not cut at the root of egoism. There is much talk of love between man and God, but when so described, love is personal and nothing personal can be free from egoism. The way of liberation looks first to the elimination of egoism, knowing that when egoism goes, Divine Love enters spontaneously.

This is why *fana-i zāt* is also called *huwiyyat* or the state in which only the One is present. All personal manifestation ceases. This is called *raf-i taayun,* the individual will becomes the Absolute Will. The Khwājagān refer also to *ifnā-i wujūdiyyat* which means the cessation of existences, i.e. the same as the Buddhist: "Rebirth is no more. There is no return" which is said of the Arahant who has attained final liberation.

Let us get back to the weaver Khwaja Nassaj of Rūmī's poem. His full name was Khwaja Azīzān Alī Ramitanī. Ramitān was a large town about twelve miles from Bukhāra. The exact date of his birth is not known. He is said to have died in 1321 at the age of a hundred and thirty which would place his birth somewhere about 1191. This would make him thirty years old when Bukhāra was taken by Chinghis Khan, whom he is said to have met through his teacher Mahmūd Faghnawī. He travelled widely both in Turkestan and Khurasan and was consulted by the Mongol Khans appointed by Mongke. According to one tradition, Mongke was convinced by Khwaja Azīzān that the Mongols should adopt the religion of Islam.

To understand what was happening we must again look at the world situation at the end of the thirteenth century. The Crusades had come to an end and Europe was once again in disorder. The Caliphate in Egypt had acquired a new strength with a great mercenary army – the Mamluks – mainly recruited from Turkish refugees from the Mongol invasion of Asia Minor. The Mongols had suffered their first major setback when the Mongol army, seeking to invade Egypt, was cut to pieces at the battle of Goliath's Wall on September 3rd, 1260. Although the Mongols were in control of Russia and even invaded Poland, their basic empire was in Turkestan, Persia and Iraq. The immensity of the Mongol conquests can be judged if one realises that even after their eventual withdrawal, they ruled from Poland to China over three great empires. Their central empire was greater than the Persian empire at its greatest expansion.

There was, however, one terrible difference. The Mongol conquest had devastated and impoverished huge areas and the work of reconstruction took nearly a century. From the stories preserved in the *Rashahat* and other accounts it would seem that the Khwajagan took an active part in organising the work of reconstruction but remained strictly aloof from political and religious quarrels.

There is no doubt that the Masters of Wisdom made a deep impression on the Mongols, who saw in them exceptionally gifted shamans, able to manifest spiritual powers. The preference shown by the Mongols for independent 'holy men' rather than for the orthodox priesthood, may account for the appearance of many teachers who imitated the Khwajagan without having received their initiation. Khwaja Azizan was often interrogated by the leaders of various 'brotherhoods'. The following stories taken from Şuşud's *Hacegan Hanedani* help to convey some idea of his influence.

A successful shaikh called Rukn ad-din Ala ad-dawlat asked him three questions.

R.A.: "Like you, we also serve those who come and go. You don't offer them meals and we do. Yet the people are pleased with you and they find fault with us. Why is this?"

A.A.R.: "Plenty of people do service as a favour; but few know how to serve as an obligation. Work to learn how to serve others as an obligation and not as a favour; until you find that no-one complains any more."

R.A.: "We have heard that you received your initiation directly from his holiness the Prophet Khidr. What does this mean?"

A.A.R.: "There are servants of the Supreme and Glorious Truth who are True Lovers. They are the ones whom Khidr loves."

R.A.: "We hear that you do your *zikr* aloud. What kind of *zikr* is that?"

A.A.R.: "And we hear that you do your *zikr* secretly: this is as if you did it aloud."

One of the best-known theologians of the time, Mawlānā Saif ad-dīn also asked Khwāja Azīzān why he taught his pupils to do their *zikr* aloud. He replied: "There is a saying of the Prophet, *hadīth-i sharīf*, to the effect that when in death agony, one should make the confession of faith in a loud voice with one's last breath. A true dervish breathes every breath as his last."

Shaikh Badr ad-dīn, a close friend of the Shaikh Hasan Bulghārī asked him: "As we are commanded by God to pray continually, we perform the perpetual *zikr*. Is this merely a verbal repetition or does it come from the heart?" Khwāja Azīzān replied: "It begins with the tongue and ends with the heart."

He gave various short counsels such as: "Watch yourselves in two activities: speaking and eating." "Pray with lips you have not sinned with." i.e. by the love that you arouse in others, you will evoke prayers that are not your own.

Khwāja Azīzān was known as a man with great spiritual gifts. He was aware of the inner state of his followers and often answered questions that they themselves could not express in words. He was also a healer credited with having brought people back from death's door. He explained that he never healed or helped anyone because he was asked to do so, but solely when he received a clear order from the voice of God. He lived to a great age, but continued to support himself as a weaver and would never agree to move from his own humble dwelling. Following Khwāja Abd al-Khāliq's advice, he deferred marriage until he was fifty years old. His youngest son was born when he was nearly a hundred. He was regarded above all as a prophet because he foretold the events of the century ahead including the appearance of two very great saints who would demonstrate the full significance of the Way of Transformation. These were Bahā ad-dīn Naqshbandī and Ubaidallāh Ahrār, both of whom claimed to have communicated with him in a vision. He also foretold the universal decline of religion if mankind failed to take the opportunity opened by the Masters.

When he was dying, he sent for his two surviving sons, Khwaja Muhammad, who was then eighty, and Khwaja Ibrahim who was thirty. He designated Ibrahim as his heir. Being aware that those surrounding him were surprised, he said: "Muhammad will soon follow me". In fact, Muhammad lived only nineteen days after the death of his father. Khwaja Ibrahim lived for another seventy years.

Khwaja Azizan's greatest successor was Khwaja Muhammad Baba Samasi. When he was dying he sent for all his followers and told them to put themselves under the direction of Baba Samasi. He, in his turn, initiated Sayyid Amir Kulal who was not only a descendant of the Prophet, but a member of the highest aristocracy of Bukhara. His father was a close associate of the Mongol Khan. As a young man, Sayyid Amir was devoted to sport and his ambition was to become a champion wrestler. One day as he was in a wrestling match, Baba Samasi happened to pass by. He stopped and said to his companion: "In that ring there is a man whose teaching will bring many people transformation". Amir Kulal caught his eye and was captured. He at once abandoned his match and followed Baba Samasi home. He was accepted as a pupil and not long after was given his first initiation. Sayyid Amir Kulal served Baba Samasi for twenty years. He afterwards said: "Twice every week, on Tuesday and Thursday, I used to ride eighteen miles each way from Suhari to Samas to take part in the Khwaja's group meetings." Under the direction of Baba Samasi, Amir Kulal reached final liberation and became one of the great Masters. He had four sons and four successors.

Amir Kulal's greatest achievement was as spiritual director of the greatest Master of the fourteenth century, Khwaja Muhammad Baha ad-din Shah, the founder of the Naqshbandi order of dervishes which was to succeed the Masters when they ceased to be active a hundred years later. There is a well-known story that Khwaja Baba Samasi was passing through the village of Qasr-i Hinduwan, later known as Arifan, when he turned to his companions and said: "This soil smells of a hero". Passing again soon after, he said: "The smell is stronger, be sure that the hero is born". In fact, three days previously Khwaja Baha ad-din

Naqshbandı came into this world.

The child's grandfather, according to the custom of the time, placed a gift on his heart and asked Baba Samasī to bless him. The Khwaja said: "This is to be our child, we have accepted him." Turning to his companions, he said: "This is the hero whose smell we were aware of. Before long, the aroma will spread though the world and he will become the *mushkil gusha* of the people of Love". The word *mushkil gusha* means one who 'opens difficulties'.* He then turned to Amīr Kulal, who was to be his successor, and said: "Don't refuse to undertake the training and initiation of my son Baha ad-dın. If you neglect, I won't forgive you." The Amīr rose to his feet and placing his hands on his heart said: "I am no man if I fail you."

Baha ad-dın did more than any other Master to establish the influence of the Khwajagan. It was said of him that the mantle of the Prophet had descended on him. When I read the story of his life, I was reminded that Gurdjieff wrote in *Beelzebub's Tales* that the spirit of Islam was not to be found in Mecca and Medina, but in Bukhara where the true significance of the religion had been preserved.

We come closer to Baha ad-dın than to any of the earlier Masters because his biography was written under the supervision of his successor Khwaja Ala ad-dın Attar by one of the latter's pupils Salah ad-dın ibn al-Mubarak from 1381 until his death in 1400. During the last twenty years of his life, Khwaja Naqshbandı exercised an immense influence in Turkestan and Persia, but he refused to accept the responsibility of teaching the way of the Masters until he was nearly fifty. I want to emphasise this because we find in the lives of the Masters, with the exception of Yūsuf Hamadanı, that they regarded a long apprenticeship as indispensable. I have read long or short histories of more than fifty of the Khwajagan between 1050 and 1530, and I could not help being struck by the retiring and modest attitude which was a common feature shared by all of them. They were able to work together even though relatively few of them were able to meet personally, because not a single one of them looked for power, fame or material benefits. Their immense influence with all classes of the population from Kings and Khans, to

---

* The suffix *gusha* in Persian means opening, expanding. For example *kishwar gusha* means a conqueror.

artisans and peasants, was due to their entire indifference to their own personal position.

When he was still a child, Baha ad-din possessed unusual gifts both of clairvoyance and of healing. From the very beginning, his spiritual potential was recognised.

"As a young boy, my father took me to Samarkand, where we went to visit the great spiritual leaders in the city. I used to share in their prayers. After a time we returned to Bukhara and settled in Qasr–i Arifan. About this time, I was presented with the dervish headpiece which had formerly been worn by that great saint Azizan Ah Ramitani. As soon as I placed this cap on my head, my state was completely transformed. My heart was filled with the love of God and I have ever since carried this love with me wherever I went."

Baha ad-din followed the way of humility and abasement. His initiation into the company of the Masters came in a vision.

"I was frequently thrown into states of ecstasy that I wanted to hide from people so I used to go to the great cemetery at Bukhara. One night I went to three tombs and at each of them saw a lamp lit and full of oil but without the finishing touches. I went to the tomb of Khwaja Muhammud Wasi. There I was told to go to the tomb of Khwaja Faghnawi. I saw two men with swords who put me on a horse. We arrived at the mausoleum of Mezdakhan at night's end. There I saw the same lamps as before. I knelt down facing the Qibla and was taken by such ecstasy that I could see right through the world. I saw the wall round the Qibla dissolving and a great throne became visible. On it a noble personage was seated, but there was a green veil that prevented me from seeing who he was.

"A multitude of people was ranged round the throne. Among others, I saw Khwaja Muhammad Samasi, that very great saint. I said to myself: 'I wonder who is seated on that throne.' Some of the people in the company said to me: 'The man seated on the throne is Khwaja Abd al-Khaliq Ghujduwani and those around are his successors and followers'. I saw a whole company of Khwajas: Ahmad Salik, Awliya-i Kilan, Arif Riwgarawi, Mahmud Faghnawi, and Azizan Ah Ramatani. 'Baba Samasi has brought you into the lives of these masters. You must recognise them, for it is they who gave you the dervish headpiece.'

"At that moment, I remembered the dervish cap that had been sent to me by some unknown giver. I looked round and there it was in the corner. It was on account of this cap that they were all showing me such extraordinary respect. One of the Khwajas said to me:

" 'Listen to what I say. The Master, the Great One, will give you two pieces of advice. No other way will so surely lead you to the Truth as to follow these two counsels.' As soon as I heard this, I stood up from my place, went up to the Khwaja and made to kiss his eyes. Those on each side drew away the curtain. I saluted him and kissed his blessed eyes. With head lowered, I stood before him. The saint spoke to me and said:

" 'Baha ad-din, the first counsel is represented by the lamp shown to you. This means that you have an aptitude for this path, but your aptitude is like the wick. You have to keep it trimmed. In order to reach the goal, the man with the necessary aptitude has to work upon himself, according to his ability. The second counsel is to hold fast to the right path as shown to us by the Prophet, the bringer of grace. Various so-called 'traditions' have been given out since the time of our Prophet. Disregard them all. Look for guidance to the acts of the Prophet and his companions.'

"One of the Khwajas present said: 'Tomorrow go quickly and find Sayyid Kulal and enter his service. On your way, you will meet an old man who will give you a loaf of bread still hot from the oven. Take this bread, but do not say a word. When you have passed him, you will meet with a caravan and, after that, with a lone horseman. The horseman will pay you reverence. You must take the dervish headpiece to Amir Kulal.'

"The following day, I set out on the road and just as they had foretold, I met with the old man and he gave me a loaf of fresh bread. I went by and sometime afterwards I met a caravan. The caravan people asked me where I was coming from.

'I am coming from the village of Ekine.'

'When did you leave?'

'At sunrise.'

'How could you possibly have come so fast?'

"After passing the caravan, I met a man on horseback. I greeted him. He pulled up his horse's head and stopped.

'Whoever are you? You have filled me with fear.'

'I am that person, before whom you are to bow down.'

"As soon as he heard this, he leaped from his horse and with tears in his eyes clasped my knees. He then went and pulled out a skinful of wine that was on the back of his horse. He trampled it under foot and made me a reverence."

Evidently the three incidents are symbolical of the powers Baha ad-din was to acquire. The loaf of bread stands for his own transformation. The caravan represents the ordinary world and Baha ad-din's journey is 'against time and space', indicating that he is free from all earthly limitations. The man cured of drunkenness stands for the power to free people from their vices in which Baha ad-din was to become pre-eminent.

After this experience, he went to Nasaf and met Sayyid Amir Kulal who welcomed him as a pupil, taught him the *zikr* and told him to follow the path of conscious choice.* He also advised him to practise the *zikr* silently. Amir Kulal, seeing Baha ad-din's sincerity and spiritual gifts, showed him special favour that aroused the jealousy of other pupils. One of them complained to the Amir that Baha ad-din performed his *zikr* silently when all the rest at their regular meetings used to chant the *zikr* aloud. Not long afterwards, Amir Kulal with some five hundred of his pupils, was engaged in building a mosque and hall for meetings. While they were resting, he said to them all: "You have not understood my son Baha ad-din. He is under the special care of God and he is wholly submitted to Him. There is no need for me to guide him." He went on carrying sacks of lime and in front of all of them he called to Baha ad-din and said: "I have brought you to the degree that Khwaja Baba Samasi commanded me. He said that I was to bring Baha ad-din to the point where he himself was ready to teach. That is what I have done. I have nourished you as my own heart. A bird has been hatched and has left the egg of the creation. Through you, all mankind will receive a blessing. Whoever is in need of help has only to get your scent."

To understand the work of the Masters in the fourteenth century, we must look at Turkestan after the first Great Khans, Chinghis, Uguday, Mongke and Hulagu had gone and the Mongol empire had been divided into a number of successor states. Although the Grand Khan was still nominally the paramount ruler, the Golden Horde in Russia, the Yuan dynasty in China, the Ilkhans in Persia and Mesopotamia, were in effect independent rulers. For a few generations, there were still

---

* The Arabic phrase is *nafi wa ithbat*, that is negation and affirmation. It is the rejection of actions prompted by egoism and the acceptance of the guidance of conscience.

remarkable Mongol Khāns but by the fourteenth century degeneration had set in.

It is worth casting a quick glance over the situation in Persia, where the Ilkhāns became, in effect, Persian emperors who prepared the way for the re-establishment of Persian independence under the Safavids. Under the rule of Abaqa (1278–1282), the Mongol tolerance towards all religions was extended into Mesopotamia and Syria. There were numerous Buddhist temples and Christian churches. Islām was but one of the tolerated religions. Abaqa himself was a shamanist and is reported to have given a grand welcome to a shaman who visited him at Tabrīz in 1278 shortly after his accession.

Under Arghun (1284–1291), who died at the age of thirty-five, great encouragement was given to the contact between religions. The Ilkhān decided to send an embassy to the Pope, whom he regarded as the ruler of Christian Europe. This was a natural mistake. Unfortunately, the Christians of central Asia, who were very numerous and well-organised, were able to send their patriarch and two bishops with the Khān's representatives. The Pope was Nicholas IV who was elected a year later after long and ignominious disputes and ruled for eighteen years with almost despotic power over the Christian west. During his papacy, the one and only opportunity arose for uniting all Christendom from the Atlantic to China, and of reducing Islam to impotence in Egypt, Iraq and India. The mission sent by the Ilkhān was received with some embarrassment. The Pope had no intention of embarking on another crusade after the disastrous failures of Louis of France and Richard of England. Constantinople had been pillaged and the eastern empire was at its lowest ebb. The Pope was concerned to establish the temporal power of the Holy See and could not recognise the spiritual opportunity presented by the Mongol interest in Christianity.

Nevertheless, a mission was sent to the court of the Ilkhān and a dialogue with the Nestorian patriarch was started. The Roman delegates demanded adherence to the Athanasian creed which, to do them credit, the eastern theologians were prepared to accept. But it soon became clear that the Pope and his satellite emperors and kings were unable, or unwilling, to embark on a crusade in alliance with the Mongols and the opportunity disappeared.

Buddhist priests in Persia came from India and a mystical form of Shiite Islam prevailed over the orthodox Sunnīs. We cannot tell how far the subsequent development of Sufism in Mesopotamia was influenced by these contacts. In central Asia, there is little doubt that orthodox Islam was strong.

Arghun was the last of the Khans to receive the secret burial that belonged to the ancient shamanist tradition. His death – alleged to be at the hands of an 'Indian yogi' who administered the wrong medicine! – marked the end of the truly Mongol era. For some time the fate of the different religions was decided by the Ilkhan Ghazan. His predecessor Baidu was a 'good Christian', who had been influenced by one of Abaqa's wives, Despoina, a daughter of the Byzantine emperor Paleologus. Ghazan was brought up as a Buddhist and while governor of Turkestan had erected Buddhist temples and encouraged the spread of Buddhism in his territory. His Wazīr Naurūz was a convert to Islam and succeeded in persuading him that he should adopt the religion of his army – mostly Turkish Muslims. On the 19th of June 1295 he made the profession of faith followed by his principal Amīrs. Soon after, he issued a decree ordering the destruction of all Jewish synagogues, Christian churches and Buddhist temples, prohibiting the practice of any religion except Islam. Christian historians* describe the ignominy suffered by the Christians throughout the empire from Baghdad to Bukhara. From the beginning of the fourteenth century, the entire region including Persia and Turkestan was Muslim territory. The tolerance of the Mongols was lost in the fanaticism of the Turks who became more and more dominant.

By this time, the ravages of the Mongol conquest had been largely repaired, though excessive taxation still made life hard for the poor and the merchants alike. The role of the Masters was primarily directed to reconstruction, as we can see from the story of Amīr Kulal's mosque-building.

By the time that Baha ad-dīn Naqshbandī came to the fore, Islam was dominant everywhere. The role of the Masters changed. They began to be concerned with the preservation of peace and the encouragement of social justice.

---

* *c.f.* Barhebraeus, *The Chronography of Gregory Abu'l Faraj*, translated Budge, London 1932 p. 507.

Chapter Nine

The Master Training

The tradition of the Masters called for a long and arduous training, reminiscent of that of the Essene Brotherhood or of the Magi. Only those who could endure through the years of training were chosen for the final initiation that brought them into the circle of the Masters. The Khwājagān have been referred to as a dynasty that ruled central Asia on the spiritual plane for four or five centuries. It is true that in many cases son would follow father; or the transmission would be through the female to a specially selected son-in-law. This did not, however, exclude any capable seeker from approaching the Master and offering his service. If accepted, the pupil was on the same footing as the Master's own family. From descriptions of the methods used by the Masters in training their pupils, it was clear that there was no fixed rule, but on the contrary, the training varied from pupil to pupil as well as from Master to Master. Some pupils would remain with the same teacher for ten, twenty or even thirty years, others would be sent from one teacher to another or sometimes even left to find their own way. Some pupils were treated with extreme severity and made to endure great hardships. Often these same pupils were afterwards taken into the Master's families and married to one of their daughters. Other pupils were treated with embarrassing attention and respect until they saw for themselves that they were being made fools of.

These extraordinary methods of dealing with pupils are liable to give a misleading impression; later teachers who attempted to imitate the Masters made many mistakes on this account.

The Masters' training cannot be understood. We realise that they called for a strict self-discipline that would bring the body entirely into subjection to the will. They also demanded a personal humility that was proof against flattery or condemnation and indifferent to success or failure. These qualities are not attained without many years of single-minded devotion. When they were obtained the Masters showed their pupils how to attain the spiritual powers that gave them their dominating position throughout central Asia and eventually spread their influence all over the Muslim world.

Not all seekers were able to reach the stages of self-abnegation that went with the title of Khwaja. We can distinguish three categories of *salik*, seeker of the truth. The first were candidates whom the Master accepted for general training. They were initiated into the *zikr*, attended regular group meetings, *suhbat*, and took part in the external activities such as the repair of buildings and the work on farms. They received very little personal instruction from the Khwaja who might have anything from twenty to several hundred *saliks* in his *halqa*, circle. The second category consisted of *khadins*, servers, who were the personal attendants of the Master. They often remained in this capacity until the Master died and then transferred to another. The third category were the *khalifas*, deputies or initiates, able to transmit and continue the tradition. The *khalifas* were specially selected from the ranks of both candidates and servers to undergo special training; usually involving attendance upon more than one Master. During the centuries of the Masters' spiritual activity, the *khalifas* were men of exceptional spiritual qualities and were mainly responsible for the high prestige in which the Masters were held.

The modern world is seeking for teachers and many come forward as guides, gurus, or shaikhs who are far from having passed through the training regarded as indispensable by the Khawjagan. It would surprise many seekers to learn that thirty or even forty years of training was considered normal by the Masters of Wisdom, before accepting the responsibility of *irshad*, guiding others, or exercising *karamat*, spiritual powers.

The procedure for accepting candidates was laid down by Abd al-Khaliq Ghujduwani and changed little in the course of centuries. The only important innovation came from Baha ad-din Naqshbandi, who was renowned as an interpreter of dreams. When a young man came to see him he would tell him to come back in three days and report on his dreams. If the dream corresponded to Bahā ad-dīn's own inner vision, he would, in principle, accept the candidate, but he nevertheless had to pass through the same novitiate as was laid down by the earlier Masters.

The foundation of the training was self-discipline in matters of diet, sleep and other bodily activities; the *zikr*, repetition of the name of God; participation in group meetings, *suhbat;* and the undertaking of practical tasks. During the years of devastation after the Mongol invasions, the Masters and their pupils worked incessantly to house the homeless, build mosques and schools and train people in practical skills. Most of the teaching was given at group meetings in reply to questions. We are very fortunate in that one of the later Khwājas, Fakhr ad-dīn Alī Husain al-Wāiz Kāshifī, has left us very detailed records in his book *Rashahāt Ain al-Hayāt,* Dew Drops from the Spring of Life. He attended the meetings of many Masters, including Ubaidallāh Ahrar and Jāmī, and heard accounts of the earlier Masters from their own pupils and descendants. He says that as soon as he heard anything, he noted it exactly as it was said without adding any commentary of his own. The following extract is an example of this which describes group meetings of Khwāja Alā ad-dīn Attār in the middle of the fourteenth century.

Q. "What is the purpose of asceticism. Is it to overcome the passions of the flesh?"
A. "No, the purpose is to break our dependence upon the physical world. It is the means whereby we are able to rise to the worlds of spirit and truth."
Q. "Why is it that some pupils have to go by way of complete obedience and devotion to the teacher, whereas others seem to be able to go by themselves?"
A. "When the seeker is at the beginning of the path, it is essential that he should bind his heart to his guide. The teacher and guide is like a mirror of divine truth and by regarding the teacher in this way, the pupil is turned towards abandonment of self, *fana,* and the longing for God, *jazba.* Without this devotion it is not possible for the eye of the Truth to open. It is for this reason that the seeker at the beginning of his path must first of all bind himself to his

teacher until he can get free from the attractions of the external world. If he does not do this, he falls away from his search and he fails to get the taste of nothingness. It is certain that it is wise to do everything in the right order. On the other hand, for the experienced seeker, this connection is no longer the answer, because the experienced seeker has come to the reality of non-identification. For him, everything has become a mirror of absolute perfection. For him, the things of this world have all the same value: the ocean is no more than a stream; the sun no more than a mote in the sunshine. For those who have come to this degree, to look through the mirror of the teacher is a limitation and a defect; they must see for themselves."

Q. "What is the visible mark of the experienced seeker?"

A. "The aim of the work is to pass beyond all interests, activities and dependencies that are obstacles on the way to the truth. Our Khwaja Baha ad-dın used, for example, to treat everything as if it had no connection with himself. If it happened that he wore a new kaftan, he would say this kaftan belongs to so and so; thus wearing it as if it was borrowed and not his own. When you see someone is free from attachment to any thing or activity, you can be confident that he is already established on the path."

Q. "What are the main marks by which one can recognise one's progress?"

A. "When you have wiped out from your vision the world of matter and the world of spirit then you have reached *fana*. When you have abandoned the sense of your own existence, then this is emptiness within emptiness, *fana-i zat*. That which holds the seeker back is his own existence. That which prevents him from having perfect knowledge is his inability to abandon relative knowledge; what prevents him from reaching his absolute spirit is his inability to give up the relative spirit."

Q. "Can one give these things up by one's own will?"

A. "It is desirable that there should be a guide with the spirit of Muhammad in him so that the heart can lose its own existence in the existence of the guide; but when emptiness reaches its final stage, then the guide is no longer required because abandonment is finally something each soul must accomplish for itself."

Q. "Is this abandonment only a matter of knowing that one's existence is really non-existent, or is it necessary to have something beyond knowledge?"

A. "It is necessary to add faith to knowledge. Muhyiddīn ibn al-Arabī in the *Futūhat* used the expression: 'The union of faith and vision'. This union is an achievement that not every wise man can accomplish. It is gained by those who are true saints."

Q. "What can the shaikh, and what must the seeker himself, do?"

A. "The great teachers have said that success comes only to those who work. The help a teacher can give is dependent upon the readiness of the pupil to work and obey the instructions he is given. Without zealous work, the deeper meanings will never be found. The accomplished man – that is the guide – can only influence the pupil for a few days. There is the saying: 'perseverance cannot be given'. When we took part in the groups of Khwāja Bahā ad-dīn, we tried to hold on to remembering our aim from morning until night. Nevertheless, among all the companions, there were very few people who were capable of holding on for one day until nightfall."

Q. "When I am doing our exercise, sometimes I find myself in a different state, but I cannot hold on to it. What is wrong?"

A. "Nothing is wrong. It can well happen that in the course of the effort to hold himself present, the pupil finds that he is in a different state but loses it at once. He should not on this account be depressed. With perseverance and effort, the transition becomes easier and finally is established. By continued effort the pupil can reach the same state as that of an angel and, when he is in this pure state, he is able both to see and to accept his own nothingness. It is in this way that the final liberation is attained."

Q. "Do you approve of visits to the tombs of the Masters of former times?"

A. "When you pay a visit to the tomb of one of the Masters of Wisdom, you benefit to the extent that you have understood their teaching and placed your confidence in them. The more there is understanding and trust, the more such a visit can be profitable. There is indeed a very great power that can be experienced when visiting sacred tombs, but you must understand that we communicate with the spirits of the dead Masters also from a distance."

Q. "We are told to imitate our teacher, but we are also told that we should learn not to imitate. How do you explain this apparent contradiction?"

A. "When you enter the path, you must of necessity copy because you do not know how to work from yourself, but, through copying, you will certainly come to find the reality for yourself. Khwaja Naqshbandī ordered me to imitate him closely, and, the more faithfully I copied him, the more certain was I to get a clear result from my work."

Every candidate was required to do hard physical work as well as practise his spiritual exercises and participate in all religious observances. The group meetings, such as have just been described, were rarely held more than once in a week, but, in most cases, there was also direct personal teaching. As an example of the way of working, we have the personal recollection of Sayyid Ahmad Bukharī who described it to Mawlānā Jāmī. He was working under his teacher Shaikh Ilāhī. With the permission of his teacher he went on a pilgrimage to Mecca, spending some time in Jerusalem and nearly a year in Mecca. He returned to his Master in Asia Minor, in the town of Simav, after two years absence. He was already in his forties. When he met the Shaikh in Simav, he was required to perform the prayer in the monastery five times every day. The first prayer was at day-break and immediately afterwards he went into the hills to cut wood and bring it to the house. This continued until the midday prayer. After this, he worked on the farm according to the season, ploughing, sowing or reaping. At other times he would tie a towel around his waist and work in the irrigation canal of the fruit and vegetable garden. After performing the afternoon prayer, he would work in the house and did his *zikr* and other preparatory exercises. The evening would be spent either in meetings or private meditation. The shaikh himself used to spend most of the night in prayer and meditation. He never slept in a bed but at night would go into the forest and, leaning against a tree, would sleep for one hour. Those of his pupils who were strong enough followed his example. They also had frequent fasts in addition to the fast of *Ramadān* required by religion. This continued for six years and after the death of the shaikh, Sayyid

Bukhari was asked by the other pupils to become their guide and teacher. They then moved into Istanbul and built themselves a centre in Galata where they had their own little mosque and a number of individual cells. These conditions of training were typical of the relationship of the *khadim,* server, with his teacher In the case of candidates it was usual for them to have their own trade or calling and to visit the teacher on every possible occasion, but not to live in his house.

As soon as the Khwaja saw that the seeker was capable of making rapid progress he would set him a special programme of work. Baha ad-din Naqshbandi describes how after leaving Khahl Ata when Samarkand was invaded and sacked by the Ozbegs, he was told to devote himself to vegetables. He was to understand vegetable life by caring for living plants and understanding also the place of invertebrates in the life of man. After this he was told to care for animals. He used to go in the streets and if he found a horse who was ill-treated or suffering in any way, he would take charge of it and nurse it to health. One day in the middle of summer, which is intensely dry and hot in Bukhara, he went out into the waste land and came upon a wild boar gazing fixedly into the sun. He thought to himself: "that creature is worshipping God in his own way" and he mentally asked the boar to say a prayer for him. The boar immediately rolled over and over in the sand, lifted himself upon his hindlegs and bowed to the sun, then trotted quietly away. When Baha ad-din returned to his teacher he was told: "You have now understood that all creatures worship God in their own way. Now you must set yourself to take care of the material world. You should go into the streets and remove all filthy things that can be harmful to man." He did this for some time, taking great care to keep himself and his own body scrupulously clean. His teacher was very insistent on personal cleanliness, beyond the requirements of the ritual ablutions. All pupils were required to wash their linen daily and keep everything spotless.

About this time the terrible plague of 1357 brought calamity to Turkestan, but neither Baha ad-din nor a single one of the pupils of the Khwajagan got the infection. Looking back on this with our present knowledge, we can see that it was due to their attention to hygiene, but it was then thought that they were all under special Divine protection.

During the plague year, the pupils, in order to alleviate the sufferings of the people and with no thought for their own danger, would take children and young people and see to it that they were kept clean according to the instructions of their teacher.

Many instances are cited in the stories of the Khwājagān of similar labours and sufferings. One day, Bahā ad-dīn Naqshbandī was seated in the mosque in the village of Riwartūn leaning against one of the columns. He relates: "There came over me suddenly a state of consciousness which spread right through my body and I felt that the whole of my being was dissolving. I became unconscious for I don't know how long until I heard a voice saying inside me: 'Know that you have reached your goal'. I came to myself and knew that I was destined to help great numbers of people to find their way out of the confusion of this world. When I was young, I prayed saying: 'Oh Lord, give me the strength to bear the burden of this path and let me go through all the labours and sufferings that are possible for me.' This prayer of mine was granted and I had to suffer very much in my days of seeking, but now that the time has come for me to be a teacher, I have been released from the burden of labour and suffering."

This soliloquy of Bahā ad-dīn Naqshbandī is reminiscent of Gurdjieff's saying: "God has given, as the means of man's self-perfecting, the way of conscious labour and intentional suffering". This, and many other sayings of Gurdjieff, suggest a connection with the tradition of the Masters of Wisdom. The tradition is closely linked up with the doctrine of the *silsila-i baraka*, or the chain of transmission of a hidden spiritual action. The action itself is called *baraka*, blessing, and this doctrine goes back at least as far as the Zoroastrian *hvareno*, and undoubtedly to the first appearance of the Masters. It is common, in one or another form, to all traditions. We have already met it in the apostolic succession of the Catholic Church and in the rabbinical traditions of Judaism. It is also to be seen in the Indian tradition derived from great sages from Kapila to Shankara. There is an important distinction between the belief in an exclusive action confined to a single line, as is held by the Catholic Church and by Judaism, and the acceptance that there is an action that is universal but takes different forms in different traditions. It is clearly the latter belief that we are exploring in the present book and it is based on the evidence that a high intelligence, the

Demiurge, which is guiding evolution on this planet, is in the process of working more and more through man as its instrument. The *silsila* is an expression of the continuity of the action over many generations. The *baraka,* grace, that works through the different traditions is a manifestation perceptible to all who can look at it with unprejudiced eyes. It is, therefore, the principal evidence upon which we base our belief in providence. It is for this reason that the tradition of the Masters of Wisdom has an importance that goes far beyond the limits of central Asia where they worked from the eleventh to the sixteenth century.

Here I should mention the belief in an unseen prophet who can appear in many forms. He is Khidr, in the green cloak. The association of Khidr with the colour green is evidence of a great antiquity, going back to the beginnings of agriculture ten or twelve thousand years ago. It is believed that Khidr can appear and disappear at will; that he has penetrating knowledge of hidden events and that he is the link between all the Masters of Wisdom. Again and again we read that a certain Master received his initiation directly from Khidr; and when a new technique was introduced as, for example, a change in the way of doing the *zikr,* this was not attributed to the Master but to Khidr who inspired it. It must be said, however, that I have not come across a single instance where one of the Masters directly asserted that he had received his initiation in this way. It was always a belief attributed by the pupils. For example, when Khwaja Azizan Ali Ramitani was asked by Shaikh Rukn ad-din whether it was true that he had received his training from His Holiness the Prophet Khidr, he said: "There are some lovers of God, Glorious and Almighty, who are beloved of Khidr". This cryptic reply was taken by everyone to mean that Azizan had indeed been initiated by Khidr, but was not prepared to say so openly.

Later writers were anxious to establish the succession of the Masters back to the Prophet Muhammad and it was usual to give a line of initiates descended from one of the four first Caliphs, particularly Abu Bakr and Ali. The earlier writings about the Masters referred only to Yusuf Hamadani as their founder and Yusuf, as we have seen, was connected with the Magian tradition. Islamic writers have always been unwilling to admit their debt to Zoroastrianism because it is not specifically mentioned in the Quran. The 'Master of Masters', Khwaja Abd al-Khaliq Ghujduwani, who expressed the principles of living to

be followed by the Masters in his eight 'sentences', was believed
to possess altogether exceptional powers that enabled him to
appear personally to Masters, not only of his own time, but also
of later generations. It was he who prepared them for the task
that was to come with the Mongol invasion. In all the accounts of
the Masters and their work the line of transmission is always
mentioned. When an outstanding man did not receive the final
initiation, he might be referred to as Mawlānā or Shaikh, but not
as a Khwāja. In the case of Ahmad Yasawī, his successors are
called Ata, but it seems that they were regarded as belonging to
the dynasty of the Masters and there were many Khwājas,
including Baha ad-dīn Naqshbandī, who went to a Yasawī
shaikh as part of their training.

We can learn much from the story of Baha ad-dīn Naqshbandī
of how an inward action was combined with training under a
Master.

"One day after a long period of *zikr,* I heard a voice from the
silence speak to me in my heart.

'You are entering this path. What do you wish from us and
what conditions do you make?'

'May what I wish for come true.'

'No, it cannot be. You must do what we command.'

'I cannot promise, for I may not have the strength. Suppose
you ask me to do hard things that are beyond my power?'

'No, whatever we command, that must be done.'

'I shall not be able to. I have not the strength.'

"At that moment, I lost consciousness. My own selfhood left
me. For ten days, I did not know where I went or what I was
doing. At the end of this time, I heard again that inner voice.

'It is well. You have accepted. Whatever you ask for will be
accomplished.' "

In another account of his life. Baha ad-dīn reports a typical
instance of his entire commitment. It is not clear whether it
occurred before or after the initiation just described. He says:

"One day, a state of ecstasy came over me. I cast off all my
clothes and covered myself with a sheepskin. With feet and head
bare, I began to wander in the desert. As I walked and walked,
my feet were pierced with innumerable thorns. Suddenly it came
to me that I must go at once to the house of Amīr Kulāl. As I
came in, the Amīr asked:

'Who is it?' Those standing by said:

'Baha ad-din, my lord.'

'Throw him out.'

"They took me by the arms and thrust me out, shutting the door in my face. My gorge rose and my soul wanted to rebel. But divine grace came to my aid. I said: 'This humiliation is a means with which to serve and satisfy the All-Powerful. That's that; there is nothing else to do.'

"With these words, I laid my head at the door of the Amir's house. All night long, I did not quit the door. When morning came, the Sayyid came out of the house to go to the day-break prayer and his foot struck against my head. When he saw me prostrate, he stretched out his hand and raised me up. He brought me into his house and drew the thorns out of my feet speaking gently to me the while. He took off his own robe and put it on me saying:

'My child, you alone are worthy to wear this robe.'

"The picture of that moment never leaves me. I see myself and my shaikh together. Whenever I go out of my own house, I look at the threshold: but I have never yet seen a dervish with his head on the ground. There are no more pupils: all of them have become shaikhs."

After his novitiate with Sayyid Ami Kulal he placed himself under the tutelage of Mawlana Arif Dikkarani who was Amir Kulal's second successor. Among Baha ad-din's teachers was Mawlana Baha ad-din Kishlaki. He was father-in-law to Arif Dikkarani who had studied with him before joining Amir Kulal. It was said of Baha ad-din Kishlaki that he was the most accomplished spiritual leader and guide of his time. He was equally proficient in science and spirituality. He was also said to possess extraordinary powers of clairvoyance and healing. Baha ad-din Naqshbandi first met Mawlana Kishlaki in the winter quarters of Sultan Mubarak Shah. He said to him: "You are a bird that flies so high that the only person to be your companion and friend is Arif Dikkarani." When he said this, there arose in Khwaja Naqshbandi a burning wish to meet Arif. Without a word, Kishlaki went to the roof of his house and facing the south three times shouted "Arif, Arif, Arif!" At that time, Arif was sowing cotton seed in a field twenty parasangs (sixty miles) away. He received the message and set out at midday. He arrived in time for the evening meal and his friendship with Naqshbandi began that very day. Baha ad-din Naqshbandi took Ārif for his teacher. In his life, Naqshbandi referred to his years with Ārif as: "a continuous search for the secret of liberation". They travelled together in Turkestan, Persia and Iraq and went on a pilgrimage to Mecca. Naqshbandi learned the value of humiliation and abasement. Ārif would never accept any kind of present, considering that to accept is a disaster for the recipient. He said: "The giver of a gift acquires the *baraka,* merit, which the recipient forfeits. Only a perfected man can have the grace that makes gifts harmless. I do not have that grace."

When Ārif Dikkarānī felt the moment of death approaching, he sent for Khwaja Baha ad-din, who went post haste from Merv to Bukhara. He was lying sick in his home village of Dikkaran. He sent for Muhammad Pārsā, then a young novice, and speaking to both of them said: "You know that complete unity exists between us. We have shared many events. Now the time of parting has come. I have watched your relationship and I want Muhammad to place himself at Baha ad-din's service to lighten his burden. He will go to the end of the path and achieve final liberation. You do not have to carry his burden." He died three days later. The *Rashahāt* states that Baha ad-din's association with Ārif lasted for thirty years and that they were ready to travel anywhere to find 'People of the Truth'.

When Ārif died, Baha ad-din Naqshbandi, following counsel given to him by Amīr Kulal, went to Shaikh Qāsim, who was one of Ahmad Yasawī's successors. He remained with him only three months, but a very close friendship was established and whenever Shaikh Qasim visited Bukhara, he made a point of inviting Baha ad-din. It does not seem that there was a teacher-pupil relationship, but rather that there were certain techniques known to the shaikhs of Chinese Turkestan that the Masters wished to investigate.

After Shaikh Qāsim, Baha ad-din attached himself to the greatest of the Turkish Shaikhs, Khalīl Atā, as a result of a vision that had come to him some years before. The story is given in the *Nafahāt al-Uns.* The vision came during Baha ad-din's novitiate: he was told to find a dervish by name of Khalīl and was also shown his face. From that time, he was constantly on the watch: "One day", says Baha ad-din, "when I was in the Great Bazaar of Bukhara, I saw and recognised him. Owing to the crowd, I lost sight of him almost at once. I asked his name and was told he was Khahl Ata. I returned home very distressed. A porter came and said: 'that dervish Khahl is asking for you'. It was a very hot summer evening and I picked up a handful of fruit and ran to the place where he was staying. As soon as I saw him, I asked permission to tell him my vision. He spoke in Turkish and said: 'What does an old dream matter now that we are face to face?' I felt so powerfully drawn towards him that I abandoned all that I was doing and asked to follow him''.

Not long afterwards, Khahl Ata succeeded to the throne of Turkestan. He was a descendant of Chinghis Khān and he ruled in Bukhārā for six years during which time Bahā ad-dīn remained in his service. Khahl is described by the historians of central Asia as a mild ruler who did not engage in wars of conquest but attempted, as his father had done, to repair the ravages of the Mongol conquest. He faced difficulties with the great landowners and merchants who had become very powerful during a time of weak central rule and were mercilessly exploiting the artisan classes and the farmers. There was also rivalry between the landowners and the official leaders of religion, who owed their authority to their superior education and experience. Khahl attempted to make a fair balance and, in this, he made use of the power of the Masters to influence the people. It was a time when trade was reviving rapidly between China and the West, and Samarkand and Bukhārā were great caravan centres. The great landowners financed the merchants and participated in the profits. Khahl was greatly loved and respected by the common people of Samarkand and Tashkent, but he aroused the hostility of the nobles and it was only the awe engendered by the blood of Chinghis Khān that enabled him to keep his place without resorting to the wholesale execution of his descendants that was customary in the Khānates at that time.

Bahā ad-dīn was closely involved in the administration. Khahl found time for his training. In his autobiography, Bahā ad-dīn writes: "He showed me great kindness. He taught me how to serve; sometimes by severity and sometimes by gentleness. I was able to make great progress in my spiritual life. Khahl Ata once said that: 'Whoever, in the name of God Almighty, sets himself to help me, will become great among the people'. He often repeated this and I understood very well what he intended to convey."

After six years, the Sultanate collapsed after a revolt by the nobility supported by the army, and central Turkestan fell into disorder. "In a flash", wrote Baha ad-din, "all the labour of so many years was destroyed. From that time, I lost all confidence in the affairs of this world. I saw that the best of men is helpless in front of the greed and selfishness of the people. I left Samarkand and returned to Bukhara and lived in the village of Riwda a few miles from the city."

It was not until he was fifty that Khwaja Baha ad-din accepted the role of *murshid*. He continued for twenty-four years until his death in 1389. During his Masterhood, he went for a second time on the pilgrimage to Mecca, this time accompanied by Muhammad Parsa. He sent Parsa and other companions to Nishapur and himself went to visit Mawlana Zain ad-din Taihadi at Herat. On his return from Mecca, he spent some time in Merv and then settled in Bukhara where he remained until the end of his life.

During his twenty-four years of Masterhood Baha ad-din gained an immense reputation throughout the Islamic world. The *Rashahat* describes the way in which influential people sought his approval in their major decisions. Once the King of Herat sent to say that he ardently desired to converse with Baha ad-din and invited him to visit Herat as his guest. He said to his pupils: "It is no part of our duty to deal with kings and sultans, but if we don't go to him, he will come to us and this will be a burden on the dervishes and a calamity for the people. So I had better go to Herat."

The King received Baha ad-din with the utmost respect. The great landowners, rich merchants and the priesthood were all present to do him honour. The Khwaja did not respond to all this show. Suspecting the purity of the food, he would not eat a morsel at the table. Even when they brought him game freshly killed and entirely acceptable according to the common law, he would not touch it. The King personally begged him to accept at least a mouthful; but he was adamant.

The King asked him some questions: "Did this Mastership come to you by inheritance?" He replied: "It is not an inheritance but a vocation. This blessing came to me as a gift."

Q. "Do you encourage withdrawal into solitude?"
A. "The term 'solitude in the crowd' is one of the sayings of one of the great ones of our path, Khwaja Abd al-Khaliq

Ghujduwani."
Q. "What does 'solitude in the crowd' mean?"
A. "Outwardly to be with the people, inwardly to be with God."
Q. "Is it possible for man to achieve this?"
A. "If it had not been possible, God would not have commended it in the Quran."
Q. "Some shaikhs say that Sainthood is loftier than Prophethood. What kind of a Saint can be more than a Prophet?"
A. "This refers to the saintliness of the Prophets themselves. Saintliness in a Prophet is loftier than the gift of prophesy."

After this conversation, the Khwaja arose and went to stay at the guest house of Abdallah Ansari. He did not accept a single present from among the costly gifts sent by the King. He said: "All my life God has allowed me to live without receiving gifts from anyone and I will not change now". The King then sent him a shirt, a scarf and a shawl that he had bought with money he had personally earned and which was, therefore, free from stain, saying that he implored the Khwaja to accept at least these tokens. Once again he refused, in spite of the fact that at that time he did not possess even one shirt and his turban was in rags.

Khwaja Baha ad-din used to fast frequently, but whenever a visitor came to his house, he would break the fast to honour the guest. One day one of his pupils refused to join a guest on the grounds that he was engaged in a fast. The Khwaja said: "That man is far from God, or he would see God in the guest and see where his obligation lies."

Some of the sayings of Baha ad-din convey a picture of the methods of transmission the Masters used.

"When I began the repetition exercise, *zikr,* I became aware that a very great secret was close at hand. I became a seeker after that secret."

"In my days of discipleship, according to the heritage of Khwaja Baba Samasi, I listened to many traditions and I talked with many learned men. But on my path, that which helped me the most was abasement and humiliation. I entered by that gate and whatever I may have found, that is how I found it."

"To deny, humiliate and annihilate oneself is of prime importance in this Way. This provides the foundation for the possibility of claiming to succeed. It is thus that I passed through all the human states and learnt their properties. I saw that all beings, in their essence, were better than I. Finally I arrived at the class of beings who had lost their value and their reputation. I found great good in them, but none in myself. I came to possess the state of a dog; and believed I would find no profit in this. But I slowly came to realise that this state contained as much profit as any other. I am better informed about myself than about anybody; I am not better than a dog, but worse. However I regard my state, it is not worth a grain from head to foot."

"I learned utter devotion to the Search for Truth from a gambler. I watched a gambler lose everything he possessed and when a comrade begged him to give it up, he answered: 'Ah my friend, if I had to give my head for this game, I could not do without it.' When I heard this, my heart was flooded with amazement and ever since I have pursued Truth with the same single-mindedness."

"Our way is that of group discussion. In solitude, there is renown and in renown there is peril. Welfare is to be found in a group. Those who follow this way find great benefit and blessing in group-meetings."

"We do not accept everyone and if we do accept we do so with difficulty."

"The conditions of acceptance as they should duly be imposed are hard to fulfill. Either a pupil with capacity appears and a Master fit to receive him is lacking, or a Master is there and pupils with capacity are lacking." This was said on the occasion of the admission of Yaqūb Charkhī to the *halqa*.

"When I was responsible for groups, my state was such that whenever I was aware of two or three in conversation, I lent an ear. If they were conversing of God, I was blissful; if they were talking of anything else, I became sad and heavy at heart."

"We are means for reaching the goal. It is necessary that seekers should cut themselves away from us and think only of the goal."

"The capacity of all hearts is the same but the practical wisdom within the heart is very different from one heart to another."

"If I were to look at the faults of my friends, I would be left without a friend. For there is no faultless friend. Everyone loves good people. The art is to learn how to love bad people."

A famous learned man asked what was the purpose of the way

he followed. Khwāja Bahā ad-dīn answered: "The clarification of practical wisdom." "And what is that?" asked his interlocutor. "There are things to be believed that have been transmitted by reliable informants but only in a summary way. The clarification of practical wisdom consists in showing people how to discover them in their own personal experience."

"It is not possible for man to attain the secret of union, *tawhīd*. To attain the secret of practical wisdom, *marifat*, is difficult but not impossible."

His son-in-law and first successor, Khwāja Alā ad-dīn Attār, used to tell the story of how in the early days of his membership of the *halqā*, he was speaking to a 'person of the way' at Ramatān, about the heart. "I said that I did not know the true nature of the heart. This person said that in his opinion the heart was like the moon three days old. I told this to our beloved Khwāja Bahā ad-dīn. At the moment he was standing up. He placed his foot on mine. At that moment a great bliss came over me and I felt myself in contact with All Truth. When I recovered from this state, he said: 'That is the heart; not what the dervish said. How can you expect to know the true heart, *qalb*, unless you have direct experience of it?' "

"Whoever is able to see the hidden faults in his own nature and take them under his control will certainly reach felicity. The follower of the way should be able to raise up his whole being in the Presence of God and test himself. In this way, he can pass from an imitated faith to the true substantial faith."

"Some shaikhs adjust their behaviour towards their followers according to the capacities of the latter. If the follower is a beginner he takes his burden off his back. He even sets himself to serve his own pupil, but from those who are more perfected he makes greater and greater demands and requires of them an ever greater perfection."

"Decision, submission, self-denial, all have their special meanings. Our aim in this path must be to enable those who follow to feel the attraction working spontaneously in them, *jazba*, but sometimes it may be necessary for us to train them by instruction. We should make use of the experience of those who are wise in the way and we should learn how to pass this experience on to others. For each follower, different things are required at different times. One moment it is service, another struggle with oneself, at another moment it is meditation and at another it is self-evaluation.

"We are the means whereby the seeker can reach his aim. Our task is to provide the seeker with everything that he needs to reach his aim. A pupil must pray but he must not do so in such a way as to strengthen his own egoism. However earnestly and intelligently he may pray, he must still always see himself as full of defects. Whoever prays with confidence in himself, remains far from the Truth. Khwaja Abd al-Khaliq Ghudjuwani and Muhammad Samasi were examples of humility and self-abnegation."

We come now to the training of Khwaja Ubaidallah Ahrar of Tashkent. Ubaidallah dominated central Asia for the greater part of the fifteenth century and all historians agree that his influence was paramount. During his boyhood, he was very poor. He says that at the time of Sultan Shahrukh, he was living in Herat and did not even have a change of clothes. The turban on his head was in rags and he could only afford one kaftan a year which wore so thin that the cotton showed through. He said: "I used to do service for many people but I never had either a horse or a donkey. On account of the thinness and shortness of my clothes, the lower part of my body never got warm. In my search for God, the whole of the time – even the middle of winter – I never had a basin of warm water for my ablutions. Sometimes I used to get up from the meetings of Shaikh Baha ad-din Umar and had to go to the town for my ablutions. I often used to wonder if the Shaikh would offer me some means of melting the ice so that I could do my ablutions, but this never happened."

During the five years that he stayed in Herat, in spite of his poverty and need, he never accepted help from anyone. According to the *Rashahat,* to the very end of his life he would never accept any kind of present.

With regard to his poverty, he himself describes how one day he went to Sayyid Qasim Tabrizi. The Sayyid gave him half a plate of food which he was eating and said: "Hey, Crown Prince of Turkestan, as suffering has been a protection for me, may it be so for you also in the invisible world." Khwaja Ubaidallah said: "When the Sayyid said these words, I was extremely poor. I had nothing whatever of worldly goods. My personal wealth and prosperity I know came from the *baraka* that Qasim Tabrizi breathed on me that day".

In later years he told his disciples of early visions and

experiences. "I saw in a dream the Prophet Jesus. I was then just fifteen years old. The Holy Lord was standing erect at the head of the tomb of Khwaja Abu Bakr Shasi. I fell at his blessed feet. He raised my head from the ground saying, 'Do not be troubled. It is well that I myself should undertake your training.' When I told this dream to some older friends, they said that it indicated that I was to follow the art of medicine. I interpreted the dream in my own fashion with the thought that if He, the Greatest Healer of souls, undertook to train one so unworthy as I, this could only mean that I would be given the power and the insight to purify the hearts of men. Very soon after, this interpretation was verified when I discovered that I was able to see into the hidden states of those who came to me and give them comfort."

In another of his dreams he saw the Prophet Muhammad, who ordered him to lift him up and carry him on his shoulders to the top of a mountain. He did so. The Holy Lord then said: "I knew that you had the strength to do this. My purpose was to prove your faith." In yet another dream he was made to witness an assembly of the followers of Khwaja Baha ad-din Naqshbandi and understand the inner secrets of the Master's teaching.

At this time, he passed through the stage of loss of personal identity, which rarely occurs even in exceptional seekers until many years of search. He says: "At that time, my inner state was invaded by such a flood of self-abasement, that I worshipped everyone I met. It did not matter if they were slave or free, white or black, lowly or great, master or servant, I would fall at their feet and beg them to help my soul." By the time he was eighteen, his zikr had become so strong, that like the followers of Abd al-Khaliq Ghujduwani, he did not hear or see anything even in the tumult of a crowded bazaar.

When he was twenty-two years old, his uncle Khwaja Ibrahim brought him from Tashkent to Samarkand to be educated. Nevertheless, on account of his passionate interest in the inner wisdom and mysticism, he could not make anything of ordinary learning. In spite of the insistence of his uncle, he would spend his time in Samarkand going to the meetings of the Masters of Wisdom and listening to their conversation. He tried to force himself to go to school, but only became ill. Finally, when he had a very painful eye infection, he realised that he could not continue learning. In later life, he used to say that his education got as far as page two of the alphabet.

After spending two years in this way in Samarkand, at the age of twenty-four he went to Herat and studied there for five years. During this time he was continually with the Masters of Wisdom in the principle centres of Turkestan, from the Gobi desert and the Hindu Kush, to the Caspian Sea and the Caucasus.

According to his own account: "Until I was twenty-nine years of age, I was a pilgrim. Five years before the plague year, I returned to Tashkent." As the plague fell in 1436, he must have settled in Tashkent in 1431.

In speaking of his pilgrimage, Khwāja Ahrār pointed to Sayyid Qāsim Tabrīzī as the most important person he had met. "In all my life, I have not met a more highly developed person. I met many of the notable teachers of the age, but when I had passed a time in their company and attended their meetings sooner or later a state came over me that obliged me to leave them. But the well-being I experienced in the presence of Sayyid Qāsim never diminished. Whenever I entered his presence it seemed that I was in the very centre of Reality and that it was established firm and unshakable." For his part, Sayyid Qāsim Tabrīzī was devoted to Ubaidallah Ahrār. In the usual way, he used not to allow visitors to stay near him very long but when Khwāja Ahrār came to his meetings he would prolong them. He instructed his people to admit Ahrār whenever he arrived.

At their first meeting, he asked the Khwāja's name. When he learned that it was Ubaidallāh (meaning the obedient servant of God) he said: "It is right that you should attain the Reality of your name." This saying is explained in the *Rashahāt* as follows: "The noble Sayyid by these words indicated that the true significance of being a servant of God, *Abdallāh*, is revealed only to those who have become worthy of knowing the reality of God's will. In every age one single man reaches that level of perfection. He is called the *Qutb al-Aqtāb*, Axis of the World." When the shaikh said that Ahrār was to 'realise his name', he signified that he was destined to become the Great Axis and the Highest Caliph.

One of the Sayyid Qāsim's associates, Mawlānā Fathallāh of Tabrīz, reports that whenever Khwāja Ahrār visited him and sat down in his presence, Qāsim Tabrīzī would begin to speak of the most profound secrets of the Divine Reality. The most amazing revelations would come in the course of the conversation. This never happened unless Ahrār was present. One day after such a conversation, after Khwāja Ubaidallāh had left, Sayyid Qāsim spoke to Fathallāh and said: "Such profound discussions are very attractive: but their virtue does not end with listening. If you wish to attain the object and to know the felicity it holds for you, my advice to you is to catch hold of the robe of that young Turkestani and never l et it go, for he is destined to become the jewel of the age. Many wonderful things will happen through him. If by a miracle the world were able to perceive the light that he sheds about him and were to become sensitive to his *baraka*, then many hearts would reach eternal felicity, and love and friendship would be established in many a heart."

One day Sayyid Qāsim said to Ubaidallāh: "Do you know why in these times wisdom and truth appear so seldom? It is because the inner foundation is lacking. This inner foundation cannot be established without pure spiritual nourishment. In our day, pure nourishment has diminished and in consequence purity of heart can no longer be found. This is why Divine Secrets must be concealed."

Khwāja Ahrār was attracted by Shaikh Bahā ad-dın Umar. This personage used to speak freely with visitors; but according to the custom of the path he followed, he went from time to time into retirement. During the five years he was in Herat, Khwāja Ahrār used to visit him two or three times a week.

It was when he returned to Tashkent that he became interested in agriculture. Following an inner vision that was given to him, he took a small piece of land and a pair of oxen provided by his family and planted seed according to the indications he had received in his vision. From the start, his crops were amazing and he discovered the secret of finding the right crop for every kind of land. The result of this was that many people developed their own land under his direction. Within a few years, he became one of the biggest farmers in Turkestan. He was responsible for introducing the system of cropping that made Turkestan for centuries the granary of Asia. In this connection he said: "God Almighty gave me such an extraordinary insight into the needs of plants and animals that I can produce three, five or even ten times more from the land than other farmers do. In the time of Sultan Ahmad Mirzād, I used to send to him eight hundred thousand bushels of corn every year."

Khwāja Ahrār's initiation into the Khwājagān was not made by Qāsim Tabrızı, but by Mawlāna Yaqūb Charkhı who was

one of the close pupils of Baha ad-din Naqshbandi. The
Mawlana had studied natural science at Herat and Bukhara and
had also gone to Egypt to learn about Egyptian astronomy.
When he returned to Bukhara on his way home, he met Khwaja
Baha ad-din to whom he said: "Please give me your blessing".
Baha ad-din replied: "How much more time are you going to
waste before coming to me?" Charkhi replied: "I am anxious to
enter your service". Charkhi then goes on to say: "This reply
surprised me because a few minutes before there was no such
thought in my mind. Baha ad-din then asked me why and I
answered without thinking: 'Because you are a great man and all
the people respect you". Baha ad-din said: 'You must find a
better reason than that'. I then said: 'There is a saying of the
Prophet that if God makes a person his friend, that friendship will
touch the hearts of those around him.' When I said these words
he smiled and said: 'We are one of those whom God loves'. At
this I was struck dumb because just one month previously in a
dream I heard a voice saying to me: 'Become a pupil of God's
beloved'. I had forgotten this dream and it suddenly came back to
me." Following this he went back to Herat and settled his affairs
and remained with Baha ad-din until his death. After the death of
Baha ad-din Naqshbandi, Yaqub joined Khwaja Ala ad-din
Attar and remained with him until the end of his life.

Ahrar had heard strange stories about this man Yaqub Charkhi
and felt that he must know more about him. He describes the
event himself in his own words: "After studying for four years at
Herat, I set out with the intention of seeking instruction from
Mawlana Yaqub Charkhi. I had heard some years earlier that
there was a person of this name who understood the subtleties of
the way of the Masters."

"When I arrived at Chiganiyan where Mawlana Yaqub was
living, I felt ill. This held me up for twenty days. During this
time I heard unpleasant things about Mawlana Charkhi and
nearly gave up my intention to visit him. However, having come
such a long distance I felt it would be stupid to return without at
least meeting him."

"I arrived in his presence and he showed me the most
extraordinary courtesy and attention. I went again the next day
and again he showered so many compliments on me that I was
thoroughly embarrassed. I felt that I could not leave without
understanding what it all meant and for this reason I put away

the doubts that his way of talking had engendered. Within an hour, he once again started speaking with extravagant praise of myself and my doings and told me the story of how he had come to meet Khwāja Bahā ad-dīn Naqshbandī. Then, stretching out his hands, he said: 'Come and make your oath'. At that moment I saw in his eyes a whiteness like leprosy, enough to give one the horrors, and I could not find it in my heart to take the oath. The Mawlānā, perceiving my inner feeling at once, withdrew his hands and, as if he were changing his clothes, he transformed his face to such a beauty that all my reservations disappeared and I nearly jumped to my feet and took him in my arms. Yaqūb Charkhī again stretched out his hands and said: 'His Holiness Bahā ad-dīn Naqshbandī took my hand in his and said to me: "Your hand is my hand; whoever holds your hand has held my hand." This hand is the hand of Khwāja Bahā ad-dīn Naqshbandī. Have no doubt and hold it.' I took his sacred hand in mine and he at once taught me the way of conscious labour. He added: 'This is what came to me from Khwāja Naqshbandī. If you wish, you can train your own pupils by the way of labour and suffering.' After spending three months in frequent meetings, Mawlānā Yaqūb gave me permission to return home. When I went to take leave of him he gave me the complete initiation into the way of the Masters. His final words were: 'You have been admitted to this sacred brotherhood and you must be constantly on your guard to preserve its sanctity. May you be the means of bringing capable seekers to the truth'."

Ahrār's teaching was recorded in the *Nafahāt al-Uns* and the *Rashahāt*. The following is typical.

"There are two kinds of pride. One is the pride we all know and this is to be rejected. The other, acceptable pride is not to place one's trust in anything but the Supreme Reality. This is a noble pride and it leads to annihilation."

"Khwāja Muhammad Pārsā told us that the continuous prayer, *zikr dawām*, reaches a stage at which the substance of the prayer and the substance of the heart become one and the same. In my opinion, the meaning of this must be that the substance of prayer is composed of letters and breath. The substance of the heart is a subtle awareness embracing both form and content. When prayer reaches perfection these two substances unite and it is no longer possible to separate the prayer from him who prays. At that moment nothing but the object (that is reality) can enter and both prayer and the one who prays become nothing with the object – reality."

The author of the *Rashahāt* reports that Ubaidallāh Ahrār once said to him: "The sum of all the various sciences is revelation, the acts of Muhammad and the law. The sum of all these is the science of Sufism. The sum of Sufism is the assertion of *Presence*. They say that at all levels, there is only one Presence; but that this is perceived according to each person's own capacity. This statement is very hard and subtle. To grasp it, reason, imagination and thought must all be brought to bear. Those possess the required intelligence who are able to take their own reality as a mirror and search for the signs that will reveal it. To this they must devote themselves entirely. In the light of the Presence, the subtle elements of the reality will little by little reveal themselves. Those who have become aware of the mystery of destiny are at peace. For they know that the visible universe is completely void and non-existent. They know also that the Supreme Reality is manifested in every light and shade of this cosmic illusion. Their peace resembles that of the waves re-absorbed into the ocean.

"Such an intimate contact with reality is to be attained that neither water can wash it away nor fire burn it up."

As the last example of the Masters' training, we can look at the great poet Mawlānā Jāmī whose prose works and poems have had an influence second only to that of Jalal ad–dīn Rūmī upon the spiritual life of central Asia. Mawlānā Jāmī was born in 1414 and died in 1492 at Herat. He was born in the year that Sultan Shahrukh established his ascendancy throughout the domains of his father Tamerlane. He was personally initiated by Khwāja Saad ad-dīn Kāshghari, but his chief inspiration was Khwāja Ubaidallāh Ahrār. In the course of his travels, he met most of the great spiritual leaders of his time.

He went with his father to Herat and studied in the Nizāmiyya School near to the Iraq Gate. In the story of his life, a detailed account is given of the Masters with whom he studied. He went to Samarkand and studied at the Academy of Mirzā Ulug Beg. Because it was the main attraction at Samarkand at that time, many of the greatest scholars of the age came and lectured in the Academy. The Principal of the Academy, Qādi Zāda, said of him: "Since this place was established, no seeker so full of promise has come to us from beyond the Amu Darya." One day the famous astronomer and mathematician Alī Kushchu came into a lecture and asked some very difficult questions. Jāmī, without stopping to think, gave full answers to each one of them. Ah Kushchu was dumb with surprise and later used to say to his own followers: "From that day I understood that there are still people in the world who receive their knowledge direct from God, for that young man could not possibly have known beforehand the things that he said."

Mawlānā Jāmī used to go and talk with Mawlānā Saad ad-dīn Kāshgharī both before and after the midday prayer. At that time, Jāmī fell in love with a young beauty. In order to get her out of his mind, he left Herat and went to Samarkand. One night in a dream, he saw Kāshgharī who said to him: "Brother listen to me, you find a beloved whom you cannot leave." This experience had a great impact on Jāmī and he went straight back to Khurasān and turned his attention to mysticism towards which he already had a strong leaning. He then set himself to fulfill Kāshgharī's 'command' and regularly attended meetings and followed his instructions. Saad ad-dīn said at that time: "Today a royal one has come on to our soil. God has sent me this Jāmī to make me rejoice". One of Jāmī's science teachers – Muhammad Jajurmī – said in this connection: "In five hundred years one real scientist has appeared on the soil of Khurasān and now Saad ad-dīn Kāshgharī has stolen him away."

When he abandoned science and mathematics in order to follow the path of mysticism, Saad ad-dīn Kāshgharī instructed him to follow a programme of strict privation and self-denial. He withdrew altogether from contact with the world and spent his time in solitary meditation. After this experience, which lasted two years, he was told once again to meet with worldly people. He found it very hard to speak at all and could not even remember the words that he wanted to use without making a special effort. This state of being withdrawn whilst still in contact with people lasted a considerable time but gradually disappeared.

About this period, Jāmī himself wrote: "At the beginning, various lights and colours appeared to me. On the orders of Mawlānā Saad ad-dīn, I rejected these visions until they ceased to come. He explained to me that it is necessary to reject visions and spiritual blessings. The greatest blessing for a dervish is to be taken out of himself and find that his self does not return." When he told the story of his training, one of his pupils asked him:

"How is it that some people receive spiritual blessings whereas others remain closed?" He replied: "There are two kinds of search. One is by tradition or transmission. The seeker who follows this way enters the world of manifestation and must return to the source by the same path. The other way is the way of purification, which is the way of the Masters. In this way the tradition counts for nothing; all that matters is to keep one's intention exclusively fixed on the Supreme Being". On another occasion he was asked: "What is the reason why you, who have such a mastery of languages, so seldom use Sufi technical terms?" His reply was: "Our aim is to have direct perception of the truth not to talk cleverly about it". Another pupil asked him to show him something that he would be able to keep for the rest of his life. He laid his hand on his breast and said: "It is here the whole business: in the heart. You will find everything there".

Although Jāmī recognised Khwāja Ahrār as the greatest teacher of the age and the support of spirituality all over the world, he only met him occasionally. He went three times to Samarkand. The first was during the time of Mirzā Ulug Beg to study with Qādī Zāda. The second was in the year 1466 and the third was in 1469. On this last visit he met Khwāja Ahrār while he was on his way to make peace between the two sons of Sultan Abū Saīd Mirzā. They had met in Tashkent and after peace-making was achieved, Jāmī remained with Ahrār for a number of days. According to the report of Ahrār's own pupils, most of the time was spent in silence. Occasionally Khwāja Ubaidallāh would say something that would surprise everyone present, making them realise that Ahrār and Jāmī were able to communicate without speaking.

These conversations lasted for fifteen days after which Jāmī returned to Samarkand. Afterwards they had regular correspondence, most of which has unfortunately been lost, but some of the letters have been preserved and show that they were able to express themselves in a form that no other reader could decipher. Ahrār used to send many of his pupils to Jāmī and praised him very highly. He used to say: "Whoever has seen Mawlana Jāmī in Khurasān has no need to cross the river."

After the deaths of Ahrār and Jāmī, the Masters of Wisdom no longer took the title of Khwāja. At this time, the Naqshbandī Brotherhood was taking shape and in the sixteenth century spread first to Turkey through Shaikh Fazl-i Ilāhī and his pupil

Saīd Ahmad Bukharī. The brotherhood also established itself in India and reached as far as Indonesia and the Solomon Islands. In the West it reached the whole of the Ottoman Empire and went beyond it into Morocco. This brotherhood has remained to the present time as the most powerful influence in the Islamic world. The title of Khwaja, however, disappeared. It was adopted by a dynasty in Kāshgharia that remained until the Russian conquest in the nineteenth century. I have been able to get information about the Khwajas in Kashgharia only from Russian sources which are prejudiced and hostile. They represented the Khwājas as power-seeking tyrants who opposed the people and dominated over the rulers. According to Gurdjieff, who visited the region forty years after the Russian conquest of Kāshgharia, the Khwājas were still spiritual leaders but withdrawn into the schools hidden in the oases in deserts north of Tibet.

Chapter Ten

The Master Peacemakers

Between 1360 and 1530, central Asia was dominated by extraordinary conquerors and rulers, beginning with Tamerlane (1336–1405) and ending with Bābur, the founder of the Mogul empire in India (1471–1530) and Shāh Ismāīl (1499–1524) who recreated the Persian empire and founded the Safavid dynasty. Nevertheless the truly great rulers of this period were Shāhrukh, Tamerlane's fourth son, who ruled in Herat for forty years and his son Ulug Beg who created the Golden Age of Samarkand. Abū Saīd and Husain Baiqara were almost equally great and wise rulers. The reason for their mention here is that all of them from Tamerlane to Bābur* were deeply religious men and nearly all turned to the Kwājagan as their spiritual guides. The Masters of Wisdom came out into the open and accepted responsibilities that would have been unthinkable in the time of Abd al-Khāliq Ghujduwāni or Bahā ad-dīn Naqshbandī.

At the end of the fourteenth century of the Christian era, all the nations from China to Spain were thrown into consternation by the devastating conquests of Amīr Timur, known in the west as Tamerlane. No conqueror has ever devastated so great a part of the inhabited world; yet he was also a profoundly religious man and believed that he was guided by divine providence. He had deep respect for his spiritual guides and was ready to change

---

* *Editor's note.* The emperor Bābur rendered into verse a tract on the *tarīqat* or way of the Khwājagān written by Ahrār. The Khwāja also appeared to him in a dream to tell him he would get Samarkand, which is reminiscent of Tamerlane's dream of Yasawī.

his plans on their advice. He was also a patron of the arts and a bon viveur, whose splendid court astounded the emissary of the king of Spain no less than the ambassadors from China and Egypt. He died in 1404 and his vast empire – stretching from China and India, to Egypt, Hungary and Poland, and from Siberia to the Indian Ocean – disintegrated, leaving a state of utter confusion. The central area of Turkestan and Persia remained under the rule of his family, but the outer regions of China, India, Turkey and Russia, soon regained their independence and, in some way, seemed to have been re-invigorated by the shock of his passage. In Turkestan, the situation looked very bad. Timur's sons and nephews disputed the succession and the terrible family wars that had for centuries been the bane of central Asia, seemed once again to threaten the lives and homes of the people who remembered the two centuries that it had taken to recover from the first Mongol invasions under Chinghis Khān.

Events took a very different course. Timur's son Shāhrukh succeeded in pacifying the country, and his son Ulug Beg – whom he made viceroy of Turkestan – created one of the highest cultures in art, architecture and science that the world had ever known. The thirty-eight years of Ulug Beg's rule were the Golden Age of Samarkand. He himself was a renowned mathematician and astronomer whose tables were, for three centuries, used throughout the world as the most complete and accurate record of solar and planetary movements. During his rule also, Bukhārā became the centre of Islamic spirituality, and an extraordinary tolerance towards all religions replaced the fanaticism of the Saljuk Turks. Jews, Christians and Buddhists were free to practise their religions and pilgrims came from all parts of the world. Throughout the fifteenth and sixteenth centuries, Turkestan was the centre of the world's spiritual activity. Its influence reached from Japan to England and Spain and the period was one of relative peace compared with the incessant wars that had ravaged the country for centuries. Though incursions of nomads from the north resulted in the periodic destruction of great buildings and works of art, the spiritual life of Bukhārā remained unbroken. When we closely examine the course of events, we can discern everywhere the influence of the Khwājagān, or Masters of Wisdom. The Khwājagān had an immense influence with the rulers, the great landowners and merchants, as well as with the common people. They were able by their mere presence to stop war; by their word alone, to remove unjust and cruel rulers. Extraordinary powers were attributed to them, not only by their own disciples but by sober and sometimes unfriendly historians. In the seventeenth century, the Masters retired from the scene, but their traditions were preserved in brotherhoods, some of which still exist. The most influential are the Naqshbandīs, who have millions of adherents throughout the Muslim world and exercise a powerful, though hidden, influence in nearly twenty countries.

Tamerlane established his empire in Bukhārā and Samarkand, which he always regarded as his home. His first conquests were in Persia and Mesopotamia. He then over-ran Russia, sacked Moscow and threatened to conquer all of Europe, which would have been defenceless, had he not turned his attention to India where he penetrated further than Alexander the Great or Chinghis Khān. He established his authority as far as Delhi and beyond. Turning westward again, he took Damascus and broke the power of the Mamluk sultans of Egypt. Finally he conquered and captured that other great conqueror Sultan Bayazīd, surnamed the "Thunderer", who had pushed his own conquests to the walls of Vienna. As Gibbon wrote: "From the Irtysh and the Volga to the Persian Gulf, from the Ganges to Damascus and the Archipelago, all Asia was in the hands of Timur."

We must see what kind of a man he was. He left two books, the *Malfūzāt* or Memoirs and *Tūzukāt* or Institutes. The former gives an account — not always reliable — of his life and doings. The latter sets out the principles on which he based his strategy and policy of government. All historians agree that Tamerlane was not only the bravest of the brave but also profoundly sagacious, generous, experienced and persevering. A combination of these qualities made him "an unopposed leader of men and a very God of War, adored by all ranks."*

Amīr Timur himself had the deepest regard for his own spiritual director Khwāja Sayyid Baraka who was a disciple of Bahā ad-dīn. Timur also believed himself to be guided and inspired by Khwāja Ahmad Yasāwī, the great Turkish Master of the twelfth century. Bayazīd was completely defeated by Tamerlane at Ankara and the battle is the one already referred to

---

* Sir Percy Sykes, *History of Persia* Vol. 2 p. 134.

where Tamerlane repeated the poem given to him in a dream by Khwāja Ahmad Yasāwī.*

Amīr Timur died in 1405 in his seventieth year. He was on his way to a final campaign in China. When dying he was occupied in prayer and asked a Mawlānā to read the Qurān until he was sure he had finally left his body. He was buried in the same tomb as his teacher Khwāja Baraka. His successors ruled in Transoxania for a century. They were followed by the Uzbeg sultans whose domination ended in 1597. Meanwhile the great Persian dynasty of the Safavids had been founded in Persia by Shāh Ismāil. All these rulers, some good, some wicked, some warlike, some artists and poets and some even Sufis and saints, accepted the Khwājagān as the source of spiritual guidance. For more than two hundred years the influence of the Masters was the pillar of social stability. Until the end of the fourteenth century they kept in the background helping to repair the ravages of the Mongol invasions and to re-establish agriculture and craftmanship. We have seen how Khwāja Bahā ad-dīn Naqshbandī avoided contact with kings and princes and yet undoubtedly exercised a great influence on their behaviour towards the common people. The merciless taxation which had done as much as war to make life unbearable, was greatly alleviated by the prudent administration of viziers, many of whom were disciples of the Khwājagān.

If we read the accounts of Persian historians we have the impression of devastation, massacre and whole countries reduced to misery. I have read all the histories that I can lay my hands on, including those of Rashīd ad-dīn and Alā ad-dīn Juwainī: the emphasis is always upon the conflict of monarchs, wars and devastation. When there are peaceful periods these are passed over with little comment, with the result that the reader gets the impression that central Asia has been, for centuries, the scene of almost continuous wars and the people in a state of wretchedness. When I turned to the story of the Masters of Wisdom as accounted in books like the *Rashahāt Ain al-Hayāt* or the *Nafahāt al-Uns,* or the personal stories of Bahā ad-dīn Naqshbandī or Mawlana Jami, a very different picture emerges: the periods of peace and the rulers who did not go to war, show themselves as the significant leaders in history.

I have seen similar differences in events of which I have been a

* *c.f.* Chapter Six pp. 129-130.

witness, such as the forced exchanges of Greeks and Turks in 1925 which were described by historians as causing great misery and loss of life. The really important feature of these events, as I saw it, was the great courage with which people overcame their difficulties and the benefit to their countries in the new blood that was brought across the sea.

The contradictions between the political and spiritual versions of events in the fourteenth-century are partly explained by the wish of the Masters to avoid public approval and fame. On the contrary, they all, without exception, understood the importance of humiliation and poverty. Khahl Ata was one of the few rulers who refused to have any court or add to his personal fortune. Baha ad-dın would not have accepted the task of chancellor to the sultan if he had not regarded it as part of his own spiritual training and, when Khahl was finally deposed, he faithfully made his way back to his village and avoided all contact with rulers and princes.

When we come to the fifteenth century, we can verify the Masters' own accounts from the records of contemporary historians; but when they filter through modern writers, almost everything is lost. The Masters of Wisdom are represented as saintly men, revered by the population and respected by the rulers. Some writers even see them as teaching a dreamy, mystical religion that was divorced from practical life. This kind of criticism has been made again and again whenever wise men have succeeded in convincing people that man's true welfare is in the spiritual life rather than in material success.

Khahl Ata is a striking instance of the indifference of historians towards the rulers who concerned themselves with the welfare of their people rather than aggrandisement. Khalıl Ata ruled for six years in Bukhārā and we know from the accounts in the *Nafahāt* that Bahā ad-dın Naqshbandı was his right-hand man through that time. Khahl set himself to create a new society based upon the teachings of the Masters and for some time he succeeded. This was about 1360 and for the rest of the fourteenth century his influence was felt throughout Transoxania. Nevertheless, I have looked in vain for his name in any of the histories of Turkestan under the successors of Chinghis Khan. It does not appear in Lane-Poole's *Mohammedan Dynasties*, probably because he did not strike coins in his own name.*

* *Editor's note.* The Arabic historian Ibn Battūta describes Khalıl's rise to power

The truth is that the past cannot be reconstructed, even from the writings of contemporaries. Gurdjieff in *Beelzebub's Tales to His Grandson* makes this point in his delightful satire of Beelzebub who had visited the earth since the time of Atlantis and had seen for himself the events which later historians pretend to describe.

In *Beelzebub's Tales*, in chapter 43, "War", Gurdjieff describes partly as fable and partly as history the attempts which have been made to remove the scourge of war from human life. He says that the nearest to success was that made by a society with the title "The Earth is Free for All" which assembled in Mosul at the beginning of the fifteenth century. The date is given by a reference to a representative of Amīr Timur who participated in the deliberations. I am inclined to believe that Gurdjieff intended this episode to be taken as historical.

In the *Zubd al-Tawārīkh*, an account is given of a visit paid by Timur to Khwāja Sadr ad-dīn who was living in poverty at Ardebil with a few disciples. Timur was deeply impressed by the sanctity of the Khwāja and asked what favour he could bestow on him. Sadr ad-dīn replied that he could give freedom to the Turks he had captured in the conquest of Anatolia. This Timur did and the Turks settled in the region, the population of which had been decimated in the time of Hulegu and never recovered. These Turks later enabled Shāh Ismāīl to found the great Safavid dynasty named after Khwāja Safā ad-dīn the father of Sadr ad-dīn.

Shāh Ismāīl was himself a descendant of the Khwājas. The time of the peacemakers ends in 1627 with the death of Abbās the Great of whom Chardin wrote: "When this great prince ceased to live, Persia ceased to prosper." The influence of the Khwājagān ceased and central Asia lost its pre-eminence as a centre of world spirituality.

The last of the great Masters was Ubaidallāh Ahrār whose training was described in the last chapter. Ahrār met and was in constant communication with the noblest successors of Khwāja Bahā ad-dīn Naqshbandī and the Masters of Wisdom in the principal centres of Turkestan, from the Gobi Desert and the Hindu Kush to the Caspian Sea and the Caucasus. He was the recognised *Qutb*, spiritual axis, of his time and one of the very

---

but makes no reference to his spiritual background. *c.f.* Trimingham *The Sufi Orders in Islam* p. 63.

rare ones to play a public role. His initiator was Sayyid Qāsim of Tabrīz to whom he attributed all his subsequent achievements.

His ancestry goes back to Umar Ibn al-Hattāf. He was received into the way by Mawlānā Yaqūb Charkhī and met with many learned men and Sufis of his time. During his lifetime, Mawlānā Jāmī wrote of him in the *Nafahāt al-Uns:* "The bond of union and the means whereby order is to be achieved in the present generation of Khwājagān and their noble tradition is none other than his Reverence Khwāja Ubaidallāh. They should place their hopes and direct their prayers to ensure that the unity and order that has been achieved through his blessed powers should continue until the end of time."

Ubaidallāh's father, Khwāja Mahmūd Shāshī came from a Tashkent family. He was a friend and supporter of the Sufis. His grandfather was Shihāb ad-dīn Shāshī. These men were shaikhs who had mastered science and wisdom, had reached states and could bestow blessings. The reason why Khwāja Ubaidallāh was, in later years, sometimes referred to as the 'Crown Prince of Turkestan' was due to the renown of his grandfather. Shaikh Shihāb ad-dīn and his followers were particularly fond of group meetings. He was both a merchant and a farmer. He had two sons: one was Khwāja Mahmūd, the father of Ubaidallāh Ahrār and the other was his paternal uncle Khwāja Muhammad.

When Khwāja Shihāb ad-dīn was on the point of death, he desired to see his grandsons. They first brought the children of his younger son, Khwāja Muhammad. He was not pleased with them and reproached his son saying: "I did not expect such children from you." Then they brought before him Ubaidallāh, still of tender age, wrapping him in a *khirqa*.

As soon as his eyes fell on the child, he became agitated and said: "Lift me up." They lifted the Khwāja up in his bed. He took Ubaidallāh in his arms and stroking his cheeks with his blessed hand began to weep saying: "See here, the child I have desired. It is well that I am alive in his day. May it be that this child will give name to the world, currency to the Divine Law and splendour to the Spiritual Path. The princes of the world will obey his decrees and bow their necks to his command. His achievements will be such as the noblest shaikhs of the past have never manifested."

Shihāb ad-dīn then recounted separately all the events that were to occur to Khwāja Ubaidallāh throughout the course of his life, once again stroked his cheeks and returned the child to his father, Khwāja Mahmūd, exhorting him to attend carefully to his upbringing.

Ahrār himself relates that when he was one year old, the time for the hair-cutting ceremony came round. According to the custom then prevailing in Tashkent a feast was being prepared, when news came of the death of Tamerlane. The population fell into a great state of agitation and terror, expecting a war of succession with resulting massacres in Mongol style. Without even waiting to eat the meal, they emptied the ovens and fled to the mountains. At that time, the Khwāja's family were living in Bāghistān, near Tashkent.

The only teacher of natural sciences and mathematics whom he was able to learn from was Mawlānā Nizām ad-dīn Khāmush – not himself one of the Khwājagān – who taught in the Ulug Beg Academy in Samarkand. His own account was: "I had heard high praise of this man's inner state, his wisdom and his goodness and this meant more to me than his reputation for understanding the secrets of the Creation. I entered the hall where he was lecturing and stood in the corner, listening without speaking. At the end of his lecture, he asked me the reason for my silence and without waiting for my answer, he turned to his pupils and said: 'There are two kinds of silence. One appears when the silent person has been carried in rapture out of the creaturely world. Such a silence is blessed. The other comes from remaining in the creaturely world, while at the same time refusing to take part in its processes. Such silence is harmful, poisoned.' "

The *Rashahāt* and other contemporary records are full of accounts of the supranormal powers and qualities manifested by Ubaidallāh Ahrār. One story from his youth became famous and has often been quoted in prose and poetry. Once he was wandering in the bazaar at Herat with Mawlānā Saad ad-dīn of Kashgar. The favourite sport of central Asia has always been wrestling and wrestlers can often be seen in the bazaars. Ahrār himself had learnt the art of wrestling. The people of those parts are great gamblers and wagers are made on every wrestling match. Ahrār and Saad ad-dīn saw a mighty great wrestler making mincemeat of a much weaker one. By a gesture the two dervishes agreed to concentrate their mental energies on the weaker one. Almost immediately, such an influx of energy poured into him that he stretched out his hands, seized the mountain of flesh and threw him over his head with such force that he was stunned. "To hear the watchers shout, one would think the end of the world had come. No-one guessed the secret. I looked and saw that Mawlānā Saad ad-dīn was standing with his eyes closed. I pulled his cloak and said: 'The job's done, leave it.' " (from the *Rashahāt*).

"We were at Firhat in the presence of Khwāja Ahrār. One day he asked for a scrap of paper and a pen. He wrote on the paper the name of Ahmad ibn Saīd Mirzā and folding it tightly thrust it into the folds of his turban. At that time no-one had heard of Ahmad ibn Saīd Mirzā. Some of the Khwāja's intimate friends begged him to tell them whose name he had written. The Khwāja said: 'It is the name of the someone that should be ruling over• you and me and all Tashkent and Samarkand and Khurasān.'

"Very soon afterwards the fame of Sultan Ahmad ibn Saīd Mirzā began to spread from Turkestan. Now it appears that in a dream Ahmad ibn Saīd Mirzā saw Khwāja Ahrār, at the suggestion of Khwāja Ahmad Yasāwī, reciting the *Fātiha,* the opening chapter of the Quran, to the Sultan. Ibn Saīd, in his dream, asked Yasāwī to tell him the name of the reciter and being told that it was Ahrār, memorized his name and face. When he awoke he asked if anyone had heard of someone of that name. Being told that such a person was living in Tashkent, he immediately mounted his horse and set out.

"He met Khwāja Ubaidallāh at Firhat where he had come to meet him. He recognised him at once as the man he had seen in his dream and fell at his feet and humbly asked him to recite the *Fātiha.* 'One recital suffices', he replied."

Sultan Saīd Mirzā was completely captivated by the Khwāja's conversation and demeanour and throughout his reign constantly turned to him for advice and protection.

A few years later, it happened that Sultan Mahmūd Mirzā attempted to seize Samarkand by force from his brother Sultan Ahmad. Khwāja Ahrār did his best to dissuade him, reminding him that to draw the sword against his brother was against humanity and against Divine Law; but Sultan Mahmūd would not listen. He marched on Samarkand and Sultan Ahmad Mirzā mobilized his army and stood on the defensive. Khwāja Ubaidallāh took three of his followers, strongest in mystical power and caused a prodigious storm and tempest from the

Qipchāq desert to break over Sultan Mahmūd and his army. The floods were so overwhelming that his generals were terrified and the army fled in confusion without even seeing the defenders.*

The *Rashahāt* contains many accounts of similar exploits and of the extraordinary influence exercised by Khwāja Ahrār from end to end of Turkestan. He was also a very profound exponent of the way of liberation.

Ahrār never consented to be a teacher, *shaikh*. He is reported to have said: "If I were to set up as a teacher, none of the shaikhs would be left with a single pupil. But my task is not teaching, but protecting innocent believers from oppression by tyrants and preventing wars and civil wars. On account of this, I have been obliged to consort with sovereigns and sultans and to win their hearts."**

---

* *Editor's note.* On a previous occasion, Ahrār saved Samarkand from an attack by Bābur Mirzā – not the Emperor – through the device of causing a murrain among his horses.
** *Editor's note.* This appears to be literally true. The most famous story – which is corroborated from other sources than the *Rashahāt* – is of the Khwāja camping between the two armies of Ahmad and his brother Umar and bringing about a reconciliation. According to eye-witness accounts, both the rulers and the armies were reduced to tears and peace ensued.

Epilogue

The manuscript of this work had been completed up to the end of Chapter Nine at the time of the author's death but there were also several fragmentary beginnings to a chapter entitled "The Peacemakers". These fragments have been brought together and integrated into the present concluding Chapter Ten. It is only in this final chapter, and in certain other places where there existed more than one version of a passage, that those of us who have helped prepare this work for publication have departed from our firm resolve to place before the reader exactly what the author had written.

We would be negligent, however, if we failed to emphasise that the work is incomplete. It is incomplete in several ways. The first is the obvious incompleteness of the manuscript. The second is that the manuscript itself was only the first draft and there are probably many places where the author might have wished on reflection to add further material or to develop or strengthen the argument. Finally, it is the nature of any effective work that it generates in the reader a certain momentum that carries him into new areas when the work is concluded. In this instance, due to the premature conclusion, it is felt there is a particular need to provide further directions for any reader who wishes to continue the search. To meet these incompletenesses, it is the purpose of this epilogue to bring to the attention of the reader additional material, which is relevant to what has been written, but which was not available to the author, and, at the same time, to share those indications of where the book might have led that are contained in early synopses of the work which we are fortunate to have.

It will be helpful at the outset to remind ourselves that we are confronted here, not with history in the traditional sense, but, as was so clearly stated in the Preface, rather with a history of significances. The fourth volume of *The Dramatic Universe* contains more fully the author's understanding of history, but it would be useful to reflect for a moment on what is commonly held to be 'the scientific approach'. It is generally thought that to be 'scientific' is to collect all the data and then to deduce from them some explanatory pattern or laws that can account for them. This, the deductive approach, as has been admirably demonstrated by Popper and others, is not the approach that has in fact led to the great breakthroughs in the history of science. It has rather been the inductive approach, where a working hypothesis or an analogous pattern often drawn from another discipline has preceded and sometimes organised the collection of facts, that has provided the heuristic power and dynamism of scientific enquiry and discovery. We need not then be alarmed when, as has been done in this work, a similar approach is applied to history, nor should we dismiss it as being in any way 'unscientific'.

In this work the hypothesis of a Demiurgic intelligence guiding the affairs of mankind and working through the agency of advanced human beings called Masters of Wisdom is tested against the known or partially known history of a vast time span — an outstanding testimony to the author's great range of knowledge and vision. One must recognise that our knowledge of much of the ground covered is far from complete, for otherwise an objective reader could justly consider some of the linkages and supporting evidence to be less than convincing. A case in point is the author's use of the Magi which might, at first sight, be regarded as a purely formal device. But what do we know for certain about the Magi? They were probably the Median priestly caste, they certainly served as priests at Zoroastrian rites and they were certainly influential and important. They were clearly not of uniform belief as there is evidence of variant sects and some were certainly Zurvanite. It is likely that some groups retained beliefs and practices dating from before the time of Zoroaster and there was probably some form of hierarchy amongst them suggestive of progressive initiation into deeper mysteries. This is little enough, but we should note that there is nothing incompatible between what we know and the author's treatment. For those who wish to pursue this matter further and find additional references, there is a good summary in Professor Frye's book, *The Heritage of Persia*.

There are instances in this first draft where the author failed to make use of all the material he could have done. Of all the Mesopotamian sects that preserved in some form the ancient Babylonian culture and traditions, it is particularly unfortunate that no mention was made of the Mandaeans. One can find in this Gnostic baptising sect just that continuity of tradition the author was seeking to demonstrate. In addition to the Babylonian legacy one finds also Iranian and Jewish connections, the latter so strong that it has long been argued they might well have had some connection with John the Baptist and with the Essenes. They have another importance also in that it was in this sect that Mani received much of his early religious upbringing before he left to launch his own faith, Manichaeanism. Much of the esoteric literature of the Mandaeans is now available in English translation thanks to the labours of Lady E. S. Drower and her book *The Secret Adam,* as well as being particularly informative about them, also contains further bibliographical references.

In this book she makes mention of another sect, the Sābians, from the town of Harrān some hundred and fifty kilometres north east of Aleppo, who were an extraordinarily interesting Gnostic sect who again preserved a great deal of the ancient Babylonian tradition together with elements of Greek gnosticism. It was members of this sect who made a substantial contribution during the Islamic period by translating many important Greek treatises into Arabic. This might seem at first a trivial task, but from hindsight it was of very great importance. Not only did it introduce quite new concepts into Islamic philosophy but it preserved many Greek works which might otherwise have been lost, so that they were later available to play their part in the European Renaissance. A useful article on the Sabians of Harran by B. Dodge is to be found in the Festival Book of the American University of Beirut, 1967.

It was only after the author's death that two books have been published that give us a much clearer picture than we had before of the Arabic conquest of Persia and its conversion to Islām. These are the fourth volume of *The Cambridge History of Iran* and

Professor Frye's *The Golden Age of Persia* both of which cover the period from the Arab invasions to the Saljuks. How it was that Zoroastrianism apparently succumbed so readily to Islām was a question that rightly preoccupied the author, and, with the sources at his disposal, he was clearly unable to find a satisfactory answer. The evidence all points to the fact that the Sassanid empire was exhausted and indeed in chaos both during and after the rule of Chosroes II and that Zoroastrianism, the state religion, was equally in decline internally and also externally due to the inroads made upon it by other faiths, notably Nestorian and latterly Monophysite Christianity. It required no miracle then for Zoroastrianism to crumble.

Professor Frye rightly stresses the important distinction between the eastern and the western Iranians. The conversion of the western Sassanid Iranians was certainly not overnight, but was an inevitable and gradual process. Due to the economic and social advantages of being a Muslim, and since the state had been overthrown which had maintained the Zoroastrian priesthood in its position of authority, the conversion proceeded steadily and relatively uneventfully.

It is what happened in Khurasān and central Asia, however, that is of particular significance to the thesis advanced in this work. The eastern Iranians in this region were, for the most part, beyond the reach of Sassanid rule and were in contact with a great mixture of sects, faiths, tribes and races. It was the political and religious revolts in this area that not only brought the Abbasid Caliphate to power, but were the main influence in *transforming Islam from an Arab to a universal religion.* Nor was this all, for it was there that the rise of the Iranian dynasties fostered the development of the new Persian language, literature and culture that the Saljuk Turks were to carry with them westwards. From this very early period one can recognise the dynamic role this region played in shaping the culture of the Islamic world.

Coming to the Khwājagān, there is an important article which was not available to the author but which suggests how a connection could be made between Chapter Four, The Time of Christ, and the Masters of central Asia. The article, *Autour du Daré Mansour: L'apprentissage mystique de Bahā ad-Dīn Naqshband,* by M. Molé, appeared in *Revue des Etudes Islamiques* in 1959. In dealing with many of the anecdotes of the Khwājagān, Molé

points out the clear Malamatī influences in the approach of the
Masters. Nishapur in Khurasan was known to have been an
important Malamatī centre and Abū Yazīd Bistāmī is considered
an important figure in both the Malamatī and Naqshbandī
spiritual pedigrees. Molé rejects a direct connection, pointing out
that the Naqshbandīs avoided many of the excesses of the
Malamatīs, but he stresses that the major traits of humility and
self humiliation, the acceptance of oneself as being inferior to all
other creatures and the refusal to make any outward show of
piety or spiritual progress, were common to both schools. It is
not difficult to see how this makes the emphasis on humility and
humiliation a very real connecting link between the message of
The Time of Christ and the way of the Khwājagān.

There is one final work which we know not to have been
available to the author, but which we strongly recommend to the
reader. This is J. S. Trimingham's book, *The Sufi Orders in Islam.*
The reason for our strong recommendation is not only that it is
the first scholarly work to recognise the great importance of the
Khwājagān and to provide striking confirmation of much that
our author has written, but, at a more general level, it will
provide a valuable broad background to Sufism and its various
orders, such, for example, as the Malāmatiyya referred to above.
It also has an excellent bibliography so that the reader can follow
up any matter he wishes further. Its only defect is that it is too
'tidy'.

A clear example of the confirmation Trimingham offers to our
author's thesis is on page 90. "In central Asia the two-century
period separating the Mongol invasion from the foundation of
the Safawid regime in Persia was a time of ferment, crucial for
the future of Islam in the region. The immediate consequences of
the Mongol conquests had been the displacement of Islam as the
state religion throughout the region. Islam now had to prove
itself and accommodate itself to non-Muslim rulers, Shamanist,
Buddhist or crypto-Christian. It was a time pregnant with
possibilities, and the outcome was the triumph of Islam as the
dominant religion of central Asia. Sufism's role was of
considerable significance, not as a Way, but through its men of
power, manifested also after their deaths from their tombs, many
of whose structures were raised by Mongol rulers."

In discussing the Naqshbandī order, Trimingham describes
how: "although so clearly Iranian and urban, it was adopted by

many Tatar tribes as a kind of religious linkage." He rightly regards Ubaidallah Ahrār as the most influential figure after Baha ad-dīn and shows how the three regional lines of the order, the central Asian, the western Turkish and the Indian, all derive from him. He writes: "The heads of all the independent states which succeeded the Mongols (except in Persia) favoured this great Sunni order, honouring its leaders during their lifetime and building mausoleums over their graves and khānqāhs to house their dervishes. Although it weakened in time, it remained the dominant regional order, with great centres at Samarqand, Merv, Khiva, Tashkand, Herat as well as Bukhāra. There were also significant groups in Chinese Turkestan and Khokand, Afghanistan, Persia, Baluchistan and India."

But although Trimingham gives much greater detail about the later expansion of the Naqshbandiyya in India and Turkey, he also enables us to reconstruct the family tree given on page 210 which shows all the orders that lead back to Yūsuf Hamadānī and his early companions. On the left we see the Naqshbandiyya which from the seventeenth century gave rise to other orders while, at the same time, remaining the major force it is even today. In the middle are the Khalwatī order, which was particularly influential amongst the western Turks, and the Safawiyya order which led to the foundation of the Safavid dynasty in Persia, and which also generated further orders such as the Bairāmiyya and the Jilwatiyya. On the right we have the Yasawiyya and the Bektāshiyya, two highly influential orders which could claim to have played a major part in the awakening of Turkish spirituality and inspiring a wonderful Turkish mystical literature.

Perhaps to the reader these are just names on a page, but even from this it must be clear that, from the viewpoint of hindsight, Yūsuf Hamadānī and the early Khwājas have been a powerful influence for peace, piety and spiritual awareness, and all that this inspires in terms of art, literature, science and architecture, for many centuries amongst a not insignificant proportion of the world's population. That such humble men could create such an influence at a time when the world in which they lived was one of turmoil and uncertainty offering constant threats of death and destruction is little short of a miracle. It is for this reason that our author has brought them and their achievements so forcibly to our attention as testimony to the working of a higher intelligence in the affairs of man.

Leaving now the Islamic world, we know from the earliest synopsis of this book that the author had, at one stage, wished to include a chapter on the European Masters and it seems right, even though it was never written, to share this barest of outlines with the reader in the hope that it might be of interest and possibly stimulate further enquiry. Although just a list of names, it provides sufficient indication of what was intended: "The Gothic Masters. The anonymity of the Cathedral builders and glassworkers. The crusades. St. Francis in Egypt and Syria. Dante Alighieri. Torquato Tasso. The German Mystics. Meister Eckhart and the Friends of God. Duns Scotus and Roger Bacon. Jacob Boehme. The Beguines and the Friends of the Common Life. The Masters in the Netherlands. The English Mistery. The Masters of painting. Massacio and Botticelli. Leonardo. The Astronomers and the Alchemists. Kepler. Copernicus. Galileo. Boyle. Newton. The search for a Cosmic Law. The Rosicrucians and the origins of Free Masonry. The Masters in Modern Times. Kierkegaard. The Pre-Raphaelites."

Finally, from this same early synopsis, we have an outline of the concluding chapter. It is clear that, had the book been written along these lines, it would have been a very different work. Nonetheless, we again share this summary with the reader to place before him the questions that our author faced. The chapter was entitled The Masters and The Future and had the following headings: "The Masters at moments of transition. The Coming Epoch. The Demiurge and the New Man. What is meant by the Second Coming of Christ. The present moment compared with 12,000 years ago. The social revolution of the Neolithic Age. The social revolution of the next hundred years. The Synergism as co-operation between man and the Demiurgic Intelligence. The psychokinetic society in a psychostatic world. A long view into the future. The next twelve thousand years and the coming of a New Race of Men."

It would be fascinating to know how these questions would have been answered. Or would it? These headings have been included because those of us who worked with the author knew that his life was devoted to awakening people to real questions and to giving hope and encouragement to those who worked to find their own answers. Few will be Masters, but this work offers hope to all, no matter how humble or insignificant, that guidance is always with us provided only that we face the questions that he quoted at the opening of *The Dramatic Universe,* itself the outcome of his own search begun so many years ago. We are sure that it would at least have met with his approval if we conclude this, his last work with those same questions which so simply summarize his constant search for the meaning and purpose of life on earth.

"How came I to be? Whence am I? And to serve what purpose did I come?"

CHART OF THE SPIRITUAL DESCENDANTS OF YUSUF HAMADANI

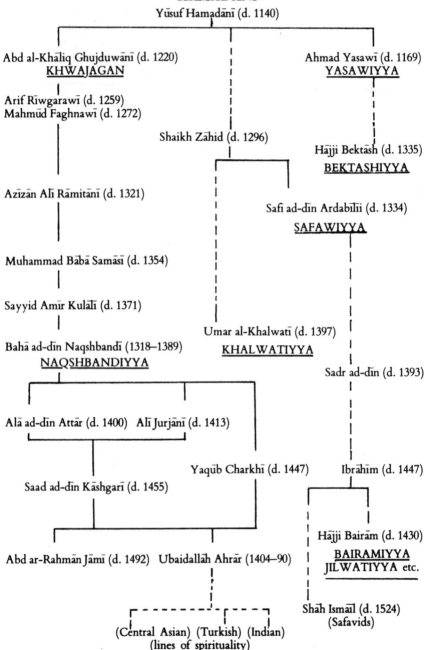

Yūsuf Hamadānī (d. 1140)

Abd al-Khāliq Ghujduwānī (d. 1220)
KHWAJAGAN

Arif Rīwgarawī (d. 1259)
Mahmūd Faghnawī (d. 1272)

Azīzān Alī Rāmitānī (d. 1321)

Muhammad Bābā Samāsī (d. 1354)

Sayyid Amīr Kulālī (d. 1371)

Bahā ad-dīn Naqshbandī (1318–1389)
NAQSHBANDIYYA

Alā ad-dīn Attār (d. 1400)   Alī Jurjānī (d. 1413)

Saad ad-dīn Kāshgarī (d. 1455)

Abd ar-Rahmān Jāmī (d. 1492)   Ubaidallāh Ahrār (1404–90)

(Central Asian) (Turkish) (Indian)
(lines of spirituality)

Shaikh Zāhid (d. 1296)

Umar al-Khalwatī (d. 1397)
KHALWATIYYA

Yaqūb Charkhī (d. 1447)

Ahmad Yasawī (d. 1169)
YASAWIYYA

Hājji Bektāsh (d. 1335)
BEKTASHIYYA

Safi ad-dīn Ardabīlii (d. 1334)
SAFAWIYYA

Sadr ad-dīn (d. 1393)

Ibrāhīm (d. 1447)

Hājji Bairām (d. 1430)
BAIRAMIYYA
JILWATIYYA etc.

Shāh Ismāīl (d. 1524)
(Safavids)

INDEX OF BOOKS AND PAPERS

Editor's Note: Where it was felt to be useful, translations od the titles and descriptions of the books have been given according to the following scheme:
Title (translation); author (description)

INDEX OF PROPER NAMES, SECTS AND DYNASTIES

Note As far as possible, the title or role of each historical figure has been added in brackets.

INDEX OF TECHNICAL TERMS

Editor's Note: As far as possible a translation or interpretation of technical terms in a foreign language has been given in an English phrase. The form of the entries is as follows:
technical term (meaning) *other references*